AMAZONS

AMAZONS

A Love Story

E. J. Levy

UNIVERSITY OF MISSOURI PRESS
COLUMBIA AND LONDON

Copyright © 2012 by E. J. Levy
University of Missouri Press, Columbia, Missouri 65201
Printed and bound in the United States of America
All rights reserved
5 4 3 2 1   16 15 14 13 12

Cataloging-in-Publication data available from the Library of Congress.
ISBN 978-0-8262-1975-6

∞™ This paper meets the requirements of the
American National Standard for Permanence of Paper
for Printed Library Materials, Z39.48, 1984.

Designer: Kristie Lee
Typesetter: K. Lee Design & Graphics
Printer and binder: Thomson-Shore, Inc.
Typefaces: Palatino and Latino

For Nel

Contents

AMAZONS

A modern hero—or anti-hero—[reflects] an extreme external situation within his own extremity. His neurosis becomes diagnosis, not just of himself but of a phase of history.

—STEPHEN SPENDER,
introduction to *Under the Volcano*

Prologue

The Cartographer of Loss

Imagine the world as flesh.

The southern continents, its meaty flanks. The oceans, its shifting faces. Rivers, veins. Dunes, its soft teats. Like you, it breathes, sighs clouds from steaming rivers, exhales oxygen from the rain forests that gird its distended belly like dispersed lungs. Each leaf, alveolus.

The symbiotic theory of cell evolution maintains that the human body evolved from a composite of relationships of which our organs bear the traces yet; that we are thus not one but many creatures, composed of other unions: symbiotic, parasitic, predator, and prey. This theory (first championed in the nineteenth century and disputed still) maintains that each body carries within it, like the bed of some ancient ocean, a history of microbial cooperation, of species that came together and formed indissoluble bonds. Like the Amazon rain forest, which has evolved slowly over millennia into a complex network of alliance and misalliance, we are each of us a world unto ourselves. Our bodies, like the Amazon, like fate, a built thing.

For a long time I could not think about my tropic life, that year I spent in the Amazon rain forest and in Salvador, Bahia, Brazil. I could not think about the women I knew there, about Nelci and Isa and Barbara, that year during which I tried for months to get to the Amazon, which I had come to study and hoped to "save."

Maybe it was fear that held me back from reflecting until now, stopping me from looking back. Fear informed by the memory of a favorite childhood bedtime story, that of Orpheus and Eurydice, read to me in the optimistic late 1960s by my mother, whose optimism like the nation's was beginning to wear thin and who sought to instill in us, her three children, in a modest suburb

1

in Minnesota, something of a classical education, the Victorian virtues, by reading to us each night before sleep Greek myths and legends, seeking to pass on to us a faith in gods and mysteries she was no longer able to retain. Weary, without the comforts of cigarettes, which she had given up to give birth to me, without the comforts of her husband who was busy elsewhere, with other women, bored out of her ever-loving brilliant mind, teetering on the brink of suicide, she read to us what seems to me now a fitting tale for her circumstance and for our time—the story of Orpheus seeking to reclaim love from among the ranks of the dead. I learned from my mother and Edith Hamilton never to look back, Orpheus my model for a forward-looking gaze.

It's a familiar story: Orpheus, the lyre player, loses his beloved Eurydice to snakebite. Grieved by her death, he descends to the underworld determined to bring her back to life with him. There he plays for Hades, the king of the dead, who is so moved by Orpheus' music that he agrees to release Eurydice on one condition: that Orpheus not look back at her until he reaches the surface of the world. He demands, in effect, an act of faith, a sacrifice to revive what has been lost. Without faith, without sacrifice, Orpheus will lose what he loves. But as he ascends to the surface of the world, Orpheus fails to hear his lover's footfalls on the path behind him and panics; overcome with anxiety, with the need to know, with the need for *certainty*, he turns around, sees her there, and loses what he loves forever.

Orpheus was granted what no one can really hope to have—the opportunity to revive what has been lost once already. Still we hope. Live recklessly. Bank on being able to bring back what we so casually squander: species brought to the brink of extinction. A world warmed to the edge of melting. But even Orpheus, who was on a first-name basis with the gods, blew it. If we insist on certainty, on an absence of doubt, we too may lose what we best love.

How do we *know* the world is warming? How do we know what the effects will be of vastly increased levels of CO_2? What happens if we fell most tropical moist forests in the course of a single century? We document, sometimes, at the risk of damage, deliberating instead of doing something. Instead of taking action to stem loss or prevent climate change, holding to a path we know to be right, we are tempted to look death in the face, to know for *sure* what will happen, more afraid of sacrifice for the sake of uncertain reward than of loss, and so risk losing it all. How do we know human activity is warming the world? When we know for *certain*, will we say, *If only we had known*?

When I first returned to the United States from the Amazon, I had lunch with my mother. I was home again on some vacation or other, spring break it must have been, and we were eating as we often did in a restaurant that adjoined a local grocery store. It was one of those boastful American grocery stores, with their vast cornucopias of produce and bread and condiments. This particular grocery chain, Byerly's, had made its mark by catering to those who hate to shop. It hung crystal chandeliers above the frozen food aisles; it made its aisles as wide as fashionable boulevards; it dedicated an entire shelf of a block-long aisle to hot pepper sauces; another to pickles from around the world; yet another to varieties of chips; each day it tossed the produce that had not been sold. The store's opulence stood in embarrassing contrast to the place I'd left, Brazil's impoverished northeast. I don't know if I noticed. Likely its superfluity was comforting.

It was over that lunch that I told my mother that I'd been raped in Brazil. Sodomized. She took a stab at her salad, looked at her plate. She said she didn't care what I did, that it was my business, but that she hoped I was using protection. I was not protected against this. I said, "Mom, I just told you I was raped and you're talking about condoms? I don't believe this. That's like my telling you that I tried to slit my wrists and your saying that you hope the blade wasn't rusty." We sat in awkward embarrassed silence for a while. When my mother spoke again, she said that she was sorry, she'd thought I was trying to shock her, trying to show her how grown-up I was. I was twenty-two by then, and I was not grown-up. I just knew a lot of things I could not understand yet. A lot of things I rather wished I didn't know about what people are capable of and what they aren't.

It would be years before I realized that my mother was merely doing what we all have done, are doing still: she was trying in the face of loss and pain and shock to bring ordinary caution to bear; she was trying to make this reasonable somehow; just as we at the National Institute of Amazonian Research, where I had worked in the Amazon, had done with our maps and charts, our scholarly papers and our studies of rain forest destruction. She was trying to apply the standards of a reasonable discourse to unreasonable acts.

In the face of loss, some document. Christopher Isherwood's partner drew pictures of him as he lay dying. The fashion photographer Richard Avedon photographed his father's last days. I took few notes that year; I retain few reminders outside memory. I did not keep mementos. I have a *berimbau*—the gourd instrument used to accompany the martial art of *capoeira*; I have three books in Portuguese. I have a single photo of myself in black and white (in it, my eyes are blank, an attempt to effect the vacuous stare of an American model, achieving instead the demeanor of one who has been mugged.) A handful more in color of me and some capoeiristas on the Island of Itaparica. Guys whose names I don't know. Disjointed images, which I return to reticently, as I imagine one must approach a corpse in a city morgue. Loath to identify the body. Loath to look at the figure stretched out before me, displayed for dissection. Loath to give this its proper name. To say, "I recognize this face. It's mine."

Fifteen years after departing the Amazon, I was living on a high desert mesa working to protect another river—this time the Rio Grande—when I accepted an invitation to write an essay about my stint in the Amazon and the images from that year began to filter back to me the way blades of light will filter through the tannic liquid of a river if you look up from beneath the surface. Filaments of light, a fan, or spines, a shape I had not recognized before came clear and the pointless chaos of that year seemed suddenly patterned and if not beautiful then meaningful at least.

I was amazed to find how much and how vividly I remembered that lost year. Amazed to find how much survived that I'd believed was lost. I found a journal that I'd kept and forgotten, among my few keepsakes, and a few sketches I'd written shortly after my return.

It was at the close of the twentieth century that I began to look back at that year, and perhaps because endings tend to make us think symbolically (in light of an ending, we can see a thing entire, discern the pattern), the people I knew then, the fate of the rain forest, the sacrifices we made and those we unpropitiously failed to make, suddenly seemed emblematic of that American century. I began to see that the logic that endangered the rain forest had endangered me as well. What had happened to the girls I knew then and what happened to the forest seemed connected, the damage done to each recalling the damage done the other, the consequence of ill-conceived development schemes, the dangerous logic of commodities.

When I made it to the Amazon twenty-five years ago, I worked as a cartographer. I spent my days in a cubicle in an office on the grounds of the Instituto Naçional de Pesquisas da Amazônia—the National Institute for Amazonian Research (INPA, for short)—deep in the forest on the outskirts of that mirage of a city, Manaus.

Now, as then, I face the cartographer's dilemma: What to map? What territory is worth recording, which aspects merit note, what can be discarded or ignored? I was no more than a flunky at INPA, an intern in the office of a world-renowned researcher and the choice of what to map wasn't mine to make though it was left to me to connect the dots. It was my job to daily chart the coordinates that marked rates of deforestation.

I was in charge of recording not what *was*, but what was *not*. Mapping absence.

I was—perhaps I am again—a cartographer of loss.

PART I
DESTINO

Maps

The map of Salvador that I look at now is unrecognizable, in black and white; Xeroxed from some tourist brochure, it covers two pages, 8 1/2 by 11 inches each. I will tape it together in the middle, trying to make a whole, but even then the image will be wrong.

It bears the names of the neighborhoods I visited and those I was afraid to, not because they were dangerous but because I was afraid then and thought that if I held still I might protect myself. I thought I'd be safe if I didn't make a move. And I didn't know, in any case, what move to make.

The map in front of me has names of neighborhoods and streets printed in bold uppercase type: Barra, Vitoria, Canela lie to the left (which is south, on this disoriented map). To the right-hand side, on the northern edge of the peninsula on which Salvador sits, are Ribeira and Bonfim; the city center lies suspended between these, in the curve of the Bay of All Saints, due west; at the bottom of the page, to the east and the interior lie Campinas, Fazenda Grande.

The original map was candy colored, bright and promising. Even in this secondhand Xerox, I can see it was meant to be cheerful, its directions clear. It is decorated with cartoon figures—giant smiling angelfish and sailboats decorate the coastal waters; each beach is marked by an umbrella, beneath which reclines a bikini-clad, long-haired blond. Capoeira schools are indicated by dancing dark-skinned men; *terreiros*—the sanctuaries of the cult of *candomblé*—by black women, their heads wrapped in turbaned scarves, bodies encased in bells of cloth, layer on layer of white cotton and lace.

I am not sure what is supposed to be indicated by the black matrons seated by a pot of boiling *dendê*, palm oil. That this is a black neighborhood? Or is she merely decorative in the mapmaker's mind? A splash of local color? Picturesque as poverty is said to be by those who needn't suffer it or sympathize. There are buildings depicted, too, in miniature, caricatures of modern hotels and the lovely confections of the baroque that distinguish the old city neighborhoods of Pelourinho and Bonfim, which perch atop a cliff above the center of town, overlooking the harbor.

I look at Avenida Sete de Setembro that runs north and south along the edge of the spit of land that is Salvador, from the city center—*o centro*—to the Porto da Barra, past the San Antonio fort to the *farol*, named for the lighthouse there, and I picture the street, the heat, the sudden interruptible shade of trees, the bus, the stench of exhaust, the school for English, the hotel where I stayed those first few days, the apartment I rented on Rua João Pondé, which later I would share with Nelci, neither of us realizing—till it was far too late—just how much it would cost us.

Development Projects

It was the third of January 1984 when I flew down to Brazil. That morning, in the Minneapolis-St. Paul international airport, I had hugged my parents hurriedly good-bye at the gate where I would board my plane to Miami, where I would in turn board a plane to Salvador, Bahia, Brazil. As I hugged my mother, I could see over her shoulder the pale brightness of a Minnesota January day framed by the massive windows that lined the concourse walls; I could see beyond her to the runway covered with plump planes. I did not cry, though I wanted to. I was twenty-one, too old to cry.

What I remember of the airport at Miami is a jumble. I remember the ebbing day, the darkness of the runway, the fear potent, haunting, ever present, that I would miss my connection. I was young then, young even for my age, and I was afraid of failing to make connections.

In those days, I wanted to belong and did not, to anyone, least of all to myself, and this was painful to me. I had had, since I was fifteen, a steady stream of boyfriends and friends but outside my parents I had loved no one, a fact I contemplated often with the extravagant despair of self-despairing youth.

Perhaps as I sat in the Miami airport, looking around at all the people I did not know, many of them speaking Portuguese, a language I was not yet fluent in, I told myself that I loved no one, as if hoping to be proven wrong. I believed then that I hadn't a clue what it meant to love, because in truth I had not yet been deeply moved by a person as I could be by a painting, a film, a strain of music; I had yet to meet anyone as lovely as a landscape or a work of art.

In the absence of love, I cleaved fervently to justice, to an almost Calvinistic conception of right and wrong, the conviction that one must do right even without hope of success or salvation; mine, a hopeless ardor.

I was the child of what was genteelly known in late twentieth-century America as a "mixed marriage"—the union of Protestant and Jew—and this shaped my sensibility, surely if obscurely, informing, I suspect, the salvific impulse that for years fueled my desire to save the Amazon. My parents had been raised in religious homes—among Orthodox Jews and fundamentalist Methodists—but they relinquished their respective faiths before they met and married. My mother converted to Orthodox Judaism for the sake of my father's mother, but they gave up on religious observance. Still the brooding shadows of their gods remained. Although my parents sacrificed the confidence of those who believe that they are chosen or saved, we lived with an oppressive sense of divine judgment. Their youngest child, I was especially susceptible. From an early age, I was on the look out for vocations, wrongs to right. At eighteen, when I first read about the disappearing rain forest, I thought at last I'd found it—my calling.

In those days, I did not want to lose my way, as I do now, but find it. I did not know then—in my twenties, as I'd learn in my thirties—how to appreciate the pleasures of an airport with its promiscuous crush of humanity, its placelessness, its promising dislocation, inviting you to believe that wherever you may have been or be you might begin anew elsewhere, transformed by this simple trinity: a gate, a gangplank, a ticket.

I was halfway through my junior year at Yale that January when I set out for Brazil to spend a year studying the environmental consequences of development projects in the Amazon. As a sophomore, I had applied for and been awarded a generous fellowship from the Rotary Foundation International, which offered fellowships to students, scholars, and journalists to fund international research. These grants typically went to graduate students, not undergrads, and on the East Coast, where I'd applied, competition was fierce. I had been lucky to get the money and I knew it. I wanted to make good use of my time.

In my application, I had proposed to work at the National Institute of Amazonian Research in Manaus, deep in the jungle, one of the premier institutions for the study of tropical moist forests. I was well versed in the literature, a student of economics and Latin American studies with a specialization in twentieth-century Brazilian economic development.

I wanted to be a part of the team of researchers whose work and names I had come to know from reading journals. I wanted to be among the biologists and zoologists and economists who seemed to me then heroic in their efforts to halt the devastation of the vast tracts of forest and rivers and communities known as the Amazon. I was ambitious of saving part of the disappearing world.

But something had gone wrong. The fellowship office's command of geography was sadly lacking and someone in the Foundation headquarters near Chicago had succeeded in sending me to Salvador, Bahia, a coastal tourist capital some 1,600 miles southeast of the rain forest I had come to study. I'd booked a hotel in Salvador and figured I'd spend maybe a week there, maybe less, getting my bearings, boning up on Portuguese, getting my money, before I arranged a transfer and headed north to the Amazon.

If you'd asked me that day who I was, I would have said that I was a student of economics with a specialization in twentieth-century Brazilian economic development. If you'd asked me what I wanted to be, I would have said an artist, a writer—in the museums my parents had taken us to as kids,

I had seen Franz Marc's *Blue Horses* and Calder's whimsical mobiles, Hans Hoffman's nearly edible colors and the haunting luminosity of Rothko's squares, and they'd made me long for something, as if the paintings were speaking to me in a private language we understood; I sensed, as poet Patti Smith would later write, "that to be an artist was to see what others could not"; I wanted to see as clearly. But I knew better: that kind of thing was beyond people like me.

People Like Me—children of the burgeoning American middle class, born of working-class parents, who had themselves been born of immigrants who'd bet on education as the ticket up and out of wherever they were, ghettos or farms—were educated in public schools at a time when Shakespeare and calculus were still taught there, not yet thought too elite for the masses, when metal detectors were not yet a commonplace at the doors (when we did not yet see ourselves, or our young, as dangerous, suspect); we expected ourselves to go to college, to move up and move on. We expected to become lawyers, doctors, professors, psychologists, critics; we talked about and analyzed what other people made; we joined the Foreign Service and worked for the USIA, bringing artists in to tour foreign countries and building amity among nations; we gave papers and luncheons and joined the Rotary Club. We read books; we did not write them. We went to museums to see paintings; we did not paint them.

People Like Me believed it was important to know what was what (reading the newspaper was a moral issue, the *New York Times* was like high mass); we believed it was important to know what one was, to know one's nature and to master it. To know what you could and could not do. To be realistic. To have perspective.

We took to heart that Delphic exhortation: know thyself. But for us the phrase was inflected by Calvinism, some vague strain of doubt in our election. Know Yourself for us meant know your limitations (I thought the two synonymous). Know them and accept. Know your nature and develop it.

Destino

It was full-blown summer when I arrived in Salvador and the city was ablaze with sunlight in the dead heat of a tropical January day. In the course of the flight from Minneapolis—at the forty-fifth parallel north—the plane had passed through the Tropic of Cancer, crossing the equator north of the Amazon, heading for the Tropic of Capricorn. Those twin imaginary lines— the Tropics of Cancer and Capricorn—demarcate the torrid zone, better known as the tropics, a term that seems suggestive now, portentous, deriving as it does from the ancient Greek *tropikos*, "pertaining to a turn." For the tropic effects a turn: as literary tropes turn words from their literal meaning to some other sense, as, heliotropic, plants turn toward the sun, turn towards that scalding light.

We had crossed into the country by night, had been awakened when we reached Belem, in order to fill out Customs cards, and had flown on in darkness. Waking, I looked out the window to my left and was moved to find a world softly lit. I still remember how the ground looked below me as dawn came on: the felty animal-hide brown of the countryside, which is known in Brazil as *o interior*—the interior—the camel-colored hills, sloping gently, as if muscles lay beneath them, recumbent, relaxed. To the east, a crack of yellow sun spread over the curved edge of the earth, sending out long bright beams of light; bands of yellow, orange, rose striated the sky at the horizon, which was blue-black with ocean.

As we approached Salvador, losing altitude, the rectangle of my window framed green, deeper than any I'd ever seen before. It was a green that seemed to suck in light, nearing black except where sunlight picked out trees. It was the dense tropical knotted green of forest canopy, clotted like clouds, quivering with palms as we approached the coastline and Salvador.

A month earlier, I had written to Senor Pinheiro, my Rotary contact in Salvador, to let him know the date of my arrival, my flight number and time, hoping he might offer to have someone meet me. But I had not heard back—mail was slow, sometimes lost, and he might well have considered it an imposition, I thought—and so as we touched down, I was prepared to hail a cab. I had a *Fodor's* guide in my backpack, and had all but memorized the tiny map of Salvador, which showed Avenida Sete de Setembro where my hotel was.

The word for destination and destiny are one and the same in Portuguese: *destino*.

I arrived at my *destino* overdressed and unable to speak the language. I was in no hurry to disembark, so I lingered in my seat, as others filed past. When the aisle was mostly clear, I stood and reached up to haul down my backpack from the plane's overhead compartment. A few other passengers straggled into the aisles. I ran my hand down the front of my ankle-length khaki cotton skirt, trying to press out with my palm the wrinkles that had settled there during the flight. A portly balding man behind me told me, in plain English, that I'd be too hot dressed like that; this was *not* the United States.

I had aimed for fashionable and failed. I wore a lightweight, tangerine-orange cotton sweater with three-quarter length sleeves, a thin cotton T-shirt, a khaki skirt made of cotton light as leaves, and that tell-tale sign of the American traveler: tennis shoes.

The sweater I wore was by a French designer, the only designer clothing I owned, and I'd bought it especially for the trip; the skirt, by an American designer, I'd borrowed from my mother. I took off the sweater, tied its sleeves around my throat so the sweater dangled like a shawl down my back, in a fashion that had not been fashionable for years, a sort of preppy, tennis-pro casual I had disdained when it had been popular years before when I was in high school. I smiled at the man who smiled at me in amusement.

We filed to the front of the plane and walked down a metal stairway to the tarmac. The hand railing too hot to hold. The heat was palpable through the rubber soles of my white tennis shoes as I stepped onto the runway. I pushed through the oppressive heat as if it were some liquid substance, some medium other than air, stunning as a vacuum, sucking the breath out of me. It seemed too hot to breathe.

I felt light-headed as I scanned the bank of bodies waiting beneath the cement canopy of the single-story building that served as airport terminal here. Palm fronds waved hysterically from the edges of the tarmac. I still hoped that Senor Pinheiro would show, but even if he did, I had no photo, no way to know it was he; I had not the least idea who he was or what he looked like or if he'd got my letter at all and if he had whether he would meet me. I squinted at signs, at faces, at the limp hands dangling at people's sides, at those who squealed and ran out to embrace some friend or family member. I looked for signs bearing my name. Saw none did.

I filed through the waiting crowd into the open, single-story concrete structure, where I would gather my luggage, pass through customs, and hail a cab. After I found my bags—this was not difficult, they were flame orange, matched my sorry sweater—I heaved my suitcases onto a table as a uniformed guard directed me to, and opened them. I looked around nervously as another guard went through my bags. I saw people waving, nodding, but no one waved to me.

My bags done, rebuckled, I hauled them down from the table and started across the marble lobby to the front door, which was really just a missing section of wall through which I could see the white haze of daylight in the parking lot beyond. Then a handsome, well-dressed man in a white suit waved to me. He raised his right hand like he was taking a pledge, dropped it—a desultory (do I imagine it?) disappointed wave.

At the time, I was impressed that Pinheiro could pick me out of the crowd. But I realize now that I couldn't have been hard to miss in my ankle-length khaki skirt, my sensible unfashionable white tennis shoes, my carefully curled hair gone flat. Besides, he had a picture of me in the file.

He greeted me with a smile and a flurry of Portuguese I could not understand. I let loose a flurry of my own corrupted grade-school French, resorting in a pinch to any language foreign.

—*Je m'appelle,* I began, and faltered, then, worse yet, butchering his native tongue, I announced, hand extended with crude American formality, *Estou Ellen,* which would translate, had I bothered to think it through, as, *I am (temporarily) Ellen.*

—*Desculpe,* I said. *Não falo portugues muito bem,* explaining the obvious— that I did not speak the language well.

—*Claro,* he said dryly—*clearly*—and he lifted my suitcase from my hand.

Pinheiro checked his watch, plainly nonplused. He wore a white linen suit, a sky-blue shirt; his thick black hair waved back from his temples and brow; he had a tanned, shapely, clean-shaven face. He was handsome, forty-ish, younger than I'd expected, younger I would learn than the other Rotarians, whose generosity had brought me here. He was an editor at one of the region's oldest and respected newspapers, *A Tarde.* A busy man. He was not a cabbie, and resented being drafted into the role; that seems clear now, though it wasn't then. I see now he had no time for girls who had not mastered his language.

He had the bored, distracted air of handsome men, who do not need to show an interest in women, especially unbeautiful ones. He did not hide his irritation, nor try to. My unfashionably long skirt was rumpled like an old Kleenex. My brightly colored sweater—meant to be attractive, *au courant*— succeeded only in attracting contempt.

—You'll be too hot in that, he said, as we redistributed my bags between us.

So I've been told, I wanted to say. But I could not; language failed me. Or perhaps I failed it: I remembered little of the Portuguese I'd studied in college the year before or during a brief, two-month summer stay in southern Brazil after high school.

Instead, I untied the sweater from my neck and stuffed it in my backpack, and then proceeded to further insult my host by reaching out to carry my second suitcase, which he took and painfully lugged toward the parking lot; I trailed him in silence.

The thin white T-shirt I wore had a round collar, not a V-neck: there was a schoolgirlish modesty to my dress that I had chosen strategically, after deliberation, aiming to impress the Rotarians as reliable, as one who would not take their money and run. I had aimed to impress my hosts as wholesome, as my mother proposed I should, but I could see that I'd impressed Pinheiro as merely unfashionable and therefore irrelevant.

I knew in that moment for the first time that I was unbeautiful and that beauty was a kind of currency here.

It came as something of a shock, his dismissal of me. In the United States I could get away with being attractive, that catch-all phrase for the compelling but unbeautiful. Tall, lanky, with large brown eyes, I'd been told I was a beautiful child, and I had always been well liked in high school, attending every prom; in college, I usually had some boy interested in dating me or some professor proposing we go to bed. I was attractive enough in the bland manner of my mother's English forbears—lantern jawed, with a broad forehead and a face open as the American plains—I had learned early on to make up in wit and aggressive intelligence, in invention and charm, what I lacked in T and A.

My sister Susan was the family beauty—older than me by three years, shorter by four inches, she was five five, slender, olive skinned, marvelously busty from the age of twelve, when not so marvelously grown men began to whisper obscenities to her when the family filed through the bleachers at baseball games, in movie theaters, restaurants. By the age of sixteen, she'd taken to wearing widow's black, dresses fashioned in the forties and pumps; she shellacked her lips bright rebellious red, tired of being ashamed and tormented for her figure, tired of being cast in the role of siren, she played the part; she wore her hair long to the middle of her back, in curls like our Russian grandmother's.

My sister got catcalls. I got asked to the prom. I was the sort of girl you married. The sort of girl who was conscious always that her boyfriends were more beautiful than she. It became one of the many bonds my mother and I shared: our handsomeness, our lack of feminine charms. It was one of the many painful wounds that bound us, my mom and me, scar tissue being the *materia prima* of family.

As Pinheiro and I emerged into the parking lot, the brightness was blinding. I was conscious of the blue sky overhead, the oily sweat on my face and dampness staining my T-shirt beneath my arms. I held my arms tight to my sides, hoping Pinheiro would not notice. It seemed to take forever to reach his white convertible, where Pinheiro in silence opened the trunk, hefted my bag into it, slammed it, unlocked my door.

As he started the engine, I looked at the intense greenery that edged the parking lot, surrounded the airport, against which the grill of the car was stopped—a forest of bamboo and hibiscus and the delicate papery pink and purple beaks of bougainvillea.

As we turned onto a service road flanked by trees, I tried to explain to Pinheiro that I could understand Portuguese, I simply did not speak the language well. I fumbled an attempt at the subjunctive, gave up, and lapsed into the startled, perpetual present tense.

—*Entendo Portuguese*, I said. *Mas não falo bem.* I understand, but I don't speak well.

—*Claro*, Pinheiro said again. Clearly. But this time, he smiled. *Tá bem*, he said. It's fine.

As we merged onto the main road, a wide two-lane open road that ran along the coast past sandy beaches and the open Atlantic, toward the center of town, Pinheiro grew expansive.

He might've been shouting because of the wind that blew through our hair or because he thought volume would aid my understanding. But I understood him perfectly.

Pinheiro spoke lightly of our prospects. As he drove me along the beach, the white sand and blue Atlantic on our left so different, in their sensual entreaty, from their northern counterparts along the Connecticut coast from which I'd come, he apologized for having arrived late at the airport. He'd had a meeting or a deadline at the paper; I was never clear which. Work, though, had delayed him. He had to get back, but he gave me a tour as we drove.

He pointed out things that only later would take on meaning for me, names I heard but did not register or note since these places, these names were as yet innocent of personal memory. Abayaté, Itapoa, Barra. He pointed to a piece of land in the bay and shouted, *Ilha*.

—Ilha, I repeated, to show I understood.

—Ilha de Itaparica.

—Itaparica, I shouted, like a deranged parrot, nodding.

Sunlight glinted off the hood of the car. As the city came into view, Pinheiro pointed out the divided city ahead of us, half of which sat atop a cliff, the other half of which lay at sea level on the beach below. He told me that when the Portuguese had first arrived here in the sixteenth century, they had built this city, the oldest of Brazilian capital cities, on the cliff top as defense against attack by Dutch ships. Now, he said, the city center had spread to the shore below, defense against attack irrelevant.

—When they drop the atomic bomb, he said, smiling, it will not matter where you are.

Praia do Sol

There is no beach at the Praia do Sol hotel, so don't arrive expecting one, as I did. The name's deceptive, as first impressions often are.[1] The Sunny Beach hotel—where I stayed my first week in Brazil, trying to get my bearings, trying to figure out what I was doing here 1,600 miles from the Amazon I'd come to study, 5,200 miles from home—has none. Located halfway between Barra and the city center on the main thoroughfare, Avenida Sete de Setembro, the Praia do Sol is fronted by asphalt, concrete, tar. There is not a beach in sight. Palm and flamboyant trees are entombed in the sidewalk

---

1. In fact, the name's mistaken—I realized twenty years later, when I returned to Bahia and that hotel, that the name, so vivid in my memory, was *wrong* (the hotel's name is actually Bahia do Sol—Bay of the Sun). But since this is memoir, not documentary, it seems truer to record memory's mistakes.

from which they are pulled from time to time, when their roots threaten to break through the cement.

Pinheiro did not approve my choice of hotel. When he asked me approaching the city where I wanted to be dropped, I fished a scrap of paper from the tourist guide I'd brought, where I'd turned down the corner of a page, and told him the Praia do Sol.

He frowned, watching the road. *It's very expensive*, he said.

I wanted to say that I didn't plan on staying long, that it was mid-price actually, neither the most nor the least expensive, that I wanted this small comfort, this modest luxury; it was safer than a student hostel after all, but I couldn't say a thing.

Instead I watched Pinheiro's face, then I watched the road.

He pulled up in front of the hotel, which was small, three-story, white-painted cement, on the main thoroughfare a few miles from the city's center, a nameless urban neighborhood of the sort that crowd the edges of cities and towns, neighborhoods that have no neighbors, no long-term tenants, just short-lease apartment buildings and ill-funded clinics and schools, mid-price tourist hotels and shops selling inessentials, overpriced restaurants catering to those just passing through.

There was no beach in sight. Pinheiro parked. He retrieved my suitcases then he walked me in. I thanked him as he let me pass first through the door, which was held open by a uniformed doorman. I needed Pinheiro. I could not afford to dislike him, that luxury. He had my money after all.

Pinheiro spoke to the hotel clerk behind the black registration desk on my behalf. Then he turned to me and said that I should phone him at his office as soon as I had arranged for an apartment. He would meet me at the nearest bank to sign over my *bolsa*—my fellowship money—then.

Until that time—it was clear—I was on my own.

I was still struggling to formulate the proper phrase in Portuguese to explain that I needed my funds *now* to depart for the Amazon, when he left. Leaving me in the lobby of the Praia do Sol, with the dull recognition that the only person I knew in Salvador, the only person I knew for 5,000 miles in any direction, did not like me.

Had I been one who read, the ensuing solitude might have been easier to bear, but I didn't then, so it wasn't. By the time I'd graduated from high school, I could count on one hand all the books I'd read, excluding those assigned for classes or read before the first grade. Once books lost their pictures, I couldn't see their point and, betrayed, had given them up. Besides, I couldn't concentrate; I often felt a nervous rapping in my brain that I was needed somewhere else. I preferred the impersonal realm of numbers, which had calmed me as a kid, when I raced through math textbooks after school, completing problems as another child might practice shooting basketball hoops. Only the tranquil aesthetic of numbers could hold my attention for long in childhood and youth, which is no doubt why I'd ended up studying economics, which seemed for a time to offer the possibility of a moral application of numeracy. It seemed a perfect marriage: enduring numerical order applied to a human realm.

Now I have forgotten the figures. How many hectares, how many species per day, lost to the ravages of deforestation. I had them memorized then as others might memorize a poem. A catalog of loss. An elegy. In those days I thought everything could be rendered in numbers. After that year, I would realize that the beautiful, comforting symmetry of numbers is sometimes a lie, that things do not always add up.

A porter in a dull brown uniform watched me openly, unsmiling, as we rode the elevator up to my room, as if I were a thing to watch. He opened the door to my room, brought in the bag, and I followed him in. The door fell closed behind us; I heard the lock catch. He crossed to the window and pulled back the curtains with a tearing sound of metal scraping metal, then he clicked on the air conditioner. It roared and blew lukewarm air. He walked over to the small waist-high refrigerator on the far side of the room and opened it to show me the small bottles and wrapped sweets and bags of nuts it contained. He closed the refrigerator door and crossed to the bed. Then he stood there. He looked at me. He leaned over and tested the bed with his palm. He seemed disinclined to go. I went to the door and opened it. *Obrigado*, I said, thanking him. He waited. *'Brigado*, I said again. He stared at me. I began to feel uneasy. There seemed to be no one else on this floor of the hotel. Just him and me. Then I got it. I pulled out an American dollar. Handed it to him. He put the key on the bedside table. Left without a word.

I crossed the room to stand at the window, looking down at the street two stories below. It was an unpromising view of a gray and ugly street. I saw no point in palm trees and sunny skies. I had always dreaded vacations, especially summer's cheerful vacuity. I had no appreciation for the sensual then. It seemed a distraction from the more serious business of setting history straight. As long as I had a map, a goal, a destination, I was fine, but I was marooned in time, lost when steeped in it, forced to linger there.

I sat on the bed, backing myself against the headboard for support, my knees pulled to my chest. The room was grim. A murky unsavory orange light filtered through the brown curtains, the carpet was short and brown. Across the room, a dresser was set beneath a large rectangular mirror which reflected the brown quilt of the bed on which I sat. I looked at myself in the mirror.

You might expect the girl to cry, to shower, to masturbate, to read a book, smoke a cigarette, go for a walk, get a cup of coffee or a drink or a meal, but she does none of those things, that girl I once was. They don't occur to her. She knows how to analyze a passage from one of Shakespeare's tragedies, how to calculate the marginal rate of return or utility for a given set of variables, how to acquit herself well in a three-hour essay exam on the subject of Stalinist Russia, *El Cid*, or the codification of social mores concomitant with the rise of the European nation state in the twelfth century, how to identify forty slides of Renaissance art and discuss an Edda.

The girl in that room (it is shocking to realize this) has never had an orgasm, never touched herself, would not—if you suggested it—have known how. Which is not to say she is a virgin. She has in fact slept with a number of young men, fallen hard with two—her first high school boyfriend and a Brazilian she met as an exchange student four years ago in Porto Alegre, the capitol of Brazil's southernmost state—both of whom proposed marriage in earnest, which she in earnest declined.

She keeps a tally of these—proposals of marriage and boys she has bedded. By the time she stops counting at the age of twenty-five, she will be four for seven, which she will consider good odds. Though what they are good for she can't imagine. Though she can't recall the surnames of some of these boys she goes to bed with, she feels the count is important to keep. She relies on numbers, though they do not tell her much. On the whole, the territory of her body is foreign ground.

Instead the girl I once was stretches out on the bed and sleeps and when she wakes hungry from bad dreams in the early evening in a foreign city in a foreign country in a foreign language she forages in the minibar so she will not have to leave this room.

She squats by the little refrigerator, with the door open, letting the cool foggy air and the light spill out onto her face and chest, and balancing on the balls of her bare feet, squatting, she eats unfamiliar sweets indiscriminately. She unwraps from its crunchy thin cellophane something reddish and fleshy, tastes it with the tip of her tongue. It is grainy and tart, floral smelling (it will be weeks before she learns this is *goiaba*—guava paste). She tears open a foil package of cashews, pours them in her palm and covers her mouth with it.

Later, she will worry that the hotel staff will notice all the candy she has eaten. This shame is eventually what will drive her out into the street a day from now. The fear, the shame, of being found out, discovered to be hungry.

Amazon Snapshot #1

I first heard the Amazon described in numbers. In volume of water. Acres of land. In measurable loss. The statistics on rates of species loss, of hectares of "virgin" forest converted to ranchland or silviculture or farmland or cut through by logging roads were a litany both impressive and appalling, frightening and compelling. It was the sort of clear moral challenge certain people cleave to in their twenties, or at least to which I cleaved. The Brazilian Amazon was a forest under siege. I wanted to defend it against ravishment.

It's easy now to question my motives. To wonder if my concern for the forest's survival was merely misplaced fear for myself.

My family was not an emotional lot. History, politics, science, and art were the only subjects worthy of emotion in our house; the personal we did not bother with, or rather, my mother, who was the standard bearer, our paragon, did not evince emotion, and so we tried to follow suit; she did not cry out when, by accident, she plunged a knitting needle clean through her palm; she spoke equanimously: "Call 911," she said.

We did not tell stories over dinner, tell jokes, laugh or cry; we debated politics and history and the relative merits of films; we discussed the lamentable loss of precision in the English language (*irregardless* substituted for *irrespective* or *regardless of*, *comprised* used to mean *composed*, *impacted* used as adjective or verb to refer to other than teeth).

It would be easy to imagine that my feelings for the forest were merely displacement then, as I sometimes thought my mother's increased interest in PBS nature shows were. After I, their youngest, left home for college I noticed that my mother watched more and more programs on extinction, and that when we spoke she often spoke of these. Perhaps it was simply an increase in public awareness of the issue in the 1980s, but I could not help but wonder—as my mother recited her litany of loss (the black rhino, the African elephant)—if this were not simply how she suffered loss, by proxy.

Cruel Dilemmas of Development

It was a full forty-eight hours before I got up the nerve to leave my hotel room and even then I left with regret. I imagine that I was driven out by hunger, but loneliness may have overtaken me instead. I was alone after all, and knew no one for 5,000 miles in any direction. I did not know how to make an international call; I did not know the language well enough.

More likely I was afraid the hotel staff were beginning to suspect me of eccentricity or worse. It was a small hotel with few guests at the time and I was conspicuous as a young woman alone will be. I imagined that my disinclination to leave my room was the subject of discussion at the front desk and among the maids who tried, unsuccessfully, to gain access to the room that morning in order to change the linens. The prospect that I might be considered odd, talked about by hotel staff, would have terrified, inspired rash action.

Then again, maybe I was merely practical. My cash would not last long. I needed to find an apartment before I could call Pinheiro and open a bank account. I could not even read the want ads. I needed to learn Portuguese; I needed help; I needed to find some.

Had I been able to learn the language from bad TV, I might have stayed in my hotel room for days, but I couldn't understand even that. It was a babble of sounds and then laugh track, interrupted by the sonorous voice of the announcer proclaiming—as if he were heralding the Rapture—*Rede Globo*, the station's identification.

My *Fodor's* included a section on language schools, which listed one on Sete de Setembro, where my hotel was. The school's address was not much different from the hotel's; it appeared to be right up the street. I sat on the edge of the bed and pulled out the pulpy phone directory from the bedside table and looked up the school in its pages.

I needed in those days a clear destination, a reason to move, or I wouldn't. I was paralyzed by my faith in utility. I wouldn't get out of bed unless I had a place to go, something that needed doing. Truth was, I was afraid of making a wrong move, wanting the wrong thing, and so had given up on instinct and desire, weaned myself, and operated solely—or so I hoped—by reason.

In college, my rational planning had been effective. I made lists and stuck to them: I kept lists of foods I could eat and list of those I couldn't; lists of calories and class assignments and library book call numbers, distances swum or run, my weight, the titles of articles I wanted to read and the volume numbers for the scientific journals in which I could find them. I was accustomed to lectures, to bells that told me when a class began and ended, to gymnasium tracks with their measured distances, pools in 50-meter lengths, calorie counting, scales, grades, exams, IQs.

I had to tell myself to shower, brush my teeth. To rise for the simple pleasure of rising into another day was beyond me then. So I welcomed the excuse the language school provided to get out.

I flipped through the phone book, located the name and number of the school. I wrote the number on a pad of paper by the phone. Below this I scribbled down a phrase in Portuguese, writing out each word, erasing, rewriting, correcting the line, working out the sequence, repeating it a few times aloud (whispering so as not to risk being overheard by a passing bellhop or maid, who might think I was talking to myself, as I was), before risking the call.

Then I dialed.

I heard an angry buzz at the other end of the line. A burr of sound. It sounded like a busy signal and I considered hanging up.

—*Pronto,* someone said on the other end of the line. Or maybe I misremember and she said, *Diga,* Speak.

I would have been caught off guard, whatever she said. It is one of the disappointments of the international traveler that people in life do not speak as they do on language tapes. No one ever asks you, *Where is the municipal pool?* or *Where is Robert?* They do not answer the phone by saying, *Allo, Como vai voce?* They bark. They say, *Diga,* Speak. And you must, and I did.

—*Is it that this is the school for languages?* I must have asked, in my most convoluted Portuguese. I mistook convolution for a sign of good breeding then, recognizing (though not consciously) that indirection is a luxury, an option only for those to whom need is remote, for whom there is no urgency, those who can afford to be misunderstood or whom others are obliged to understand.

—*Não falo ingles,* she said, no doubt recognizing my accent.

—*Quero saber,* I pressed on, *a hora de fechar, por favor.* What time do you close?

She got the gist and told me, *Dezasseis.*

—*Repete, por favor?*

—*Dez-e-seis,* she said.

I broke the word down: Ten and six. Sixteen. Four o'clock.

—*Obrigada,* I said.

—*De nada,* she drawled, It's nothing. Her tone suggested that I, not it, was nothing.

It was about two in the afternoon, when I set out for the English school, hoping to find someone there who could help me.

The hotel clerk in his tan uniform behind the registration desk may have raised a hand and called out, gently, Senhorita, as I passed. He may have waved to me and said, *Por favor, momento,* Please, a minute with you. He would have been a small man, with dark hair and brown face, perhaps a pencil-thin mustache; he would, I am sure of it, have been tiny (Bahians were—their heads came to my shoulders, their bodies seemed child-sized, or rather I—among them—seemed a hypothalamic freak, a giantess).

He would have been easy to miss, in any case. And I did. If the desk clerk waved to me, I did not note it. If he tried to signal to me to leave my key, to keep my valuables and documents in the hotel safe, if he tried, in short, to *warn* me, I missed it, as I so often missed the warning signs in those days, as we tend to miss such things when we feel ourselves insulated from consequences, remote from harm. When we do not feel we will suffer from our ignorance, it is easy—convenient even—to remain so.

I pushed out through the double doors of the Praia do Sol into the brilliant too-brilliant light of a tropical Brazilian January day. I experienced a sudden flashbulb blindness and then the world around me began to take shape. A cobblestone sidewalk lay directly in front of me; beyond it lay the street; the hotel awning spread over my head. Along the sidewalk were palms, and flame trees, and *oitizeiro.* The broad two-lane boulevard of Avenida Sete de Setembro, the main thoroughfare through town that traced the coastline like a black magic marker from the city center to the beachside suburb of Barra, was clogged with cars.

Across the street stood cement buildings of a modest height and boxy modern design that once had been called modular and thought a sign of progress. By the 1980s, when I saw them, they had a grim hard cast, sooty and worn, reminding passersby that the hope that prompted their construction had faded now, worn thin.

The street reeked of diesel, city smells. I could not smell the sea, could not glimpse it from here. From where I stood, I wouldn't have known it was there, that vastness, just the other side of the buildings I faced, just beyond those tired structures.

In 1967, five years after I was born, Thomas Skidmore had written of Brazilians' abiding faith that their nation would become a first-world power, a status they sought to secure in part through development of the Amazon. In 1980, shortly before I arrived in Bahia, Sylvia Ann Hewlett published *Cruel Dilemmas of Development,* describing the process by which the developing nations of Latin America, in the twentieth century, had ravaged their citizenry and land in order to industrialize. Hewlett argued that capital is a necessary prerequisite for industrialization. For the empires of Europe, industrializing in the eighteenth and nineteenth centuries, the necessary capital had come from wealth shipped back from colonies abroad. Raw materials, plundered treasures, and the slave trade made it possible to industrialize the capitals of Europe. For the United States, which lacked colonies to exploit, that necessary capital had come from the American frontier and the forced labor of slaves.

For Latin American nations trying to industrialize in the late twentieth century, Hewlett claimed, the only way to capitalize was at the expense of their own people, to siphon off surplus from an already impoverished populace, and by borrowing from international banks. If the necessary surplus could not be stolen abroad, extracted from colonies or slaves, it would come from the citizens themselves. A nation ambitious of industrialization and development would sell whatever it had to sell—a forest, a generation, its people, the future.

But I wasn't thinking about Hewlett or history then. I was thinking about getting a snack, a late lunch. But first I would go to the language school, where I hoped to find someone who spoke enough English to help me arrange for a tutor in Portuguese, and maybe a newspaper, and, with any luck, a restaurant catering to tourists like me.

Language Lessons

As I walked north along Avenida Sete de Setembro toward the city center, the late afternoon breeze was hot in my face and stained with diesel exhaust. The wind was flecked with soot and grit that got under my contacts, so that I had to blink and then stop and blink some more. I could hear cars and trucks driving by in the street and the slap of palm fronds overhead.

When I could see clearly again, I walked on, passing under the dangling leaves of the oitizeiros and the red floral streamers of the flamboyant, through the cool darkness pooling beneath them and into brightness again. Around me, people talked and called to one another, but I did not understand them.

I should have known the language better. I had been to southern Brazil three years earlier as an exchange student on a brief summer program after high school. My interest in Brazil, which in time would give rise to my study of the Amazon, had been forged that first stay, where I'd lived with a fatherless, educated, middle-class family—a widowed mother, grandparents, daughter, son—in a three-bedroom flat in Porto Alegre, the capital city of Brazil's southernmost state, Rio Grande de Sul.

The Simões family, with whom I'd stayed, were kind, devout, intellectual, dry, and though I'd liked them, I felt in their midst the loneliness of one who is among strangers intimate with one another. I discovered there the loneliness of those who do not know or like themselves. Solitude is tolerable only for those who enjoy their own company, which I did not yet. I was treated with the courtesy shown a guest; I was not beloved; I was not known. I did not know myself.

My boyfriend that summer—a handsome Brazilian named Paulinho—had proposed to teach me Portuguese, but I was a lousy student; it was not that I lacked facility, but I was afraid to care. Or rather, I could care deeply about distant matters—as later I would care about saving the forest—but I was reticent to want something for myself, having seen how caring had undone my mom, whose devotion to my philandering dad had trapped her in a marriage and motherhood she openly regretted.

Paulinho had the eagling Mediterranean beauty I'd expected of Brazilians but which I'd later learn was untypical in the southern part of the country, which had been settled—like the northern United States—largely by immigrants from Europe. His skin was the color of hazelnuts, his eyes dark as wet river stones; he looked East Indian, maybe Spanish; he had jet-black hair cut a military length, glossy as an animal's pelt, and the body of a tennis champion, which he was.

We'd met at a soccer banquet at the family's church, one early evening in mid-June, approaching the winter solstice, when the evening sky was a Prussian blue and radiant, as if there were a light on the other side of evening, behind that scrim of sky. I had been to church before in Minnesota, where the Christians I knew were Protestants and most of those were Lutheran; Catholicism was utterly foreign, glamorous, a thing I associated dimly with JFK and Ireland, Renaissance art, Saint Augustine and martyrs.

After the service, my host sister Luciene had led me toward the front of the church and through a door to the right of the chancel into a fluorescent-lit back room, where it appeared a dinner was to be held. Folding tables filled the room, covered in red-and-white checked tablecloths, surrounded by folding chairs. It had the feel of a rec hall, the bright bars of the overhead lights, the cement floor, the pale tint of the walls. (This was how I would think of Catholicism after that—as a series of hidden rooms that you were led to by initiates; it seemed a secretive religion to me then and lovelier for this.)

I had been asked to present Paulinho with a medal that evening, and standing close to him, I could smell his cologne, faint and tart. I didn't know boys who wore perfume then and it surprised me. He was my height or an inch shorter, five nine or eight. His lashes were so thick it looked as if he wore eyeliner.

I raised my arms over his neck and hung the ribbon on his chest. My face was hot.

—*Obrigado,* he said, gently.

—*De nada,* I said, It's nothing.

I had turned away to head back to my table, relieved to have my duty discharged, when the others began to shout what sounded like the name of a movie theater, *Bijou, Bijou,* which later I would learn had been *beijo,* meaning, "a kiss."

I turned back in confusion to the dark-eyed guy I'd given the medal to and saw that he had resumed his seat. He held up a hand, palm forward, to silence the others. He shook his head no, his face canted toward the table, away from me. But the blue-eyed guy next to him mimed a loud smacking kiss and pushed his dark-eyed teammate up out of his seat and so, seeing that I was still there, he stood, reluctantly. He set a hand on each of my arms and said, in clear, accented, very good English,

—They want you to kiss me.

He looked strained, as if he were delivering sad news—your fly is open— something as embarrassing for him to explain as for me to hear. It was a relief to hear English, though his smile was stiff; he seemed as mortified as I to be the focus of this spectacle. I could see his Adam's apple bob as he swallowed.

—*Como assim*, he said, Like this.

He leaned toward me, stiffly, and kissed my right cheek, then my left, then kissed my right cheek once more.

—*Tres*, he said, *pra casar*.

I must've looked confused.

—Three, he translated, for marriage. Then he released a smile perfect as caps, pure as pheromones.

Later that night, Paulinho told me that he ran each day and asked if I would like to join him some morning. He could draw up a series of calisthenics for us and we could run a few miles. I was not an athlete, and had been dead last and nauseated at the conclusion of every cross-country meet my senior year of high school (though this may have had something to do with our math-teacher coach, who insisted on driving his sedan slowly alongside us as we ran our route, shouting instructions and encouragement through his open car window, demoralizing for all concerned).

I did not need to train, as Paulinho did, in preparation for competition. But I liked the idea of training. It sounded purposeful. We sought out rules and regimens in those days, Paulinho and I. We believed that they would bring us all we wanted.

Ordem e Progresso is the motto on the Brazilian flag—Order and Progress. Someone presented me with a flag that first summer in Porto Alegre, and I have it somewhere, folded, the way flags are folded and given to the widow of a soldier. The motto of the nation was our motto on the cusp of adulthood—as we stood on those rickety untried porch planks. We believed in this simple credo: Order and Progress.

And so it was that we began to run. Paulinho pulled out a map and traced a route for us, clocking the precise distance in his car. He made up a list of calisthenics for me, based on those of the Air Force, and these I did each morning before I went to see him. I did jumping jacks, sit-ups, wimpy push-ups, bent in half.

In the mornings, around 8, I would walk to his apartment building, which was four or five blocks from that of the Simões, just beyond the church, and find him suited up in nylon sweat pants and a jacket, color coordinated, with some sort of racing stripe. Dapper even to sweat.

We would start out slow, jogging through the neighborhood streets, past the corner grocery, past the rec center with its cracked cement basketball court, out to the river that was channeled through town by cement walls between highways. We ran on sidewalks, among cars, exhaust in our nostrils, the water beside us glinting brown, the sky white. I usually felt light-headed, faint, as we ran, a slight buzzing in my forehead and sinuses from what I assumed was monoxide poisoning. My face grew red, and my body's temperature showed through my skin as I sought to release heat, but I liked the exertion.

Discipline was our watchword. *Order and progress.* I didn't grasp the irony of the slogan then: Brazil was ruled by a military dictatorship at the time, as it would be for twenty-one years after a 1964 CIA-backed coup overthrew the democratically elected President João Goulart in order to stabilize the country for economic development; I didn't yet see how costly such logic could be. When I arrived at Paulinho's house for our morning run, I often found him at the dining table memorizing a list of vocabulary words. I admired this. His regimens. His constant efforts at self-improvement. I didn't yet know that there were lovelier ways to live.

But Paulinho did not seem rigid then. He radiated sensuality, the athlete's ease. His body gave him pleasure; he delighted in it. With him, I began to take delight in my own.

It is odd to think of him now—now that I know him well—and to remember when I did not yet know him at all, when I did not yet know the soft sandy texture of his tongue in my mouth, the feel of his teeth against mine, the way he looked surprised when he laughed, startled by happiness, his eyes crinkling at the corners with delight.

It's odd now to think there was a time when I did not know the hard planes of his chest, the swell beneath his jeans that he knew to draw against the ridge of my pubic bone as we stood nights fully clothed, oblivious of our clothing, in the kitchen of the Simões' around midnight, the house seemingly asleep except for us, my back against the counter beside the kitchen sink, our hands tangled in one another's hair and clothes, as Paulinho drew his hips up into mine, over and over, till we were both breathing fast and a little faint and one or the other of us, usually him, said, *I have to go, It's time to go.* I would walk him to the door then and open it and trail him into the hall and down the five steps to the foyer, our hands clasped, kissing his neck as I trailed him, kissing his mouth, till we reached the outer door which I'd unlock and he'd pass through, stepping into the drive, and I'd watch him walk to his car, watch him turn back to wave to me, blow me a kiss, and then I'd go back in and close and lock the doors and slip into the kitchen and stand in front of the fridge, tug on the metal door handle, hoping to keep its hinges quiet, and feel its cool refrigerated breath pour over me, as I stared into the anemic glow, finding there on the metal grates that served as racks nothing to satisfy this hunger.

Somewhere, in a box in a closet in my childhood home, there is a photo of Paulinho; probably the Brazilian flag is there as well. I have just one photo of him, taken on the last day of that first summer together. He leans against his red VW bug, his left elbow propped on its roof, his head tilted fetchingly against his left fist. His right arm bends to clasp his slender waist. The outline of his pecs is visible beneath the cream tennis shirt he wears.

He grins hugely, as if he were about to break into a laugh. His eyes fold at the corners in delight. His hips sway to right, like Praxiteles' famous sculpture of Hermes; his left leg crosses in front of his right, balancing on the toe of a tennis shoe. His short black hair has grown out a little from its military cut and is maybe half an inch long, lustrous and glossy.

Paulinho is smiling out at me, giving me his lopsided smile. And why not? He is young, beautiful, promising, happy; he is a state champion and his life is before him and he is—we both are—so hopeful. He looks like he is advertising something: youth or promise.

In the three and a half years since I'd seen Paulinho last, I'd lost track of my desires, eating and bedding indiscriminately. I'd grown accustomed to sleeping with boys I felt nothing for. My eating had become pointlessly regimented, then at times indiscriminate. In desire's absence, I swam and starved and studied with a numb rigor.

Desire and the body's pleasures were foreign ground. I never considered that I might live there, call it home. Perhaps that's why I always needed a destination—like the language school I was walking toward.

Whatever else I'd come back to Brazil to do, I'd come hoping to see Paulinho. I had come back to Brazil to revive desire. I had returned to save myself as much as the forest, though I didn't know that then.

The English language school in Salvador was brown and blockish, four stories tall, with smoked-glass walls enclosing its ground-floor. I entered through glass doors and stepped into a chill, dim, air-conditioned lobby.

It was shadowy and hard to see inside after the bright light of the day. There seemed to be no one there. As my eyes adjusted, I could see glass-enclosed classrooms and a broad flight of stairs that led up to another floor.

To my right was a reception area, a reception desk, a few chairs, and a table covered in Brazilian magazines—*Veja, Manchete.*

The receptionist seated behind the desk seemed shadowy and insubstantial, like a figure from Greek myth, gatekeeper to some chthonic world. She looked bored.

I told her in my pidgin Portuguese that I wanted to take lessons. She told me that I couldn't. It was a holiday. The staff—if I understood her correctly— were on vacation. She was the only one there. I wanted to ask about a private tutor, but I didn't know how to ask. I didn't speak enough Portuguese for that.

It was clear that I would have to seek my teachers elsewhere.

Or learn the hard way—by error and by trial.

Prufrock in Paradise

In the space of my first five days in Brazil, I would be robbed; I would be poisoned.

But that day in Salvador, I knew none of this. None of it had happened yet because I had not left my room. Since arriving in Brazil three days before, I had hidden there (except for my brief trip to the language school the previous day), afraid to venture forth, dining on candies in the minibar as if waiting for someone to invite me out, a girl waiting for permission to enter the world.

But the morning after I visited the language school, I woke fortified by a good night's sleep with the courage to go down to breakfast: I dared to eat a mango. I rose a little after seven and pulled open the curtains, letting in a watery white light. At this hour, the air outside in the street was still cool. The sun was a soft angled glow, not the hard brightness it would gain as it rose in the sky toward noon. The sky, above the buildings that faced my hotel, was a robin's egg blue, delicate, almost friendly.

I showered quickly and dressed in khaki mid-thigh-length shorts and a gauzy shirt. I put on my tennis shoes and cinched around my hips a money belt, in which I tucked my passport, my driver's license, and $150 cash (the remainder of my money—$250 in traveler's cheques—I stowed at the very bottom of my suitcase beneath the orange sweater I had worn so proudly two days before). I planned to carry this pouch of cash and documents with me whenever I went out, in case someone should break into my room. I carried my camera too, just to play it safe.

The travel guides I had skimmed warned of the danger of theft, and just before I'd flown down here there had been a much-publicized murder in Rio, in which a German tourist was killed after he was found to have no money to give the thieves who had held him up at gunpoint. They were children, as I recall. They had shot the man for spite.

The *Times* had run the story on the front page. In Salvador, where poverty was among the most severe in this impoverished nation, I had been warned to carry a small amount of pocket change wherever I went so that, should I be held up, I'd have something to offer. If you had nothing, you could get hurt: thieves had been known to cut faces with a razor blade, enraged to find their mark without money. Like the mad money young women of my mother's generation kept on them in case they got angry at their dates, this money had a nickname too, in English: mugger money.

I took the stairs down to the lobby, where the cafe was separated from the main lobby by folding screens. There were eight or ten small tables there, covered in white linen. Only one was occupied, by a couple speaking a language I could not make out, neither Portuguese nor English. Breakfast came with my room, and I was glad to take advantage of it, but I was embarrassed to eat alone. I stood at the entrance a little uncertainly until a waiter came over and extended his arm toward the room in a gesture that suggested I could choose my place. I took a table by the window, far from the entrance and lobby.

As I took my seat, the waiter gave my chair a little shove toward the table, which, though meant to be a courtesy, felt like what it was—a shove from behind.

—*Quer café?* he asked, when I was seated.

I nodded, pleased to understand the offer of coffee.

—*Por favor,* I said. Please.

—*Americano or com leite?* he asked.

I was not sure what he meant by *americano,* which translated literally as "one who is American," but I was sure he couldn't mean me, so I opted for *com leite* (with milk).

—*Temos também sucos,* he said. *Suco de laranja, de abacaxí, de manga, de maracujá, e de tomate. O que quer?*

I was stumped by his flurry of words. *Laranja* was orange, *tomate* was tomato. I could not make out the rest.

—*Repete, por favor,* I said, embarrassed to have to ask him to repeat himself.

—*Pois não,* he said. Of course. *Temos sucos . . .* He spoke slowly and loudly and I felt ashamed to be subject to this speech, but I listened, watching his lips as if that would help me comprehend. I hazarded a guess, like a game-show contestant.

—*Quero laranja,* I said.

—*Suco de laranja, 'ta certo?*

—*Suco de laranja.* I nodded, unsure what I was agreeing to. The waiter, apparently satisfied, turned and left me there.

I thought I had secured coffee with milk and orange juice and I waited, braced to weather egg options, when, to my relief, the waiter returned with a lovely cup of milky coffee, fresh-squeezed orange juice, a basket of warm fragrant rolls and a plate of sliced fruit—pineapple, mango, bananas, slices of pale green melon.

—*Obrigado,* I said, thanking him.

—*Número de quarto?* he asked.

I looked at him. Clearly this was not an egg option. *Número* was number. *Quarto,* room. But why would the guy want my room number? What did he think I was?

—*Número,* he repeated, loudly, as if I were deaf. The people at the other table looked over as if I were causing this commotion. He pointed to the ceiling, poking at it. *Quarto,* he said, louder still. *Pra pagar,* he was shouting now. He pulled out the check, showed me the place on it where he must write the room number.

—*Preciso. Número. De. Quarto,* he said again, slowly, loudly.

I nodded. I knew now what he was asking, but I didn't know how to say it in Portuguese, or rather, I did, but I had temporarily forgotten how to count. Me, the student of economics. Me, the girl in love with numbers.

—*Entendo,* I managed. *Mas, não sei como dizer.* I pointed to the pen in his pocket. *Por favor.* I couldn't remember the word for pen.

He handed it to me. I wrote on my napkin three numerals. My room number.

—*Obrigado,* he said, sighing, with an almost imperceptible wag of his head. And then he went to gather the dishes from the table of the other guests who had left their chairs and me alone here.

I opened my cloth napkin and lay it across my lap, conscious of each move I made and how it might look to others were they to observe me. I felt observed even when I was not. I felt observed even though there was no one there to observe me but me.

I tried to focus on the things before me: the shiny heavy stainless cutlery, the white tablecloth, the thick plain china, the pads of iced butter set out on a plate, the basket of rolls. I reached across the table, careful not to drag my sleeve in my coffee or fruit plate. I clasped a small hard roll. I put it on my bread plate, stabbed a pad of butter with my fork and scraped that onto my bread plate too. I cracked the shell of the crusty roll as if it were an enormous yellow egg. I set half of the roll on the plate; half, I held in my left hand. I lifted my butter knife, cut half a pat of butter, slathered it on the soft white interior of the roll in my hand. I proceeded slowly, carefully, unhurriedly, as if I were conducting a public service announcement on how to butter a roll.

I chewed slowly, conscious of each clench of my jaw, each swallow, each tumbling crumb. I ate, conscious of the waiter in the corner loitering by the coffeepot. I ate, self-conscious to the point of anguish. Each bite, a drag. I cut a tiny square of fruit with the side of my fork, fearful of cutting inexpertly and sending a slice of mango or melon onto the floor. I cut and chewed, cut and chewed, cut and chewed, cut and chewed.

After two rolls and a glass of juice, a cup of coffee and maybe a dozen bites of fruit, I was exhausted. I was relieved to push back my chair and leave. I considered pocketing a few rolls to eat in private, but I was afraid that the waiter, who had temporarily abandoned his post by the coffee pot, would catch me. I comforted myself that at this rate I was sure to lose weight. As I took the stairs back to my room, I calculated calories burned.

Amazon Snapshot #2

In 1984—the year I flew down to Brazil to study in the Amazon—scientists at the National Institute for Amazonian Research calculated that the rain forest had half a century to live, roughly what actuarial tables at the time gave as my remaining life span.

Precise figures on the rate of rain forest destruction were difficult to come by, but predictions about the future of the world's tropical moist forests were uniformly grim. A 1980 report for the Committee on Research Priorities in Tropical Biology of the National Research Council stated that "all tropical moist forests could be destroyed within less than 40 years," given the loss of almost 50 hectares per minute. Dr. Peter Raven, chairman of the committee was "convinced that 95% of the forests will be converted within 25 to 30 years," expecting the remainder to persist only for a few more decades.

The Amazon was especially at risk: *Science* magazine reported at the time that "an area the size of Massachusetts was being permanently converted every month." And *National Geographic* claimed that "if deforestation continues at its present rate, the equatorial rain forest ecosystem of the Amazon Basin might disappear almost entirely by the year 2000." (A fate temporarily avoided in part by rain forest activism, which temporarily slowed deforestation in the 1980s and early 1990s. Some 83 percent remains as of this writing, though recent leaps in deforestation rates suggest that the Amazon is in grave danger—again.)

Sixty-five million years of evolution might be destroyed in the course of fifty.

The greenhouse effect was not part of popular parlance in the early 1980s, nor was global warming. (The National Academy of Sciences undertook its first major study of global warming in 1979, at the request of President Carter.) Global climate change—that misleadingly quaint phrase, which suggests we're in for nothing more than a change of weather (and who, in America, doesn't like a change?)—hadn't come into usage. (In the margins of my college research paper, my professor asked, "Will [a two-degree rise in average global temperature] be <u>enough</u> of a change to melt polar ice?")

But those of us who'd heard of global warming knew it meant this: increased fossil-fuel burning, coupled with massive deforestation, could result in a shift in the balance of the world's stock of oxygen and carbon dioxide, raising the level of heat-trapping gases in the atmosphere, which in turn could trigger a disastrous warming of the world.

Before the turn of the century, the argument went, 40 percent of the land surface along the equator had been forested: tropical rain forests served as both a sink for carbon dioxide and a source of oxygen. Increased burning of hydrocarbon fuels and wood, coupled with rapid deforestation, had resulted in a rise in CO_2 over the last century from 290 to 330 parts per million, with more than a fifth of the rise occurring in the previous decade (the 1970s) alone. By the turn of the next century—that is, by 2001—CO_2 concentration was expected to rise 30 percent higher than its 1960 level.

"For many," I wrote in a term paper in 1981, "these figures are alarming . . . A major rise in CO_2 level of the atmosphere conceivably will raise the average global temperature by a degree in two decades, and by two degrees within 70 years. . . . Polar ice masses might partially melt, raising sea levels by five to eight meters, inundating coastal areas currently inhabited by a large portion of the world's population. Such a rise in temperature could lead to expansion of the world's deserts pole-ward . . . Changes in global patterns of . . . precipitation could trigger an irreversible process of desertification, affecting even the grain belt of the American Midwest."

There was debate about the role of tropical moist forests in the equation. But few scientists debated global warming's potentially disastrous consequences.

The Beach

When I got back to my hotel room, I put on my bathing suit, over which I pulled a T-shirt and khaki shorts. My skin prickled with the unfamiliar feel of air against it. At the time I was tall and relatively slender, coltish at five feet nine, 135 pounds, but I felt ungainly—fleshy and pale; I dreaded bathing suits almost as much as I dreaded nakedness.

But today, I thought, I will be brave; today, I will go to the beach.

As a rule, at twenty-one, I did not like beaches. Or rather, I liked to walk along them but I had never gotten the hang of sunbathing, which seemed to me at twenty-one an inordinately dull form of recreation (recreation itself being a category I found inordinately dull). Sunbathing—like sex (it seemed to me then)—was hot, sweaty, and boring, an uncomfortable stint on one's back, a waste of precious minutes that might better be spent in more fruitful pursuits, but I reasoned that in no time at all I would be in the Amazon, where there would be no coastal beaches, some 1,000 miles inland from the Atlantic coast; I should take advantage of this opportunity.

Taking advantage of one's opportunities was a watchword of my clan and the American middle class from which I'd come. It was among the principal tenets of our secular faith, along with the edifying aspects of painful experience. We believed in making the most of what we were given; we believed in learning from our mistakes (this last at odds with the tenet that said we shouldn't make any: education, solid reading, and forethought should obviate these).

I laced my feet into tennis shoes and cinched my money belt once more onto my waist. Then it occurred to me that perhaps I shouldn't take *all* my money with me. For a moment I debated the options: if I hid my money in my suitcase, it could be stolen while I was out. If I carried it with me, I could be held up and lose it all.

I decided to outwit my prospective assailants by settling on a compromise. I would carry a beach bag (stuffed with a towel and suntan oil) and a plastic bag (containing my room key, passport, and student ID)—nothing of interest to thieves. In my money belt, I placed only enough *cruzeiros* to pay bus fare and pay off any muggers. The rest of my cash and traveler's cheques I hid in the sole of my tennis shoe. Should I be mugged, I could hand over my *cruzeiros* without anyone ever suspecting that I was carrying $400 dollars in my shoe!

And I was ready for my day at the beach.

At the hotel front desk, I leaned my elbows on the black marble counter and asked where the nearest beach was. The clerk—another tiny man—told me that Barra had a nice beach and was nearby, just a few kilometers from here, down Avenida Sete de Setembro. I remembered the name as one Pinheiro had mentioned as he drove me here.

I asked if I could catch a bus to Barra, though I said this wrong—using the verb *tomar* instead of *pegar*—and it came out sounding as if I was asking if I can drink or seize the bus. I tried again, more simply.

—The bus goes there? I asked.

He nodded. *Vai,* he said, his voice gaining volume, like the waiter's. *Mas tem pegar no outro lado;* he pointed across the street where a small crowd is gathered.

—*Lá,* he said, there.

I thanked him and pushed out through the doors and crossed the street to where the crowd awaited the bus. At the stop, I asked a woman next to me whether I could catch the bus to Barra here, just to make sure I was in the right place and because I knew now how to ask: *Posso pegar o ônibus pra Barra aqui?*

The woman was short, the crown of her head on level with my small breasts. When she looked up at me, I saw she had tiny eyes.

—*Pôde,* she said. The word, in her mouth, sounded jointed, two-syllabled: it sounded like *paw-gee,* drawn out, like a hen squawking. I wondered if she was from the interior, one of the numerous poor who came from the countryside—the vast *sertão*—to the coastal cities to find work but often didn't. She had the slightly vacant expression of people who have spent a long time looking out across empty spaces, as if it were hard to focus the eyes on nearby things.

The skin of her face was lined and tanned. Her dark hair was pulled back in a loose bun, threaded with gray. Perhaps thirty-five, she looked already old. Her face had the softness of age, like apple flesh. A basket hung from her arm, and she wore a thin cotton dress printed with blue flowers, gray from wear. The shelf of her bosom sagged over her sash to meet the soft shelf of her belly. It's odd how vivdly she lingers in my memory, the sort of figure—as James Baldwin once said—that the mind fastens on when more crucial matters are at stake.

—*Obrigada,* I said.

—*Nada,* she returned, and squinted once more into the street.

As the bus pulled up, streaming a plume of black diesel smoke, the matron set her palm on my forearm.

—*Este,* she said, looking up into my face. *Este vai pra Barra, entendeu?* Understand? she asked, and I did: This bus goes to Barra.

The others at the stop formed a neat orderly line when the bus pulled up, and unhurriedly we boarded at the back. At the turnstile, the cashier asked me for my fare, but I didn't know how much it was, unaccustomed as yet to the unfamiliar currency.

—*Posso?* the matron asked, May I? She opened my palm and picked among the change and then we pushed into the crush of bodies already crowding the seats and aisle. I clasped the metal handrail overhead and hung on. A man stood to offer the woman his seat.

I felt almost heroic as we rode along the wide avenue. Each small exchange, a victory: discovering which bus runs to Barra (only later would I learn that all buses bound west from here go through Barra), getting on, fishing out coins for fare, riding.

Over the heads of the other passengers, I could see out the windows. I watched the buildings go past, the low stucco structures and the unpromising cement; grim girls—age ten or twelve—in uniforms filed out to play ball or study behind the bars that enclosed the cobblestone courtyard of an ornate white stucco building that bore the words *escola* and *convento*; palm trees, the flat blue sky.

And then we dropped down a hill, winding through a narrowed street. An elegant new high-rise apartment building filled the view on the left; an old three-story cement building, worn out and lined with cracks, was visible on the right. The driver had to honk, taking each turn, to clear the road in case someone should happen to be coming from the other direction, and I held on, trying to keep my balance, swinging lightly into the passengers beside me, falling against them with a dull doughy weight.

And then the view broke to the right and there was open water, the whole lovely lapis lazuli of the Atlantic—

And I thought, it will all work out all right: I will get to the Amazon, I will do something that counts here, help save that fragile irreplaceable forest. There is this, after all, this ocean and beauty, and call it what you will, it is the same thing I love at home—the blue magnificent Atlantic. Glistening with sunlight. And out there an island. Ilha, I said the word in my head. Ilha de Itaparica.

The bus shuddered and smoked down the curving avenue past a long white cement balustrade with vase-shaped posts. To the left, the land rose steeply into hilly neighborhoods; to the right, it fell away sharply to the sea. I could see waves breaking on black rocks. Below was a club, boats moored at a dock and a glistening aqua pool. There was a smell of salt and the sea and diesel.

Abruptly, the bus swung toward the curb, then stopped to let people off across from what I could see—by the street sign posted on the other side of the avenue—was Avenida Kennedy.

The matron tapped me on the arm, urgently. *É próximo,* she said. *Barra é o próximo.*

—*Aqui?* I said. There was no beach in sight, but I grabbed my bag, ready to get off.

—*Aqui não,* the matron grabbed my wrist and shook her head vigorously. *O próximo.*

I stayed on the bus, uncertain and afraid of missing my stop.

The bus rumbled on down the hill, swaying around each turn, until we took the last S-curve—past a *farmácia* on the right, a few shops on the left—and made a final sharp turn to the right around a small mosaiced *praça* of black and white marble, a near 180-turn that sent those of us in the aisle gently arcing.

The matron seated in front of me placed her hand on my forearm and said, loudly, "*Aqui oh. Barra é aqui.*"

I nodded and thanked her and then pushed anxiously to the front of the bus, trying not to get trapped inside with the others.

When I stepped down into the street, the smells changed. To the scent of diesel was added coconut suntan oil, fish, salt, shit, and the seductive scent of boiling palm oil—a smell of ground nuts and smoke, and of the onions left to boil in the clear flame-orange *dendê,* a staple of Bahian cuisine.

As the bus pulled away, I stood on the sidewalk facing the street, the beach at my back, surveying for a moment this place. Directly across the street was a laundry, with a window at which one could deliver clothing to have it washed; there was a *farmácia* and a juice and snack bar, with small round metal tables and chairs overlooking the street and ocean.

In front of the *lavanderia,* a large corrugated refrigerator box lay flattened on its side, a pair of bare human feet sticking out. Directly across from me, an old woman sat beside a boiling pot of oil in which little pale fleshy balls, like matzoh balls, floated and hissed. Her face was the color of bittersweet chocolate, gaunt and shiny with sweat, her body hidden under layers of white lace, her head wrapped in a white turban. She called out in a nasal singsong, *acarajé, vatapá,* hawking her wares.

To my left was a *praça* of marble cobblestones. There, young kids with rasta hair sat on blankets on which they'd spread jewelry made of bent wire, beads, and shells. A small wooden hut housed a magazine vendor, his offerings clipped by clothespins to a strand of wire alongside bunches of red bananas. A clothesline strung with tie-dyed shirts and cotton dresses swayed in the breeze.

Behind the vendors was a building more beautiful than any I had seen here—two stories tall, built of glass and white marble. For a moment I wondered what it was: then I saw the sign, Banco do Brasil. In the sixteenth and seventeenth centuries, the Portuguese crown lavished colonial wealth on God, and churches were Brazil's architectural gems; in the late nineteenth century, the newly independent nation built fabulous opera houses and theaters, laying claim to Old World culture by building palaces to house it in the New. At the end of the twentieth century, Brazilians built beautiful banks. Beyond the *praça*, bright white apartment buildings lined the broad avenues that led up into the hills.

On either side of me, people loitered, watching the street, watching the waves, leaning on the balustrade above the beach that ran the length of the promenade for miles. I leaned my elbows on the railing, and for a moment I was happy here.

But the beach was a disappointment: small and semicircular and smelly, redolent of shit and fish, enclosed on the right by rocks, on the left by a fort, bodies were strewn everywhere. You had to step carefully to pick your way around arms and legs and backs. There were skiffs beached at one end; sun-bathers were everywhere else. The waves slopped in, like bath water. There were no palm trees. It was less a beach than an enormous ashtray.

Nevertheless, when I saw stairs leading down to the sand to my right, I took them. Bottle tops and cigarette butts littered the beach, but these grew fewer as I walked closer to the water. I chose a place halfway down the beach, modestly distant from others. I flapped my towel out and took a seat, slid off my shoes and shorts and shirt, then folded my clothes and placed them on top of my shoes to form a pillow. I pulled out my suntan oil from my bag and rub it on my arms and where I could reach on my back. I brushed my hair, then stuffed the brush and oil back in the beach bag.

Vendors of fruit and *sucos*, no more than kids, scuffed through the sand carrying Styrofoam coolers of sodas on ice, the coolers larger than the children and borne on straps around their slender necks. I lay back and close my eyes.

When I felt someone near me, I looked up and found two women laying out towels a few feet away. A few minutes later, I opened my eyes and saw a man—in shorts, sandals, a three-day stubble, and ratty shirt—seated on his heels a few feet from my head. I worried that he was some sort of creep, but others ignored him and he ignored me so I ignored him too.

When I felt sand flicked at me a few moments later, I turned and saw the man digging what seemed to be a reverse sand castle—a sand pit. He looked uninterested in me though, so—after a moment—I closed my eyes, and when I again felt flecks of sand on my face, I brushed them away. Either because he stopped digging or because I was inured, I stopped noticing the flecks of sand and dozed.

After maybe an hour, I woke with the tender raw puffiness that signals a burn. I sat up and pressed a thumb into the flesh of my thigh and watched the skin go white. A bad sign. When I reached for my bag, I found it was gone. I patted the sand; I stood and looked around.

—*Falta alguma coisa?* One of the women seated behind me asked if I'd lost something.

—*Minha bolsa,* I said. My purse.

The woman stood up to help me look, but the woman next to her said, *Já foi embora.* It's already gone. She had large Jackie O sunglasses and thick curling chestnut hair. She told us that she had seen the whole thing. She had seen the man with the three-day stubble slowly bury my beach bag under sand until he could slip his hand inside and remove the contents without notice.

I wanted to ask the woman in the sunglasses why the hell she didn't wake me, but her friend beat me to it.

—*E você não fez nada?* The first woman asked. Why didn't you do something?—He could've had a knife, Jackie O said.

She was right, of course. Money is not worth dying for. Still it was rough to lose my key, to be locked out of my only refuge.

The first woman told me that I must go immediately to *o centro.* Have you been to the lower city, the city center?

I shook my head no.

Well, you must go there, she said, immediately. You must go to the police station and file a report. You can take a taxi.

She rested a hand on my back. Do you have money? Do you need some? She offered me cab fare, and began to reach for her purse, but I remembered that I had my money in my shoe.

—I have money, I said. Thanks. I told them that he got my key, passport, and ID, but no money.

—He can sell the passport, the kind woman said. You'll have to report it.

I sat on the sand, the beach blurry now through my tears, the two women crouched beside me. My mouth tasted salty.

—He could be dangerous, Jackie O observes. If he has your hotel key, he could come back for more. He knows where you're staying, who you are.

I did not want to hail a cab and spend money I could not afford in order to tell a cop in broken Portuguese that my passport was gone. I was tired, I was hot, I was exhausted, I was scared.

—You have to go to the police, they said.

So, tired, hot, exhausted, scared, I thanked them and I did.

The Cop

In 1984, the police station in Salvador was small and white and stucco, a single-story building in a forgotten section of the lower city, and the cop I spoke to did not seem optimistic about the chances of recovering my passport. Like the woman at the beach before him, he noted that there was a market for such things. Like the hotel clerk I'll speak to later, he was incredulous that I would bring my passport and key to the beach.

—Why did you have them with you? The cop asked.

—I was trying to protect them, I said.

He laughed.

I did not tell him that I thought I was supposed to carry identification on me at all times, that I had read this somewhere, in some misguided guide-book.

He told me that was nuts.

—Leave those things in your hotel safe, he said. You should carry only a little money on you, just in case you are robbed.

He told me to go to the American embassy and get a new passport. He gave me the address. He wished me luck.

I told him I'd need it.

The Ambassador

In the cubicle-sized lobby of the American embassy in Salvador (red car-pet, white walls, blue chairs)—in an affluent residential neighborhood, south of Barra—I explained to a clerk through a tiny bullet-proof window that I have lost my passport and need to get a new one.

She explained that I could not get a passport today, it would take weeks. I could fill out an application here but they would have to send it on to Texas, where it would be processed by an office there, which would send it back here, at which time they would call me to let me know it was in. I could fill out an application here, but first, she said, You must bring the following items.

She pushed a Xeroxed sheet of paper toward me through a hole at the bot-tom of the bullet-proof window. On it was a checklist of items required for a passport application—two recent black and white photos, a current valid ID, $45 cash or travelers checks or cashier's check. She explained the fees to me, $45 for the reissuance, an extra $15 if I wanted to have it sent express mail.

—But you cannot apply today, she said. She looked at the clock above me. You're too late. We accept passport applications only until 2 o'clock each day. You'll have to come back tomorrow.

I asked if I might simply fill out the paperwork while I was there, to expe-dite the process, since it would take time, and since I had come a long way.

—She asked if I have brought my photos.

—What photos? I asked.

—The photos you need for your passport application, she said. You can-not get a passport without photos or proper identification.

—But my identification was stolen, I told her. That's the problem. That's why I am here. I was robbed.

—You need identification, she told me, in order for us to issue a passport. Or how do we know you are who you say you are? And you need two pho-tos, she said, closing the subject.

I had no photos of myself and no idea where to get them. I had had a hell of a time simply getting here. I was near tears when I asked if I might speak to someone else, someone in the embassy itself, someone who might perhaps bend the rules, who had the power to bend them. The clerk said that everyone had gone for lunch; they wouldn't be back for awhile.

—You might as well come back tomorrow, she said.

—May I wait? I asked.

—You can do what you want, she said.

I took a seat in a blue chair, and stared at the limp flag in the corner, the smiling face of an aging B-grade actor framed on the wall, our president. I was still in the chair twenty minutes later when a woman resembling Gertrude Stein—short-haired, with a square face and blocky build—came through the front door with a paper bag. She greeted the clerk, who buzzed her in.

—Do you work here, Madame? I asked, in Portuguese.

She looked at me.

—Yes, she said, in English. May I help you?

—I need a passport, mine has been stolen. Please, can you let me fill out the forms?

—I told her she is too late, the clerk said.

—I'm afraid that's not my area, the woman said.

—Please, I said. I must have looked desperate, near tears. I was.

—One moment, she said. I'll see what I can do.

A buzzer sounded and Gertrude Stein pulled back the heavy metal door that separated this lobby from the embassy offices beyond. She disappeared behind the heavy fireproof door, beyond which I glimpsed stairs going up.

I waited. After a few minutes the phone rang, and the clerk said, You may go up now, and buzzed me through the door.

I ascended the staircase, and following the clerk's directions found among the empty offices plump Gertrude Stein, seated in a leather chair behind an impressive mahogany desk, eating her lunch from a bag.

I recall that she was eating yogurt, and that the walls were covered with photos of dance troupes and framed posters of traveling exhibitions. I remember the tasteful, soothing decor of a therapist's office, and I remember being relieved and comfortable there. I took the seat she offered across the desk from her. Gertrude Stein, it turned out, was in charge of USIA in Salvador, the branch of the foreign service responsible for cultural and artistic exchanges; the booking agents, as it were, for embassies.

She asked me what she could do for me and I told her.

She was kind. She asked if I speak Portuguese and when I said that I understand better than I spoke, she spoke in a Portuguese so slow and simple that even I could understand. She assured me that it would be no problem to get a new passport, though it would take time. She would get me the forms I needed, told me where I could get photos, suggested I come tomorrow with these and it would be done right away, she'd see to it.

Then she leaned back and asked me what I was doing here.

I told her I was down from Yale and on my way to the Amazon.

She told me there was another student here from Yale, a Fulbright scholar, and asked if I knew her.

I told her that I didn't.

She leaned across the desk and told me that she liked me better.

—The other girl is stuck up, she said. She doesn't talk. She is very arrogant. But you, she said, talk. You don't know the language well, but you try.

I was grateful that she saw my failings as a strong suit and admitted that I'd been trying to find a language tutor. She told me that she could recommend one. She wrote the woman's name and number on a square of paper and pushed it across the desk to me. She said she should be able to help. Then she wrote down another name and number, that of the girl from Yale.

—You should call her, she said.

I smiled and thanked her. I told her that I would call.

Outside the embassy, the heat of the day had cooled and there was a breeze that smelled of salt water and tar. The sky was blue and beautiful and the palm fronds overhead were clattering like beaks striking, an obscurely exciting sound, a reminder that I was far from home, in the Tropics, and so because I had nothing better to do—and had time on my hands and no one waiting for me back at the hotel or anywhere really—I decided to walk to Barra; I figured it was a few miles from the embassy, a clear shot along the winding cobblestone promenade.

It was a beautiful afternoon and the walk would do me good, I thought. I needed exercise after days in planes and cars and buses and the hotel. I could walk to the bus stop in Barra and ride on from there. Truth is I was afraid of getting on a bus, afraid it would take me somewhere I did not want to go. A five-mile walk seemed easier than asking directions in a foreign language.

By the time I got to Barra, almost two hours later, the sun was setting and my calves were cramping and I was light-headed with hunger. I had not eaten since breakfast. I thought about stopping in the café I'd seen earlier, but I'd have to sit alone at a table; I thought about buying a candy bar from a magazine vendor in the port, but I was sick of candy, having eaten little else for days; then I saw the old Bahiana dressed in lace and seated by her pot of boiling oil and decide on that.

I crossed the street and asked the woman in the turban how much. I didn't ask her what it was, because I wouldn't understand the answer and I didn't need to know. The smell was intoxicating. The scent of onion and cashews and cilantro and palm oil filled my nostrils and my mouth watered. She named her modest price and I paid it.

I watched her scoop a hot bean ball from the pot, its surface crisp and orange from frying. She held it in a wax paper napkin. She asked me if I liked it spicy, and I said yes and watched her slit the bean ball's white belly with a knife and spread on red palm oil laced with red pepper seeds. Over this, she spread a thick layer of cashew paste flecked with shrimp and spices, over which she sprinkled dried shrimp, their pink heads and eyes still attached, observing me, as I received the *acarajé* she handed up.

This was my first taste of *acarajé* and *vatapá*, which I would later learn to make at a cooking school in the old section of town, foods that bear the traces still of their West African origins, as so much of Bahian culture does. *Acarajé* is a fried bean ball made of black-eyed-pea paste ground with garlic and spices then fried in palm oil, a staple of the cuisine for which Bahia is famous. *Vatapá* is a thick, salty, cashew paste blended of garlic, onions, dried shrimp, tomato, coriander, and palm oil. Both are supremely good. Eating them, the horizon going pink, I was happy, even hopeful, as I waited to catch the bus to my hotel.

Around midnight, I woke with terrible cramps and struggled to make it to the bathroom, only to find, when I stopped shitting, that I was bleeding from my rectum. It will be months before I learn that you should not buy *acarajé* from the vendors in the street, that the water in which the beans are washed is often filthy, the same water in which clothes are washed and sewage dumped. And sometimes, in the bean paste, there is broken glass.

The local man who will tell me this will not explain if the glass is accidental —simply a fact of life among the poor who make these foods at home and sell them in the street—or intentional, but I cannot help remembering that slaves used to grind glass into the food of those who forced them to labor, slowly killing those who were slowly killing them.

Amazon Snapshot #3

Of the few memories I have of childhood the most vivid are of wild places—forests, oceans, great lakes. These places inspired in me an excitement and delight that I rarely felt in the company of people. The natural world—even our domesticated suburban backyard with its beds of wild violets in a thin crescent of woods that curved around a duck-weed-green pond—held my attention as other children rarely could. Watching trout hover under the shadowed overhang of a river bank in Vermont, or stalking thumbnail toads by moonlight on a gravel road; observing moths and butterflies in a summer field or gathering milkweed pods and bittersweet from Minnesota woods in autumn—compelled me as people did not.

The people I knew then, even those I loved, seemed a shade less real than landscapes. The passion the rain forest inspired in me was emotion I could not muster on my own behalf.

What was so great about nature? Perhaps it was the act of observation itself. Sitting by a pond watching wood ducks cut through the green algae, or crouched over unfurling violets to study their purple veins, I was engaged in what poet Elizabeth Bishop once called, apropos of writing poetry, "a self-forgetful, perfectly useless concentration." I was delighted by the act of observation itself as much as by what was observed.

The dense, moist, mineral scent of moss; the coarse sandpaper hide of an oak tree; the soft pliable too-slippery fabric of a maple leaf; the sharp-sweet musk of a pinecone—all this compelled me as later sex and art, music and literature and a good martini would. By contrast, people seemed to me then both too complicated and too simple. But the natural world—a walk through woods or watching crabs in a tidal pool—was like a book I couldn't put down.

Of the few memories I have from childhood are these: I remember foraging for acorns at the age of six with my father in our grassy yard, digging among the carpet of liver-colored oak leaves until we had filled a grocery bag with acorns, which my father and I proceeded to heap at the base of a tree for the resident squirrel, a rodentine version of meals on wheels; I remember fishing with my parents after we had dropped my older siblings off at summer camp, the sickening heave of the swells as I stood below deck praying with childish faith to Poseidon for a catch, which I subsequently got (the largest of the day); I remember next to nothing of Girl Scout camp

44

save one sunset, which I glimpsed through spring-bare trees and watched in awe, saying, *Beautiful, how beautiful,* while my best friend, Sue Hoy, observed, *Geez. It's just a sunset. What's the big deal?* My first clear memory of shameful attachment.

My parents were avid travelers even before my father became—in his fifties—a financial success and we went from collecting Green Stamps to going abroad. My mother was a talented photographer and returned home from these trips with dozens of rolls of film of the places they'd been. But her photos contained few shots of them or us. My mother's photographs are almost entirely of unpeopled landscapes. Lava flows in Hawaii. Elephants on the Serengeti. Zebra herds in Ngorongoro crater. Dik dik.

For a long time I thought that we'd failed her somehow or failed to hold her attention as Aztec temples and tropical blossoms could. Now I think my mother and I shared a common sense of proportion—or its lack: we did not see our lives as worthy of being preserved on film. Her photos reveal my psychology as well; they seem to say what for years I too believed: We will pass, but this, *this* magnificent world endures.

On the cusp of adulthood, I'd begun to realize that the natural world I loved might not after all endure.

Che

Just before noon, the front desk rang my room to tell me that there was a woman waiting for me in the lobby, and when I went down, I saw a slender willowy figure standing in the shadows. As I approached, I noted that her hair was cut blunt above her shoulders, that her frame was lithe and delicate, and that though not tall—perhaps five feet five—she had uncommonly long legs. This was Barbara, the Fulbright from Yale, whom the woman at the embassy had phoned on my behalf; Barbara had in turn phoned my hotel earlier that day to say, *It can be difficult to settle in; would you like to meet for lunch?*

Even from across the room, her uncommon grace was evident. She stood with her hands folded over her abdomen, hips slightly forward, her shoulders back, like a piece of patient sculpture, wingless Victory. I'd learn later that this is a pose she struck often, but even then its artificiality would not diminish its charm, as artifice does not damage art.

When I reached Barbara, I saw she was wearing a denim miniskirt and a T-shirt featuring the face of Che Guevara, the Cuban revolutionary. (I did not know at the time that Che was big business in Latin America. Tchotchkes featuring Che were everywhere, on every sort of trinket—beer cans, T-shirts, key chains; in the 1990s, Swatch will even come out with a Che watch, on which the Cuban government will corner the market. I did not know at the time that politics, especially revolutionary politics, could be a marketable commodity.) But I understood that for Barbara politics could be an accessory, a fashion statement, a lark, and I admired this, that she was apparently above the earnest debate of poli sci majors and aspiring economists like me.

It's hard to say precisely what impressed me so about Barbara, though certainly physical beauty played its part. She was easily the most beautiful person—male or female—I had ever met.

She had the heart-shaped face of a young Vivian Leigh, a broad brow, long thick graceful eyebrows arched over moss-green eyes, a delicate slightly pointed nose, an intelligent and ironical gaze. Her hair was the color of gold coral, a brown that hinted at gold, bobbed just below her jaw and parted on the right to fall an even length. Her skin was the color of polished maple, golden, poreless. Her neck was slender, perhaps a little too long. She had an almost childlike body, small breasted, smooth bellied.

But it was more than her beauty that arrested me. She seemed at ease, at home in the world, as no one I had ever met before did. She appeared perhaps a little bored but kind, observant, quick. What impressed me most was a certain quality of detachment that I perceived immediately, even at that first meeting, even across a room. Barbara seemed not to take anything personally; she seemed above personal concerns, and that seemed heroic to me then, marvelous.

Probably I fell in love with her on sight, though I'd not have known to call it that, not then.

Beauty, like great happiness, is hard to describe. Everything one says on the subject sounds like a cliché. And perhaps this is because beauty, like great happiness, is an experience more than a thing, a momentary immersion in radiance, or a momentary self-transcendence, a moment of recognition that lingers between the beautiful and its admirer.

Years later, I will not be surprised when a professor of East Asian studies at NYU where Barbara is a professor will say of her, "She's very exotic, isn't she?" I'll wonder if what seems exotic to this professor, who hails from Delhi, is Barbara's extreme beauty.

That day Barbara greeted me warmly, as if we were old friends. She placed her hand on my shoulder, standing on tiptoe, and kissed me on one cheek, then the other, then again: one, two, three times. When she smiled, her lips seemed to stretch all the way across her face.

—*Tudo bem?* she asked. Her pronunciation was flawless.

—*Two-do-bone,* I said.

I flinched to hear myself. The words did not drift like smoke from my nose, as they were meant to, but fell off my tongue, heavy as marbles, Americanized.

Barbara appeared not to notice, which struck me even then as a sort of regal discretion. As far back as high school, my friends and I had taken note of one another's failings, measuring ourselves anxiously against those we knew and loved. Barbara seemed to prefer to imagine that I was as graceful as she.

—Are you ready to go? she asked, as if I might have other plans, a busy social schedule.

—Delighted to, I said, and I was.

Barbara was what I had expected people at Yale would be like before I got there. I had expected the remarkable, the uncommon. I'd found something altogether else: a mix of the exuberantly ambitious, the high-IQ-endowed, heirs to food fortunes, grandchildren of presidents, celebrities' progeny, movie stars, the wealthy and neurotic, the hard working and the merely very bright.

I had expected more, though I couldn't have said precisely what it was I'd hoped for or why I felt disappointed as I often did when I met people from Harvard or Princeton or Yale. As a child growing up in Minnesota in the 1970s, I had sometimes heard people on TV introduced as having received a degree from Oxford or Cambridge or the Ivy League, and I'd imagined that they were a different breed than we: smarter, better, the American elect. In the Midwest, where I grew up, these colleges did not have the same *social* import as in the East: they did not connote blue blood and great wealth or hint at an American aristocracy, but still we were impressed. I was. And more than impressed, I was hopeful that somewhere out there people were living up to my best expectations, even if in my clan we were not. I wanted them to be better; I needed them to be.

Barbara and I walked up the street toward Barra, away from the city center, to a restaurant she liked, a place next door to the convent school I had passed the previous day. The sun was high and the sky white overhead and though we walked in the heat it did not seem oppressive now that I was in Barbara's company. People watched Barbara as we passed and I felt, as I often would in the coming months whenever we were together, proud and contented, as if, for a moment, I was a part of her more beautiful world.

As we walked, I asked Barbara, by way of making conversation, what college she was in at Yale, and learned that she had graduated the previous spring but would be returning to New Haven in the fall to enter the PhD program in comparative literature. She had been an English major as an undergrad, specializing in comp lit.

At that time Yale was what some called "the Ellis Island of deconstruction" —the place where Continental scholars came to be deloused, or rather to be stripped of their politics, before their ideas entered the rest of the country. De Man was there, and Derrida, Harold Bloom and J. Hillis Miller, along with Geoffrey Hartman. I knew nothing about it, except the names, which, like Gauloises, signified cool.

Barbara said she'd been in Salvador since September and would leave in June. I was relieved that she would be around for a while, and I relaxed a little knowing this. I asked her what she was studying here and she told me that she was writing about *literatura de cordel*, literally, line literature, little pamphlets of poetry hung out on cords in the street and sold for a penny. She was looking at the ways these lay poets translated history and protest into poetry, the way pop culture and political critique met in their work.

I had taken only one college English course—a freshman seminar on Shakespeare that examined the major tragedies through a lens inflected by Jungian psychology and the professor's own libidinous exigencies—and I had not thought that politics and art could meet in so colloquial a fashion.

Art, like Culture, was forever capitalized in my mind in those days and always qualified by the adjective High. I believed that artists were a different breed of being and that people like me had politics because we could not aspire to create. Barbara's project suggested another possibility.

I told her that her project sounded marvelous, and I meant it.

She seemed pleased, and then she said, I'm glad you're here.

I was flattered and for a moment tongue-tied.

—I'm glad you called, I said.

Barbara watched the street ahead of us, and began to speak confidingly, as if she were speaking to someone she knew well, or as if she were talking to herself.

She said she had been lonely in Bahia these last six months. It had been hard to make friends among Bahians. The women saw her as competition, and the men only wanted to have affairs. Even the woman at the embassy did not seem to like her; she was surprised when the woman called to tell her I was here. She was glad she had.

I was flattered that she told me this, admitted to loneliness, and I felt I should confide in her too. It seemed to me then that confession was often the bond between young women, as competition typically was between young men.

So I told her how unprepared I found myself, despite my prior study of the language, and I recounted my current dilemma: how the Foundation had sent me to the wrong part of the country, how Pinheiro had withheld my funds, how I needed to secure lodgings here before I could get my money and go north to the Amazon, how I had been robbed and gotten sick. I tried to sound game, unafraid as she seemed.

—That's terrible, Barbara said, with genuine sympathy, and it occurred to me, for the first time, that it was.

—I guess so, I said.

We stepped through the white-enameled ironwork gate that separated the restaurant from the sidewalk and took a seat at a round, white-enameled table, beneath a green-and-white-striped umbrella at the edge of the patio that served as the restaurant's dining room. Sounds of traffic reached us from the street a few yards away as did the shouts of girls playing in the school-yard next door. Barbara was a glamorous companion; with her, even simple things seemed uncommonly vivid, bright even now in memory. Barbara sat in the sun; I sat in the shade. She tipped her face toward the sunlight; after a moment, she turned to me and smiled, evidently pleased with everything.

I was pleased too and I was feeling almost brave with Barbara there until a waiter came and gave us menus and I realized that I did not understand the words and felt again the slight panic that accompanied me everywhere like a stray dog. I scanned the prices, nervous about what I could afford. I had not brought much money, both to economize and to insure that I stuck to my perpetual diet.

I scanned the words, looking for familiar elements: *pão* (bread), *suco* (juice), *limonada* (lemonade), *queijo* (cheese), *café*. I made up my mind to order a basket of bread and coffee, a pathetic idea of a meal but one I could both afford and pronounce.

But when the waiter returned, Barbara graciously ordered for us both. (Do you mind? she asked, eyebrows raised, smiling, as if I were doing her the favor. Delighted, I said.) She ordered foods she thought I should try: *aipim*, fried yams, some sort of sausage, *sucos*.

The food was wonderful—sweet yam strips cut thick and deep fried then sprinkled with salt, the yeasty tuber of *aipim*, slathered with butter, spicy sausage bursting from its skin—but I ate shyly, afraid of getting fat.

Barbara, who was slender, delighted in each bite. Her lips were buttery and glistened in the sunlight. I knew very few women who ate like that then, with pleasure, and I admired her unembarrassed appetite. Most of the women I knew at school lived on cottage cheese and egg whites, miserable as martyrs, penitential, swallowing guilt with each bite. As if hunger were humiliating.

As we ate, I asked Barbara about her apartment, where she lived, how she found her place, whether she could recommend neighborhoods. I was afraid our conversation might lag and relied on the bond of advice to carry us.

She said she was living in Barra, on Avenida President Kennedy.

I was relieved to know the name, the street, to be able to say that I had been by there (I didn't mention that Barra was where I was robbed).

I said I might try to find a place there as well, but she warned me against it.

—Don't, she said. Don't live in Barra. It's full of tourists. Only Americans and Europeans live there. If I had it to do again, she said, I'd live in a more interesting neighborhood. She mentioned Amaralina, Rio Vermelho—poorer, tougher, local neighborhoods—not, as Barra was, a colony of exiles.

Looking back now, it seems curious that of all the things Barbara might've warned me against, of all that would befall us in the year to come, that she should have warned me against comfort, bland, desacrilized comfort. But it occurs to me now that perhaps that was the only thing we had to fear—comfort and all we'd do for it, sacrifice, risk, in its pursuit.

It was somewhere in this conversation about the various neighborhoods of Salvador that Barbara mentioned again the difficulty she had had making friends among Brazilians and how Bahian women mistook her for a threat and I said, what perhaps she had heard all too often, that she was beautiful. Or rather, I said that I could see why women might be threatened by her, and she looked offended and in order to clarify I blurted out that she was uncommonly beautiful after all, she must know that.

She did not look pleased so much as interested in this assessment, as if she had not considered before that she was beautiful though surely she must have known it.

Thinking the point of interest to her, I continued.

—Have you ever thought of modeling? I asked.

Barbara's face went blank. She looked as if I'd suggested she turn tricks.

—No, she placed the word on the table between us like a stone.

—I mean, I said, thinking to clarify my point, would you consider it? You could certainly do it. You could make a lot of money, I imagine.

—No.

She seemed deeply offended by the idea, by the mere suggestion, and I wondered at the time if she misunderstood me, if she thought I was proposing that she pose nude. But hers was not that kind of beauty. She was not voluptuous, not the sort of woman you'd imagine naked on a bed—plush rump and full thighs, sloping belly and round breasts exposed. She was in possession of none of these. Her body was childlike, like that of a girl of twelve, almost breastless. Flexible, slender limbed, hers was an esthetically— not an erotically—compelling figure.

Besides her arresting face, it was her legs that distinguished her, her uncommonly long legs. They gave her that slight imperfection that makes for real beauty, the peculiarity that in models makes us stare at photographs but which later confuses us on the street when we see them in person and think, *He or she is prettier in pictures than in life.* The imperfection, the flaw, is what distinguishes the truly beautiful; it, ironically, is what confers beauty on a being or thing.

I did not understand how I had insulted her, I understood only that I had managed in the course of lunch to offend into monosyllables the only person I wanted to call my friend here, the first person I had met in years whom I liked.

I pondered my mistake all the way back to my hotel. I pondered it as I walked Barbara to the bus stop, where she caught a bus downtown to buy line poetry. I pondered it as I walked home alone. But try as I might, I could not understand her outrage.

It did not occur to me that Barbara was refusing to traffic in beauty, to commodify it, to sell out or name a price. I was studying economics and did not realize yet that one could do that, hold things above price, refuse to name or have one.

The Exile

When I got back to the gloom of my hotel room after our lunch in the sun, I pulled the scrap of paper from the pocket of my shorts and phoned the tutor recommended by the woman at the USIA.

A woman answered with the customary Brazilian salutation, *Pronto.* I introduced myself or tried to in careful Portuguese but I was cut off by a flurry of British-accented English. Yes, she said, quite right to have recommended her, she'd be delighted to conduct tutorials but she didn't come cheap. I should know that.

She said that she'd charge me $20 an hour. I had never heard of anyone charging $20 an hour for anything legal, and I told her frankly that I didn't have much cash, that after paying my hotel bill, which was mounting fast, I would have about $100, which I would need for food, for transport, for emergencies until the Rotarians saw fit to bestow on me my fellowship funds.

I told her that receipt of my fellowship was contingent on my getting an apartment.

She said that she could help me get one. She suggested that we meet at her apartment that afternoon and asked me if I had a car.

I told her I didn't, but that I could take a cab.

—*Don't* take a cab, she said. She had errands in town anyway; she could meet me in the lobby of the language school near my hotel. It was 2 o'clock. She could meet me at 4. For an hour. For twenty bucks.

When I walked into the language school, she was waiting in one of the lobby chairs, flipping through a magazine. She did not stand when she saw me. We exchanged greetings and I sat down.

The Englishwoman was one of those people who seem to get stranded in a place—never making a home in their adopted land, never returning to the place from whence they came, neither adapting nor withdrawing, stranded between homelands, as if survivors of some cultural shipwreck. I was never entirely clear about how she landed here in Salvador though it seemed to have to do with a love affair gone awry, perhaps a husband who was no longer around. It was ludicrous to choose an Englishwoman to teach me Portuguese in Brazil, but I was comforted to have a native English speaker, someone who seemed as awkward and in exile as I.

Her British accent was strong, her criticisms numerous. The Brazilians, she said, Bahians in particular, were late, unreliable, will rob you blind. *Robar,* she said. *That's* a word you need to know. It means to rob. Never, she cautioned, take a taxi alone. You never know what they'll do. She told me about a girl who had been killed some months before: a tourist who'd caught a cab and was found raped and dead on a remote beach north of town days later. They do not respect their women as the English do, she said. She was like something out of a book, it seemed to me then, though I was not a big reader and knew that characters in books did not charge you $20 an hour. And there she was in front of me, for $20 an hour.

She spoke airily of how long she'd been here, mentioned ten years or a dozen; it didn't seem a fresh wound whatever it was that had brought her to

Salvador. She had the weary undone aspect I'd come to think of as vaguely fortyish, a certain helter-skelter cast that seemed to me to overtake women in their forties, a collapsed quality, as if they were giving in to some force within or without that they no longer had the energy to resist. She was buxom, very pale, with wispy blond hair. Like everyone here, she was short. I towered over her, huge and unnatural.

At our first session, she translated want ads from *A Tarde* and equipped me with the proper questions to ask landlords, phrases that like a parrot I repeated, honking through my nose in an effort to emulate the nasal sing-song of the Bahian.

Back at the hotel that night, I phoned several places—two boarding houses and several landlords—and arranged appointments for the next day and the one following. Then I lay back on my bed and wondered how I would get through the time that stretched ahead of me and how I would ever get to the Amazon, to the place I believed I belonged.

O Interior

I had been in Brazil for a week by the time I visited the boarding house in Barra, and by then I was desperate to find a place. My cash was running low, but I could not call Pinheiro to obtain my fellowship until I had a permanent address. I went looking for a home that sunny Monday; I found Nelci and Isa instead.

The day before, I had toured several apartments with the Englishwoman, but I found none satisfactory. Following Barbara's advice, I'd sought out places in interesting neighborhoods—Ribeira, Rio Vermelho. In Pelourinho, the baroque cobblestone heart of the old city, I'd answered an ad for a boarding house where rent was cheap and the location interesting, but when I'd arrived to tour the place, I discovered it was straight out of Dickens. A gaunt young woman led me down a grim and narrow corridor, past cracked door after wooden door. The warren of tiny rooms was dimly lit by bare jaundiced bulbs; the whole joint resembled a brothel more than a residence for young women, as I'd been led to believe on the phone. Probably, given the neighborhood, it was.

By the time I got to Barra that morning, I was desperate to avoid another day skimming want ads, desperate to avoid seeing places I'd rather not ever have seen.

West of the old city, Barra—in those days—was a fashionable, faintly seedy, beachside neighborhood. Favored by foreigners, it was home to all manner of *flâneur*—the rich, the poor, the would-be-artist, the tourist. It had a pretty mosaic promenade and wide boulevards that led away from the beach into hills. Its streets were lined by tall apartment houses, bright as salt licks, with ironwork gates enclosing private gardens.

It was early Monday morning when I stepped off the bus in Barra. The sky was the thin blue of early summer, hard and bright as blown glass. I was nervous that morning, as tourists will be. I made my way away from the beach and into the green hills that ringed the bay, following the broad tree-lined Avenida Isabella.

I passed two banks in the space of a block, each with a large chrome name-plate bolted to a marble facade. Flamboyant trees dotted the sidewalk, and as I walked I passed through the shadows they cast. Their branches brushed my cheeks. Their red flowers hung like streamers, seedpods dangling like razor strops.

The sky seemed bluer glimpsed from the bottom of the suburban canyon, a sharp shard wedged between rooftops. Barra had none of the charm of the old city or outlying neighborhoods where narrow single-story houses were painted indigo, emerald, yellow, flamingo pink, extending uninterrupted in a band along narrow cobbled streets. Barra was starched, dentifricial, blazingly white.

The boarding house where I had an appointment that morning was about a block from the beach, and anomalous among the high rises: a squat, two-story house with thick, stucco walls painted pink.

The man who let me in was large—broad and tall, plump and thick chested—and my first impression was of an aging American beatnik. He greeted me wearing knee-length rumpled khaki shorts, flip-flop sandals, and a Hawaiian-print shirt that strained at the buttons to contain his ample Buddha belly. He was in robust middle age: white bearded, florid faced. He had a massive head and wore his shirt unbuttoned to mid-chest; gray and white hairs curlicued out from his open collar. He had peculiarly delicate, pale legs, slender as a woman's and turnip colored.

—Miss Levy, he said in English, swinging the door wide. Come in, come in. He gestured me into the cool dark foyer.

My sandals slapped against the tiles as I stepped inside.

He closed the door, clasped his broad hands over mine.

—I'm Senhor Oliveira, he said, reverting to Portuguese. It was you I spoke to on the phone the other day?

—Yes, I said, and smiled. It's cool in here, I said. It's nice.

He patted the wall affectionately.

—Oh, yes, he said. These walls are a foot thick. Come, I'll show you the house.

He was delighted to find I was American and eager, at first, to talk. As we toured the kitchen and the sitting room with its mismatched furnishings and old Zenith TV, Oliveira explained that he was a sculptor. He'd begun letting rooms a few years ago for extra income. Only to girls though, he said. He told me repeatedly that he *liked* Americans.

He asked what I was doing in Salvador, and I told him about my grant. He seemed delighted by this and told me that he'd been in Italy years ago on a Ford Foundation grant to study sculpting. Now, however, he could not travel; he had his boarding house to run.

As he showed me around the courtyard, the cool, dark kitchen, Oliveira's mood seemed to deflate. The place—or perhaps I—appeared unable to hold his interest, and after five minutes of strained conversation about philanthropy and Ford (who was, I pointed out unthinkingly, among the first to ravage the Amazon, for rubber to equip his automobiles), Oliveira showed me upstairs and into a large room with windows open to the street, where he turned me over to two young boarders—leaving me to them.

—This is Miss Levy, Oliveira said, ushering me inside. She's considering moving in with us.

I glanced around the room, embarrassed to openly appraise it. The place was like a barracks or a YMCA dorm room, absent of personal decoration. I remember wood floors, pale stucco walls, wooden shutters, windows open to air. I smiled insincerely.

—*Tudo bem,* said a pretty girl by the mirror. She spoke without interest, without turning to look at me. She was tying her hair up in a handkerchief; looking in the mirror, she raised her chin a bit and cocked her head to the left, then right.

A second, plainer girl watched me from the bed.

—*Tudo bom,* I said.

Oliveira—evidently satisfied—pulled the door closed behind him to give us privacy, and for a moment we listened to the slap of his sandals against the cement stairs as he descended.

—I'm Nelci, the plain girl said, extending a hand from where she sat on the bed. It was a formal gesture I'd not often seen among kids our age. I reached for her hand and shook it. This is Isa, she said.

—*Prazer,* I said, Pleasure. I'm Ellen.

—Helen? The girl with the handkerchief said, still facing the mirror.

—No, I said, Ellen.

—*Tá bonita, seu nome,* Nelci said. It's pretty, your name.

I shrugged. I hated my name, Midwestern plain as a picket fence, but I appreciated the gesture. I nodded at the room and said, *Tá bonita.* The place is cute.

—It's not bad, Nelci said. You can look around if you want.

—Thanks, I said. But there wasn't much to see: the room was large and unprivate, with four plain beds, an armoire, several dressers.

—*É horrível,* Isa said. It's horrible. Isa had the diva's impeccable sense of timing. Everything she said sent a rustle of drama into the room, as if birds had been released.

But the room didn't seem horrible to me, just plain, impersonal, borrowed, and sad because of that. I felt awkward standing by the bed with my arms hanging, so I walked over to the window and leaned out over the courtyard, though there was nothing really to see there, just green branches of the trees behind the house and the cement tiles in the courtyard below.

—You're not from here, Nel said, evidently noting my accent.

—No, I turned my back to the window; the sun felt heavy on my shoulders. I'm from the United States.

Isa turned from the mirror to look at me for the first time.

—*Americana?* she smiled; her eyes widened with a look I would later see her turn on handsome men and expensive cars.

—*Sou,* I said. I am.

Isa crossed her arms under her breasts and studied me. *É feio, né, teu nome? Naõ acha?* Your name's kind of ugly, don't you think?

—*Isa,* Nel hissed.

—Well it *is,* Isa said. She stared at me. I'll call you Elena, all right? *É um nome bem Bahiana, viu?* It's a very Bahian name. She had a radiant smile.

Isa was a dead ringer for the Brazilian actress Sonia Braga, Brazil's Grace Kelly. She had almond-shaped eyes that tilted up at the corners, purple black hair that fell in thick waves past delicate shoulders. Her cheekbones were high, her skin flawlessly smooth. Even I, who wasn't used to appraising other girls' bodies, could see hers was terrific.

—Come, Nelci said, patting the bed next to her. Sit here.

I crossed to the bed and sat on its edge, facing Nel.

—So what brought you to Salvador? she asked.

I told them about my grant, how the foundation had sent me here by mistake, how I planned to study at the Federal University for a term then go north, as soon as I could arrange it, to Manaus in the heart of the Amazon rain forest.

I rattled off my lines with ease, pleased with myself for these few phrases I'd memorized. It felt good to be able to converse.

—Are you both from here? I asked.

—*I* am, Isa said with evident distaste. She yanked off the handkerchief that held her hair and dropped it on the dresser, then she gathered the glossy black mass of hair off her neck and began to twist it in a chignon, pinning it up, bobby pins held between her lips.

—I'm from Feira de Santana, Nelci said. In the interior.

It was the first time I'd heard the countryside west of the coast referred to as the interior. It seemed a poetic phrase, a romantic place to come from—*the interior*—but Nel didn't think so. She said she couldn't wait to leave.

Nelci, like me, had come to study economics at the Federal University, where the term would begin in a few weeks' time. It would be her second year there. She was clearly very bright and had won some sort of scholarship to cover her expenses while in school.

—I used to have an apartment in Amaralina, Nelci said, referring to a neighborhood farther down the beach, but my father cut me off, so I live here. It's only temporary though, until we find another place.

—Yeah, I nodded. Me too.

From the first, I liked Nelci better. Nel was the intellectual, the sidekick, the one with plans and brains, but Isa was the one who dazzled.

Isa pulled off her shirt and reached behind her back to unclasp her bra then stood before the bureau mirror, naked to the waist in the cool dim bedroom, the lush plum-colored aureoles of her breasts bunched like unopened blossoms in the chill of the room. She held up to herself a chartreuse bikini top, then one of neon-orange terry cloth, admiring herself in the mirror as she held up first one outfit, then another, while Nelci and I sat on the bed discussing the university faculty.

I could see from the corner of my eye the cinnamon curve of Isa's breasts, her smooth belly. I could see the shapely bands of muscle as she arched her naked back. And I could see just as plainly that she was watching me to see if I was watching her. She stood dangling a bikini top in her hand. Then she smiled and turned away to fit herself into the suit.

—*Por favor, Elena,* she said, holding out to me the strings of her bikini. I stood awkwardly to tie them for her.

There are certain people you know only by their first name, know them well and still that name is all you have and is enough. As if they were disburdened of paternity and history, some completely modern thing, as if they moved without relation to a past, to parents, family, could not be traced. Isa was like that.

Later, familiarity would make her ugly to me, but I try to remember what it was like to see her that first time. In the boarding house that morning. The thick walls of the upstairs room, where the young women slept in narrow beds without screens or any sort of privacy. The cool plank floor of the room. The windows open to the tree tops and the sound of squirrel monkeys in the trees. The pale tint of the walls. Outside, the blaze of January light filling the street like a river.

Black violet hair. Skin the color of burnt sugar. Something about her made me think of white summer sheets, of palm oil, *cravo e canela,* clove and cinnamon.

—O Gordo is horrible, Isa said, calling the landlord by their private name for him, The Fat.

—He's not so bad, Nel told me.

—He seemed nice, I said.

—He seems nice enough *now*, Isa said, but if you live here, you'll see. Isa spoke of O Gordo with the eager condescension that young women lavish on old men who court them and the young who don't merit serious consideration—men whose attentions are discussed as if they were an insult but which are nonetheless entered in the ledger of self worth. Isa's tone suggested that O Gordo had taken an undue interest in his tenants at one time but had failed to interest them.

Isa pulled an enormous array of clothes from the armoire and set them at the foot of the bed beside us.

—Did I *tell* you, Nel, that I found cockroaches in the refrigerator on Saturday?

—It's not so bad, Nel assured me.

Isa pulled out a denim skirt and wide lavender belt from the pile of clothes.

—What do you think? she asked, holding up the outfit.

Nel shrugged. It's cute.

—You think? Isa looked back at the mirror. She bit her lip.

—Where are you staying now? Nel asked me.

—The Bahia do Sol, I said.

—That's expensive, Isa said. She looked up from the mirror.

—It's only temporary, I said. Until I find a place.

I told them about the places I'd seen and that I had an appointment at eleven to see an apartment on Rua João Pondé.

—That's just up the street, Isa said. We can show you when we go out.

—You can afford a place of your own? Nelci asked.

—It's just a kitchenette. Not too expensive.

—I wish I could get a place of my own, Nel said. She lay back on the bed and stared at the ceiling. She sighed.

—How much do they want? Isa asked. Her voice was sharp and it occurred to me that she was annoyed that I, not she, was the center of attention. Clearly this was not often the case.

—The rent is 80,000 *cruzeiros*, I said. This was roughly $40 dollars per month. By U.S. standards, this was tremendously cheap, and I could easily accommodate it with my grant (some $15,000, in addition to a few thousand for travel, as I recall), but in Salvador that year the average annual income was CR 200,000—about $100 American dollars—and $40 was a small fortune.

Nelci whistled through her teeth in admiration.

—You can afford that? Isa asked. She looked at me as if she thought I might be lying.

—When they give me my *bolsa*, I can.

—It's your money, Isa said, matter-of-factly. They should give it to you.

She pulled her hair out of its bobby pins and ran a brush through it, hard, over and over and over and over.

—They will, I said, trying to sound sure.

I admired Isa's certitude. Certainty was not a thing I possessed. Perhaps because I'd never had to fight for my place, I'd never had to figure out what—if anything—was mine, and how to claim it.

—If you can afford a place of your own, Nel asked, why would you want to live here?

—I don't know anyone in Salvador, I said. I thought maybe I'd meet people at a boarding house.

—You know us, Isa said, her eyes met mine.

I understood that this was an invitation, though I wasn't sure what I'd been invited to.

—If you can get your own apartment, Nelci said, with feeling, sitting up on her elbows, *Don't* live here.

In the single photograph I have of Nel—taken perhaps six months after we met, a head shot, too close and slightly out of focus—she wears a yellow bikini top. You can't tell from the shot, which shows only her head and shoulders, that she is tall and lanky, perhaps five feet six. Though shapely, she considers herself too thin; *magra* is the word she uses, its very sound suggesting strain, onomatopoetic as *gaunt* is.

I can see in the photograph that Nel had all it took to be pretty; I can see that she almost is: she has fine high cheekbones, intelligent brown eyes. But I can see from the photo that she is not: her gaze is unfocused; her lips pursed in a prissy way, as if she were holding back some unkind phrase. There is something off-putting about her face. Perhaps it is her almost handsome jaw, her broad shoulders drawn back, her direct gaze, the absence of tenderness in those eyes turned on the camera. The refusal to smile. The anger evident in that photograph. Evident even now.

But I did not notice that anger the day we met. Perhaps it wasn't there yet.

As Nelci and I sat conversing on the bed that morning, Isa dressing and undressing beside us, I saw only Nel's kind face and the hope—still in her then—that things would only get better.

—Didn't I *tell* you, said Nelci, sitting up. Didn't I *say* something was going to happen today, Isa? I *felt* it. *Didn't* I? I *felt* it.

By the time the three of us stepped out the front door of the boarding house into the bright mid-morning light, I knew I wouldn't live there, though I wanted to. I didn't want to live alone; I never had, and the idea frightened me, but I was embarrassed to admit this, as if feeling were a fault.

Nelci and Isa were heading to the port to catch a bus to visit Isa's family, but they offered to walk me to Rua João Pondé first, to the apartment building where I had my appointment. Out on the street, Isa adopted a carefully blank expression, slipping on dark glasses, like a movie star.

I was aware, as we walked up Avenida Princesa Isabel, as I would often be aware in her company, of the calculations she was making: whether she was the prettiest woman present, who had money or power, what she wore and bared.

As we walked, Isa spoke of her family in Salvador, her mother and sisters, and I got the impression that her mother was worried about her. She wanted Isa to live at home, worried about her daughter living by herself in the city. She wanted Isa to marry, to have security, children, but Isa disdained her mother's ambitions. Children would ruin her figure, she said, stretch her belly, leave marks, make her breasts hang. She liked to be admired by men, did not want to limit herself to one. She wanted to find a handsome man to support her, but she wanted to be free to choose and choose again. She did not want to be tied down.

Contrary to popular mythology, in our experience men were the ones who wanted to marry. Young women hardly ever did. Nel, Isa, and I had all been asked by the time we met; we had all declined our offers. Marriage seemed a poor prize to us, an end of possibility. It seemed the amorous equivalent of being a company man: signing on for a lifetime of labor in the hope of retiring with a fat pension. We were twenty-one then, and couldn't imagine making it to the lofty age of thirty. We didn't want security; we wanted to *live*, to know the world, to have adventures and our independence. We wanted to make something of ourselves.

The kitchenette I visited after the boarding house that morning was small but new and very clean. A single room with bright white walls and a tiny kitchen and bath. Two large sliding windows took up half of one wall and overlooked a window box of shriveled stems that once bore flowers, and the quiet curve of the street. Across the street was a similar apartment building, less new, behind which rose thick green trees.

The landlord was a small, pink man; he watched me as I looked around. He walked me into the closet-sized kitchen, showed me the brand-new faucet fixtures in the bath. He wore a white cotton shirt; he looked like a priest or a schoolteacher. Mild, shy, suspicious.

I told him about my grant, and about myself—that I was a student, an American. I told him that I'd like to rent the place, that I hoped to be departing for the Amazon soon, but that I would pay the rent even then, unless he found another tenant. He seemed pleased but said nonetheless that he'd require a countersignator for my lease. I told him I'd ask my fellowship sponsors.

Downstairs the landlord introduced me to the doorman as the new tenant. The doorman was slender, handsome, young, with a long ebony face and an easygoing smile. He wore black slacks with a neat crease, a short-sleeved white shirt, a tie, and a name tag that read Egberto. He sat behind a desk inside the glass entrance, and when he stood to greet me I saw that he was very tall, mantis-like, all limbs; it seemed remarkable that he could be contained behind that tiny desk, a feat of origami, careful folds. We exchanged smiles, names, shook hands; I liked him immediately. I hoped I would be, as the landlord said, the new tenant.

When I arrived at the bank in Barra the next morning, I was relieved to step inside, to pull back the heavy glass doors and slip into the cool, comforting, air-conditioned patter, the familiar retort of typists coming to the end of a line, the smell of cash and carpeting, the bright surfaces of polished marble and glass coffee tables, solid mahogany desks, the beautiful clerks with powder-blue eye shadow and red lips, to immerse myself in that reassuring sameness, the emotional détente declared by money.

Senhor Pinheiro helped me open an account and countersigned my lease. Then I took a cab back to my hotel and paid my tab, and by week's end I'd moved in.

In the weeks that followed, I often ran into Nelci and Isa in the street on my way to and from the beach or bus stops or shops. The threads of our lives seemed meant to tangle then and these chance encounters delighted me.

Isa would greet me with extravagant affection, briskly kissing me on both cheeks, singing my name as if it were a favorite melody, languorously, slightly mockingly. There was an unmistakable mix of admiration and contempt in her voice, as she transformed my name into her language—*Elena*. The emphasis always on the surprising second syllable, eh-*lane*-uh. With a smile that lingered like bright light.

I seemed slow and heavy by comparison, as I had that first day when I'd watched Isa dress in her brilliant plumage, and undress, trying on and discarding a series of wild blouses in chartreuse, neon orange, denim miniskirts, wide belts of lavender and black. Outrageous and improbable combinations, a postmodern Carmen Miranda mocking the tropical tropes she employed. Dressing herself as if she were some wild blossom, a bloom of the flamboyant trees in the Rua João Pondé, or some brightly colored bird.

PART II
SALVADOR

Amazon Snapshot #4

Long before I saw the rain forest, its mist-draped banks, its canopy-like green clouds; long before I knew its distinctive scent—a smoky mix of tea and loam, mulch and bog and blossoms; before I stepped from a low dugout canoe onto its soft bank and felt the earth give beneath my feet like a body; before I ever saw an enormous, iridescent, blue Morpho butterfly glide by like a mobile jewel (broad as my open hand) over tea-brown water or woke to the eerie, haunting cries of red howler monkeys, their roars like a fierce wind raging down a canyon then dying back (or like powerful gusts over the American prairie as they must have sounded to my maternal grandmother when she homesteaded on the Dakota plains a century ago); long, long before I walked beneath the rain forest canopy dense with bromeliads, vines, strangling fig, kapok, mahogany, hundreds of varieties of trees, birds, insects and saw the luminous white bark of the *manguba*, its fruit raised above the river like red paper lanterns; long, long before I saw any of this, I loved the forest. I was moved by its measurement—the descriptions of its vastness and its peril.

Making a Life

Those first few weeks in Salvador, while I waited to go to the Amazon, I made a life for myself. I made plans with a lowercase p. But I always thought of myself as on my way elsewhere, destined for bigger things: the Amazon.

Waiting was nothing new for me. As a child, I'd often felt that I was in the wings preparing to make my entrance, that my real life was yet to begin. I remember vividly the horror I felt one afternoon in fourth grade as I stood in line with the other children in a hallway of my elementary school, waiting to be let out for recess. There in the waxed linoleum-tiled hallway, the light of midday distorted through the warped surface of the block glass wall that formed the hallway's only window, I stood with the other kids—who like me were buckled into rain slickers of thick shiny plastic in red and yellow, our galoshes huge on our little feet—and thought with lucid horror, "I am a fully adult consciousness trapped in a tiny body." I waited to grow into what I knew I already was but could not as yet be.

Like lonely kids everywhere, I felt growing up that I was destined for some remarkable end, future greatness compensation for a present lack. I felt I was meant for something important, though I didn't know what that might be. At twenty-one, I thought at last I knew.

The Cabby

At Barbara's suggestion I had bought furniture at a secondhand shop a few blocks away and had it delivered to me, so I had a mattress to sleep on, a *guardaropa* (an armoire), a small coffee table, and an end table (an oddity given that there was no couch for it to sit at the end of). In those days it didn't occur to me to buy or build bookshelves. The few books I had I kept with my jewelry on a shelf of the armoire.

Why I thought to forgo a dining table and chairs of any kind is harder to explain. I suppose I thought it vaguely Japanese to seat my guests on a mattress on the floor, a Zen minimalism that was gaining currency in America in the 1980s (like Hellenized Rome, we absorbed postwar what we had conquered). More likely I simply thought comfort not worth spending money on. I wanted a life of the mind; the body could make do with less: what did I need with a kitchen table, a couch, a lamp, or chairs?

By the end of that first day, however, it became clear to me that in order to eat I'd have to buy a fridge, a stove, and the tiny tank of gas called a *bujão*. The British tutor—whom I continued to pay for advice, though it had long ago become apparent that she could not teach me Portuguese (she was neither a native speaker nor a skilled teacher, and I was a lousy student)—recommended that I go to the hypermercado, a massive grocery and home furnishings store in an outlying neighborhood, to buy a fridge and stove. The *bujão* I could have delivered by the gas company, whose name she gave me.

The tutor had already warned me against taking cabs. But given the distance and the number of bus transfers involved and that it would be broad daylight, it seemed—we both agreed—safe enough.

The trip from Barra to the hypermercado was a long one and the cabby's silence as we drove seemed ominous, so I chatted, practicing my Portuguese. I was trying to be engaging, trying to ward off harm in the only way that I knew then—by being pleasing, a nice girl with my mother's good Midwestern manners. (I'd have fared better had I relied on the bracing and abrasive honesty of my father's New York clan.) I asked if he was from here. If he'd driven a cab for long. I admired Salvador's beauty then we lapsed into another awkward silence while the meter ticked and I worried whether I'd have enough to pay the fare.

His was not an intimate cab as cabs sometimes will be: there were no saints medals, no ribbons from the Igreja do Bonfim, no photos of family or a girlfriend or pets, no plastic flowers, no dice.

There was only the Playboy bunny emblem—a white rabbit head in a bowtie, against a black background—hanging from the rearview mirror. Thinking perhaps to show I was not intimidated by such sexist paraphernalia, thinking perhaps to make conversation to keep the ride friendly and therefore safe, or perhaps simply not thinking at all, I *leaned forward and admired the bunny ears.*

I said they were nice or great or something equally insincere. For the first time the cabby took an interest in my comments. He volunteered that he lived not far from here, naming a beachside area on the outskirts of the city of which I'd heard nice things and said so. He said we could go by there, if I wanted to see it, it was on the way, and I understood (or misunderstood) that he needed to pick something up at home, so when he asked if I wanted to stop by his place on our way to the hypermercado, I said *Fine*, thinking how strange it was that Barbara had complained of having a hard time meeting Bahians. They seemed to me a very friendly bunch.

About ten minutes later the cabby turned onto a gravel drive that led into an open garage, above which a small, wooden bungalow stood. Boxy and new, it seemed to be on stilts, rising over the garage as if for protection against a rising tide.

To the right and left of us was sand, and in the distance the edge of blue water. There were only a few other structures around, a few isolated houses like this one, and the gravel drive and the asphalt we'd turned off. I waited in the backseat for the cabby to run in and retrieve whatever we'd come for.

He turned around, leaning his arm on the seat between us. Do you want to come in? he asked.

I was, in fact, curious to know how people lived here, so I said, Sure, but just for a minute.

I had, after all, errands to run.

At the front of the garage, by the grill of the car, was a door, which the cabby opened to allow me to pass through. Inside, a steep set of carpeted stairs led up to an apartment above. I mounted the stairs through the narrow hallway—uneasy but not wanting to be, not wanting to imagine myself vulnerable, as if by ignoring danger, I might not be in any.

In front of a second door at the top, I stopped. The cabby squeezed past me and opened this door, and I walked casually past him and into a dimly lit room, which contained, like my own apartment, only one significant piece of furniture: other than the rust-colored shag carpet on the floor, the curtains drawn against the midday sun, the only bit of furnishing evident or memorable lay to my right—an enormous bed, above which, glued to the ceiling, were dozens of one-foot-square, mirrored tiles.

Behind me, the cabby closed the door. I could hear him cross the carpet toward me. I braced as if before a blow and said, You have the wrong idea. I said this firmly but casually, as if I weren't afraid, merely annoyed, the way I'd heard my mother speak to telemarketers who called during dinner: polite but dismissive.

The cabby did not say a thing.

It occurred to me that the door he had just closed behind us might well be locked, and that, even if *that* door *did* open, the one below might not. I might run down those stairs I'd just come up and find myself trapped at the bottom of a stairwell. Locked in.

It occurred to me that if I went for the sliding glass doors in front of me and ran out onto the little veranda I'd seen from below, I'd have to jump from twenty feet in the air onto hard sand, gravel, concrete.

It occurred to me that the laconic cabbie might get mean, might get violent, might be armed or nuts.

It occurred to me that no one knew where I was, not even me.

So I spoke dismissively, authoritative intonation my only hope, trying to talk my way out of this mess I had talked my way into.

—Não quero fazer isto, viu? I said. I don't want to do this. Quero ir. I want to go.I moved toward the door, as I spoke, moving slowly, casually. But when I passed the cabbie, my skin ached with the knowledge that he could, at any moment, stop me. I reached the door, grasped the knob; it turned in my hand. I opened it.

—I want to go, I said again, sensing that he was not following. He stood by the curtains looking out into the heat of the day.

—*Tudo bem*, he said, without looking at me. Fine. He didn't seem particularly disappointed.

The cabby charged me for the detour to his house and I paid it, thinking I'd shown him by giving him a smaller-than-usual tip. The stove I bought at the hypermercado was bright red, like a child's fire engine, small and square, like a toy a kid would buy to play with, if a kid were playing with fire.

Avenida John F. Kennedy

Not long after I moved into my apartment, Barbara invited me to lunch at hers. (Evidently the offense I'd imagined I'd given hadn't offended her, or perhaps she was as lonely as I.) It was hard not to notice the difference between our two places. Though they were just a few blocks apart, Barbara's had character and charm; her apartment was in an older building on Avenida President Kennedy.

The apartment was pale blue, with parquet floors and a set of multipaned windows looking out onto tree tops. It was soothing to enter, cool after the walk through the hot, bright streets. On entering her apartment, you passed through a short hall that led to a square living room, separated from the kitchen by a counter; from the living room, a door opened onto the bedroom and from there another led to the bath. There was a blue enameled table at the far end of the living room beneath a window, and two poems she'd written taped to the windowpanes. There was a hammock, a bookshelf, and several carved figures; a woodcut and a mandolin hung on the walls. Wonderful books: Levi-Strauss' *Tristes tropiques*, poetry by Fernando Pessoa, Elizabeth Bishop. It gave the impression of casual harmony. I'd never known a poet before and I came to think of this intentionality as a poet's—her belongings arranged as carefully as words on a page.

She noticed me admiring the mandolin and told me that she'd bought it that morning at a *praça* in the center of town. I held my hands behind my back, admiring the delicate inlay of its surface while Barbara went to fry aipim and sausages for our lunch. When I went to use the toilet, I saw a delicate macramé bikini hung up to dry on the shower curtain rod.

Her apartment was splendid. Everything about it was. The full-sized bed. The pale blue light. The poems on the window panes. The sausage, the buttery aipim. Her books. Everything about her fascinated me. Like a dress pattern I wanted to copy, I studied her to know how I too might live a more beautiful, vivid life.

· · ·

By contrast, the architect of the building I lived in aimed for and achieved the bland and sanitized neutrality of a shopping mall; the place had all the charm of a mid-level hotel chain. At the time, I found its lack of particularity comforting. I mistook the generic then, thought bland sameness a kind of common ground.

The building was of poured concrete, with four apartments on each of its five floors. Its ground floor was taken up with a glass-enclosed lobby, where the doorman sat, and a parking garage; an elevator and cement stairwell led up to each floor.

I lived on an upper floor. Down the hall from me lived Luisa; across the hall was Zé; next door were two, young, beefy guys, affluent drunks whose names I never knew, though one of them would come to my door late one night, waking me out of sleep with his insistent knocking, blind drunk and amorous, swearing that he loved me, begging me to let him in. We didn't exchange more than half a dozen words that year, save for that single declaration of love.

Nelci

My first weeks in Bahia, Nel and Isa made a habit of coming by in the afternoons to gossip and chat. They'd sit on the mattress that served as a couch and I'd brew us coffee or make them *sucos* by cutting open the hard purple husks of *maracujá*—passion fruit—and straining the juice and pulp through a sieve into a glass over ice, a glass I'd later fill with water and sugar to make the tart floral drink, a cross between pineapple juice and lemonade.

I suspected that Isa did not approve of my apartment, though she never said this directly. I suspected, after their first visit, that she mocked my lack of furnishings, the odd collection of mismatched things—a mattress, a coffee table, a guardaropa, no chairs.

So I was relieved when Nel came alone one day.

She arrived with a magazine tucked beneath her arm, *Veja*, Brazil's equivalent of *Newsweek*. She sat on the mattress, and I sat across from her on the floor, cross-legged, and listened to her talk about politics, about her hopes for her future. I was flattered that she wanted to talk to me, flattered to be someone's confidant. She was studying economics and hoped to be a professor, maybe enter politics someday.

She talked about the books she was reading and about the exams she was taking—to be a bank clerk, an office worker. She was tremendously bright, a voracious reader (she was always carrying a book or magazine), and proud of her intelligence. She scored impressively high on these exams, but positions were not open. Not long before, she'd accepted a job as a jewelry store clerk. But it hadn't worked out after the boss had wanted to sleep with her. Sex—it was plain to us both—was the real hard currency.

When I asked if she ever thought about returning home to the interior—
the Bahian countryside—she shrugged it off. She was vague about her reasons.

Though we never said it, we both knew that she could find a patron here,
some wealthy man to keep her as Isa was seeking, but Nel disdained dependency. She wanted to leave the boarding house; she wanted a place of
her own. She wanted her independence, to make something of herself, to
develop her potential.

Amazon Snapshot #5

The word for "development" in Portuguese is *desenvolvimento*, a telling term. From *envolver* (to involve, to envelop, to cover, to comprehend), and the prefix *des-*, implying its opposite: it means, literally, to uncover, to uninvolve, to un-include, to uncomprehend. In our quest to make good, we rarely think of this other possibility, this correlate—what we are un-making.

The reasons for "developing" the Amazon have been various—political, geopolitical, economic. (From the eighteenth-century attempt to deport U.S. slaves to the Amazon, to Henry Ford's twentieth-century rubber plantation, Fordlandia, to the folly of the Trans-Amazonian Highway, which continues today, the history of development has been a long and peculiar one.) There was money to be made in mining, logging, even through significant tax breaks to distant landlords who could claim to be "improving" the land by clear-cutting and stocking a cow or two. And there was the myth of the Amazon, the appeal of vast tracts of unclaimed land to which the disenfranchised poor could flock in search of a better life. It promised release from the pressure of rural migration to the cities and the ever-expanding ranks of the *favelados*.

Most of all, perhaps, there was money on loan from foreign banks eager to help Brazil "develop." The extravagantly costly construction of the Trans-Amazonian highway was instrumental in launching Brazil into its devastating cycle of debt to First World banks. The highway opened veins into the forest, and people followed. But the roads led nowhere. Asphalt ended on the edges of cliffs. Still, the highway had its uses: it was arguably a distraction from Brazilian political repression in the seventies. The War on the Jungle—presented as a war on ignorance and backwardness—was partly a cover for the war on the citizenry.

The reasons for wanting to save the forest are perhaps suspect as well. We cared, of course, for the forest and its creatures. But there was also a career to be made in the field, documenting the devastation. There were grants to be had. Papers to be published. My own grant, I imagine, was modest by comparison with the salaries of the internationally known researchers at the National Institute of Amazonian Research. One could win an international reputation documenting this loss our government and banks had helped effect.

Amazon Snapshot #6

I was a freshman in college when I first took an interest in the disappearing Amazon. I had enrolled in a seminar on U.S.-Latin American history, taught by Professor Gerald Cardoso, a handsome, affable man with the face of a Portuguese explorer. Cardoso had a massive and heroic head, a pale face with a full, black, silky beard, moustache and lustrous hair; he looked like something out of another century, straight off a ship from the age of exploration; his head belonged on a coin, in a history book or on a box of cigars.

Cardoso had been educated in Rio by Jesuits, who were—he led us to believe—a tough bunch, intellectually rigorous and stingy with their communion wine, which he, as an altar boy, had nonetheless nipped on the side. He had a charming habit, after his Jesuitical tutors I supposed, of pitting his students against history in a sporting debate of fact. Was the Panama Canal an infringement of sovereignty? Did the United States have a Manifest Destiny? Was the overthrow of Arbenz justified? The installation of Somoza? The military occupation of Haiti in 1913? Did the closing of the frontier destroy democracy in America? Had Kennedy?

Cardoso made history seem like a puzzle we could solve, a riddle whose answer one could discern with effort. The world—which had seemed to me in childhood to be a jumble of baffling sensation—began, marvelously, to make sense. The various habits and conventions that had constituted the better part of my personality until then seemed at last to cohere into some more sincere and significant form in the presence of concentrated effort, a consuming interest to know more. Cardoso was the most demanding professor I had in all my years of schooling, and although in my senior year at Yale we would, in another seminar, excoriate his only book as romantic in its view of Brazilian race relations, it was with him that I learned to learn. (And it was he who suggested that I apply for the fellowship that would eventually take me to the rain forest.)

When I think back now on that freshman year of college, I recall days defined by blue. The cold aquamarine of the pool I swam in each morning, the midnight blue of the sky outside the library windows where I studied each night. The almost erotic pleasure in the pursuit of understanding. When an answer—*the* answer—seemed within reach.

I had read very little growing up, and I was experiencing that autumn and winter the first thrill of literary absorption, discovering a world inside my head to which I could be transported by words. I was not among the ranks of waif-like girls in black or flowing paisleys in thrall to Woolf, Duras, or Plath who populated college campuses in those years (alongside boys with John Lennon glasses and a cultivated pallor who boasted allegiance to Nietzsche, Derrida, DeMan, or Barthes). At eighteen, I was captivated by reports in the Bulletin of the Atomic Scientists and by the Committee on Research Priorities in Tropical Biology of the National Research Council, the Tenth Annual Report of the Council on Environmental Quality. I read these with the fervor with which others (I imagined) approached the works of Austen and Shakespeare. These reports told a tale every bit as compelling as that of any French novel or Greek tragedy, in which a heroine is ruined by an unworthy suitor, a hero robbed of his birthright by unscrupulous foes, false friends, or vengeful gods.

I remember three things clearly from that first winter in New England:

First, the vivid image of a human body torn in half, the delicate stem of the spine rising from still-belted pants like some strange flower stalk, cast off by a dusty roadside in an unnamed suburb of Nicaragua circa 1975, when the American-backed Somoza dictatorship still ruled and his sadistic guard left these bodies as a warning to locals, as we sat at a seminar table in soft upholstered chairs, snow falling gently outside the windows onto green pines;

Second, a few lunches with Cardoso, though there could only have been one or two all term. Still they mattered to me, proof that I might be taken seriously, further evidence of erudition's pleasures;

Third, the weighty pleasure of library research late into the night as I sought clues to unravel the Gordian knot that was history, seeking out among the stacks obscure journal articles and legal precedents that I took pleasure in citing, mistakenly imagining it was only knowledge we lacked.

Amazons

Stuck in Salvador, I planned how I would get to the Amazon: I'd attend the Federal University in Bahia for the autumn term that would begin in a few weeks' time, then apply for an internship at INPA for the winter break in June. If all went well, I'd stay on there. I had a letter of recommendation from a man at the Bronx Botanical Garden and planned to write to INPA to inquire about a position.

Each day I planned to write the letter to INPA, but each day, somehow, I didn't. Days passed, and still I did not write it. Probably I was afraid of rejection, but I think now that I was equally afraid of acceptance, of having to leave behind the perfect abstract dream of the forest I'd read about—like the dream of romantic love—and step into the messy actual, to see both the forest and the trees.

Instead, while I waited for the university to begin, my formless blue days took shape around a few familiar figures—Nelci, Isa, Barbara—and the routines I developed to navigate from hour to hour.

Each morning, from my apartment, I would walk to the corner pharmacy to weigh myself. My weight, like the empty blue sky, was all but invariable. Still I liked the chalky smell of the pharmacy, the glass windows, the ritual; I liked having someplace to go each morning while I waited for school to begin, while I waited to get up the nerve to request an internship in Manaus.

Like a lot of young women, I was mapping the territory of the body, monitoring its forms, charting the landscape, laying claim to the vast tracts of it—skin and muscle and fat and hair—through diet, weight, relentless measurement. I liked the sherbet green scale. Its blank round face. The way the needle swung round like a clock hand only to shimmy to a stop at 61, 60, at 59 kilos.

The daily calculation of loss was oddly comforting.

Boa Gente

It was largely from loneliness that I agreed to study capoeira when Barbara invited me to take classes with her at a school in town. I was flattered when she phoned one afternoon to ask me to join her.

Capoeira, she explained, is a Bahian martial art; part dance, part fight, it was first practiced by West Africans who—brought to Brazil as slaves and forbidden to fight—took to disguising their martial training as dance. It was only when their Portuguese captors—at war with Spanish colonial neighbors in Paraguay—sent slaves to the front line to meet the advancing troops and draw off fire that capoeira was revealed to be martial and lethal. Folklore has it that the capoeiristas won that battle, beating back the armed Spaniards with only their feet as weapons.

Capoeira is an art of inversion in many ways. Because it was developed by slaves whose hands were shackled, because it had to be disguised as a dance, capoeira is fought with the feet alone. Unlike such martial arts as karate and aikido, capoeira uses the hands only ornamentally (to circle the body in a ginga) and for balance (as when holding up the body in a cartwheel). The feet are everything, and if you *joga bem*—play well—if you are a real capoeirista, your heels are often over your head.

The secret of capoeira is not balance, as you might think, but the ability to go out of balance and regain it.

The capoeira school bordered a large, public park that lay halfway between Barra and the city center. The park—named Campo Grande—was the centerpiece of an older elegant neighborhood, once fashionable. At its edges, one could still see mansions of marble and limestone with the ornate facades typical of the turn of the last century tucked in among the more modern apartment buildings, low and squat with balconies suggesting modest elegance. In the course of the twentieth century, the park had become, it appeared, less a destination than a stopover, a weigh station between other points. Now it served mostly as a site for various bus stops for the crowds heading into or out of the center, traveling to or from outlying neighborhoods. In the park, kids played and businessmen sat on benches. Everyone on their way somewhere else.

We had trouble finding the school. But finally we did. At the far end of the *praça*, facing the park, it was unprepossessing, a single-story building constructed of cinder block wedged between two others. The side facing the park was open to the street, the roof supported by pillars. The floor was gray cement, the interior walls white. This was Mestre Boa Gente's capoeira school, where each Saturday morning in the coming ten weeks I would arrive early to embarrass myself.

Mestre Boa Gente was a small and handsome man, his skin dark as a coffee bean; that first day of class, he was dressed in what I would learn was the uniform of the school—white drawstring pants and white T-shirt on which was printed the school logo (a pair of figures dancing). His body was muscular. Even his face was: he had interesting folds around his mouth from smiling, furrows in his brow. It was impossible to guess his age. His hair was cropped short, close to the head. He had the radiance of the religious, the light saints are said to have and movie stars do. Even with my limited command of Portuguese, I understood that his name meant Master Good Guys. Despite his martial gravity, the name seemed apt.

Everything about Boa Gente suggested compression, as if a much larger man had been distilled into this small figure. His long, lithe muscles bulged; he seemed to glow. He made me think of coal turned to diamonds, of the density and gravitational pull of black holes. Or rather, he did not make me think of any of these things then, but I do now, recalling him. That was the sort of presence he had as he stood before us that first Saturday morning in February, dressed in his white cotton drawstring pants and the white shirt printed with the logo of the school. He seemed denser than the rest of us, more solid than we; beside him, before him, arrayed around the cool cement floor, waiting for his instructions, we seemed insubstantial as clouds.

Barbara had not told me that she was a dancer when she proposed I sign up for capoeira class with her. She made it sound anthropological, an outing into Bahian pop culture. To study capoeira in Salvador, she said, would be akin to studying break dancing in Harlem (breakdancing had just come into vogue in 1984). It was a main line to the culture. The A train.

I had no idea that she could dance, that she had in fact trained as a ballet dancer (though perhaps this was only as a child). As soon as I saw her in class, as soon as anyone did, it was obvious. She was a natural.

From a raised platform at the front of the long training room, Mestre Boa Gente explained each pose to us, then took us through them, calling out moves we were to execute. He strolled among us. I could hear Boa Gente admiring others' postures, complimenting their improvement from the year before. I could hear him—indeed, I listened for him to—praise Barbara.

When Barbara gingaed—the opening moves of capoeira in which one brings the right arm around in front of the body while the right foot drops back, then reverses this, much as a speed skater moves, the torso leaned low to the ground, as close to parallel as possible—it was clear she would surpass me. Had.

Barbara's body seemed made for the long graceful arcs that are the constituent elements of capoeira. When she drew her left arm around in front of her, dropping her left foot back—continuing to ginga—she seemed to be gathering water, drawing it to her. When Boa Gente called out *meia lua*—half moon—Barbara pivoted on her right foot, her torso angled back as if she were reclining on her right side in midair; she raised her left leg, knee bent, foot forward, and then extended her foot, so that she planted a blow to the air in front of her. For a moment she stood there, balanced on a single long leg like an egret or a crane, before drawing her raised foot through a clean arc to the floor.

By contrast, I was a clod. My hamstrings tight, I could not raise my leg into an elegant arc, could not draw it up to eye level to strike an opponent's head with a graceful *meia lua*, tracing a half moon's curve from midair to floor. My pivot was more like a beleaguered hop. My arc more of a teetering, an effort to keep my balance as I raised a leg into the air, my torso stretched in the opposite direction.

I had been athletic only once in my life and then fleetingly as a swimmer my first two years of college. With an anorectic's urgent fervor, I swam one to two miles before breakfast each day of my freshman and sophomore years, after which I ate a bowl of bran cereal with skim milk and a cup of hot lemon water with saccharine. Mine was a brief solitary acquaintance with the bodied, a private fluidity. In public—playing childhood b-ball games or in high school gym, running a cross-country meet, playing volleyball or the dread softball game—I was, indubitably, a clod.

When Boa Gente reached me, he grabbed my left leg, mid-arc, in one powerful hand and held it. He raised my outstretched leg higher, forcing me to lean back farther. He raised it, raised it. He watched my face. He did not smile. My hamstrings ached; the seams of my drawstring pants strained, then Boa Gente slowly guided my foot through the proper arc before bringing it to the floor.

By the end of class, I was exhausted and demoralized and relieved it was over. I was accustomed to doing well in classrooms; I had forgotten about gym class. All I could hope for was to get home, take a shower, get a cool *suco* to drink. I tried to calculate calories burned in the hour-and-a-half class, calculation my only source of consolation, the only pleasure I could take in our morning's labors.

I was headed for the doorway where we'd left our shoes when Boa Gente called out from the platform at the far end of the room for us to come over for a moment: he had an announcement to make. The class gathered, sweating, breathing hard, around the platform where Boa Gente stood.

—We have several new students to welcome, he said. He named two girls and spoke of their past training. Then he introduced a tall, lanky blond, a Paulista. Then he said that two North Americans had come to train here and asked us to give our names.

—I'm Barbara, Barbara said in her perfect Portuguese.

—Elena, I said, as if it were now my name.

Chequinho

I first met Chequinho on my way home from capoeira that day. I was dressed in the cotton sweatpants and T-shirt still wet with perspiration from the morning's training. Barbara may have stayed after class that first day or perhaps we took the same bus home and she got off earlier, at Avenida Kennedy, where she lived. I don't recall how it was that I ended up alone in the street that day, but I was alone, under the bright February sky, sweaty and ridiculous and feeling immense in my thin cotton drawstring pants and T-shirt (an outfit that Barbara managed to make flattering with her tiny waist and slender flexible frame. That first day of class, she had accented her outfit with a red bandana that she tied across her brow. She looked like a bandit, like a street kid, tough and smart. I looked like a *blanc mange*, a mobile marshmallow).

I was walking up Avenida Princessa Isabella, halfway to the Rua João Pondé where my apartment was, when I saw him coming toward me on the other side of the street. A small and compact man, tanned and muscular, attractive in an edgy way that I liked then (like those tough boys I dated in high school, playground smokers who came to physics class high on coke or pot but passed their classes anyway). He was wiry, street tough, handsome in the way that cigarette ads promoted then—a slight stubble at his cheek, dark eyes, an angular jaw, tanned with muscular arms. He smiled at me and I reflexively smiled back and thought, as I did, that his was an appreciative glance.

I was delighted to be subject to even this casual flirtation, to have someone pay attention to me after the hideous class where the only attention I drew was Boa Gente's evident dismay. In the misguided social calculus of adolescent girls, I equated being liked (especially by boys or men) with being worthy. The man crossed the street to me and asked if I lived around here. I hesitated, said, Not far. He asked if I knew where a certain address was, and I said, apologizing, that I didn't know it.

—You're not from around here, he said. It was not a question.

—No. It was obvious from my accent I supposed.

—You practice capoeira? he asked (the name of the school was on my shirt).

—I'm trying to learn.

—You're very beautiful, he said.

—Hardly, I laughed, gesturing to my outfit, my T-shirt stained with sweat, the ill-fitting sweat pants.

—I'm Chequinho, he said.

—Elena, I said. As I started up the street toward my apartment, away from the port he was headed for, I felt cheerful and yelled back to him, *Chau*, and he said, *Chau, Boneca.* Bye, Doll. And both of us laughed at that.

Amazon Snapshot #7

We have long dreamed of Amazons.

Apollonius of Rhodes, the third-century BC poet, described them as warrior women; the Greek dramatist Aeschylus called them "the warring Amazons, men-haters." According to Ovid they were the daughters of the peace-loving nymph Harmony and Ares, god of war, a nation of female warriors who lived in Scythia near the Black Sea in what is now the Ukraine.

Some say the Amazons cut off their right breast to aid them in throwing the javelin (keeping the left to nurse their children); others say that they removed the hand or leg of sons. Some say they worshipped Artemis, goddess of the moon. Statues and pictures of the Amazons attest to their place in human imagination, but little is written of them. "Familiar though they are to us," Edith Hamilton writes, "there are few stories about them."

The earliest accounts claim that the Amazons of Libya waged war on Atlantis. They are said to have defended Troy against the Greeks under their queen Penthesilea. Achilles is said to have fought them there and to have fallen in love with their leader after having killed her. Still others say that the Amazons were simply warrior women who took power in Themiscyra and assigned domestic duties to men. Their decline began with the expeditions to their land of Heracles and Theseus.

According to the *Random House* dictionary beside me, "Amazon" is a noun that can refer to a river in northern South America, to a race of female warriors, to "a tall, powerful, aggressive woman," or to "any of several green parrots of the genus Amazona . . . often kept as pets."

The *Oxford English Dictionary* gives the root as Greek—*a mazon*, meaning "without breast"—in reference to the women warriors' practice of removing a breast so as to shoot better. Robert Graves maintains that the term more likely derives from an Armenian word meaning moon women ("since the priestesses of the moon goddess on the South-eastern shore of the Black Sea bore arms, as they also did in the Libyan Gulf of Sirite").

The source of the Amazon River's name is more certain: according to the *OED*, the river takes its name from the "female warriors there seen by the Spaniards."

It was a scribe on the earliest European expedition down the Amazon River in 1542 who first called the women warriors seen on the river's banks the "Amazons." Perhaps he was referring to the women of Classical mythology, or perhaps the Spaniards were merely repeating what local Indians had said (a similar word in Tupi-Guarani means tidal bore, a name applied to those living in the area as well). The scribe described the women warriors he saw as "very white and tall . . . [with] hair very long and braided and wound about the head . . . very robust and . . . naked . . . with their bows and arrows in their hands, doing as much fighting as ten Indian men."

According to one captive's report, those river women were warriors who remained unmarried but bore children. When men were needed for mating, they were captured and brought to the Amazon village (where no men were allowed to live); once the women were pregnant, the captured men were returned home unharmed. The Amazons' houses were said to be built of stone; guards patrolled the roads that connected their villages, demanding tolls. They are said to have ridden long-haired, camel-like animals as big as horses (alpaca perhaps, a camel relative), and to worship in places adorned with gold and silver idols fashioned in the form of women.

No one ever recorded another encounter with the Amazons. When the expedition, led by the Spanish explorer Francisco de Orellana, emerged from the river (then known as the Marañón, later as the Orellana), the scribe could not have known that in time the great river would take its name from the mythic women he claimed to have once seen there: the Amazon.

When Brazil's military government first undertook "Operation Amazon," a large-scale colonization project that relocated impoverished Brazilians to infertile farms in the forest—one of a number of a disastrous policies intended to develop the Amazon basin in the 1960s and 1970s—the Amazon they dreamed of conquering was not a tribe of women but a place, a rain forest in whose mythically verdant expanse they saw an answer to pressing national problems that beset the new government in the wake of a military coup; they saw, in the vast rain forest, a distraction from political repression, an answer to rural poverty, a means to fund industrial development. It was also a possible base from which guerrilla and international threats might come, a wilderness to be feared and conquered.

An Education

The first week of March, much to my relief, the university term began, classes started, and I had somewhere to go each day. The economic faculty of the Federal University of Bahia was located on a high hill overlooking the city and bay, in a tony neighborhood behind the American embassy. I took a bus to the base of the hill, got off there among fashionable houses with wide driveways, and walked up a narrow path to class through dense trees heavy with the massive oblong forms of green jackfruit whose sweet yellow flesh smelled like Juicy Fruit gum.

I could understand more than I could say, but still the classes were challenging. I enrolled in two: a course in Bahian economic history and a second in macroenomics. I'd studied both subjects before, which helped, but still I found it an effort to follow lectures.

Nel was not in my classes, but I saw her on my way into school one day and we agreed to go home together. As we walked home that afternoon from the bus stop, under the flamboyants, the glinting fronds, Nelci explained that lots of girls here were kept by men. Even Nelci, who knew she was not beautiful, had had her offers. A dentist, she said, a married man, had offered her an apartment not long ago. She wanted to leave the boarding house; she was tempted. She frowned. Shook her head.

—*Feio,* she said. Ugly.

I did not know if she meant the man or the offer or the situation.

Luisa, my neighbor, was the first kept woman I'd ever met; she lived at the far end the hall, where a small glass window looked out onto the rooftop of a neighboring building. She came by to introduce herself not long after I moved in. She knocked on the door and when I opened it, there she was— very pretty, a little plump, dressed that first day, as I would learn she always was, in a satin robe that barely closed, a robe that ended high on her thighs, crossed over her shapely hips and breasts, a robe always—it seemed—on the verge of falling open.

I never once saw Luisa in street clothes; I never saw her leave the second floor of the apartment building where we lived. She was like someone exiled from the larger world to this small place. She was sweet tempered, gentle, bawdy, motherly, flirtatious, underneath it all a little shy, perhaps. She had lustrous black hair that curled wonderfully as it fell to her shoulders. From that first day we met, she made me think of 1940s movie stars—Rosalind Russell, Ingrid Bergman—she had that same kind of glamour, the opulence those women had, a voluptuous innocence.

When she entered my apartment that first day, she brought with her a scent of floral talcum that I would later come to associate with her visits. That day, as later, she came in full makeup, wearing slippers and her robe, as if every hour of the day she were readying herself to go out, as if each time I saw her she was caught midway through her toilette.

I invited her in, apologizing that I had nothing to offer by way of a drink or food.

—*Não me importa.* No problem, she said, smiling as she came in. I showed her my rooms with their spare furnishings—flipping on the light in the bathroom, walking her into the closet-sized kitchen. The apartment looked shabbier when I saw it through the eyes of a stranger, and I felt embarrassed that I had made of it no more than this, but Luisa was reassuring. She said that her place was exactly like mine, the same layout, just reversed.

After our brief tour, she took a seat on the coffee table beside the phone, and I sat on the mattress, and we chatted a bit. She asked what had brought me to Bahia, and I told her, and I asked what she did here. She was vague about her work, said only that she wasn't working now. Her family, she said when I asked, didn't live in Salvador.

Before she left, she gave me a big talcum-scented hug and said I should come up the hall and knock on her door if I ever needed anything. She was always home, she said.

I visited her apartment only once and then briefly. She seemed nervous about inviting Nel and me in and did not invite us to stay. I recall being impressed by the apartment's opulence—how full the small room was. There was a little dining area with a table and chairs, a television set and a few comfortable overstuffed chairs set with lace-edged pillows, lace doilies on good polished furniture that looked old and costly, a massive bed with a down comforter and heaps of satin pillows in pink and red. The whole room seemed to be made of lace and satin, in pink, white, red. Like a child's room, or a doll's house.

The Monkey

The day I went looking to buy a companion, there was only one monkey vendor in the market. He was set up at the far end of the small cobblestone *praça* between Pelourinho and the Ladeira, known as the Terreiro de Jesus. The *praça* was always crowded with vendors and on that day there was also a small *roda*—or circle—of capoeiristas performing awkwardly for French and American tourists who did not know the difference.

I made my way among the tables to the monkey vendor. The man sat curled on his stool beside a staff from which tiny squirrel monkeys walked about on chains. I thought it was cruel to take them from the trees to sell to tourists like me, but at least I would not keep it on a chain. I could not pretend to be a simian liberator, but I told myself I'd treat my monkey better than this. I wanted someone to come home to, something to love, and I imagined an exotic pet might lend me a daring and romantic air that I too plainly lacked.

Micos—as the little squirrel monkeys are called—fill the trees in Salvador, looking like something designed by Dr. Seuss: small, furry, with thin striped tails and quizzical faces; white tufts of hair spring from their cheeks and a small pad of white fur lies between their brows, above grave bright eyes. They travel in groups, squat together in the trees in city parks, screaming in high shrill calls. (I didn't yet know the Brazilian expression—*pegar um mico*—which literally means "to grab a monkey" but is slang for getting in trouble, making a mess of things.)

The squirrel monkey I chose was small, with brown-gray silky fur and a tiny old man's face. The runt of the litter. The others had the unfocused gaze of animals, wild and abstracted. The monkey I chose had a vengeful glare, intelligent, furious. The vendor assured me that the little mico would grow if I fed it well, so I paid him and took it home on the bus, a string tied round its neck, his soft body cupped in my hands.

I named him Tiago for a character in a film, *Bye Bye Brazil*, about a down-on-their-luck circus troupe in the Amazon; Tiago was their ringleader. The name sounded Brazilian, exotic. It didn't occur to me to name him for someone I knew or loved; movie characters were more romantic to me then than people I knew.

But it didn't grow as the vendor said it would. I brought it bananas, expensive apples, peeled grapes, but it only sniffed the chunks I set before it and jumped to the windowsill, at the end of its rope. On the sill, it screamed. *Screamed.* Then it waited. A shriek would come from the forest behind the apartment building across the street. The mico screamed again. I fancied sometimes that his was a cry for help and I cooed to him that I could not let him go, that he would only die in the trees, that he wasn't strong enough, his body was too frail. One fall and his bones would snap like toothpicks. But he only looked at me with moist green eyes, stared into my face, opened his mouth, and shrieked.

At night, I tried to set him on my stomach beneath the blankets to keep him warm and calm, but he would crawl away to the other end of the mattress.

Occasionally, though, Tiago came to me and climbed into my lap. He would sit and clean himself like a cat, licking his paws and bringing them down over his face again and again. If I sat motionless, when he was done cleaning himself, he might stretch out along my forearm, his face buried in the crook of my elbow, beneath one paw, and sleep. Only after his body was still, just the fur on his side parting and closing, parting and closing in rhythm with his breath, could I reach over and scratch the back of his neck, stroke it slowly, dreamily, feeling the silky ruff, the tiny ribs, and rest my eyes unfocused on the windowsill—less alone.

Focco

Not long after I'd bought the monkey, Nel and Isa came for a visit. They were talking, as was their custom, about men. Isa was dating several, choosing among them like fruit in a market. She seemed unimpressed, never mentioned names. No one evidently merited a proper noun. She spoke not of the men themselves but of the places they took her.

When Isa saw Tiago on his tether by the window, she clapped her hands in delight and trilled, *Que joia,* Elena. What a joy. I was proud for a moment to possess something that had the power to impress her. (She had met Barbara and greatly admired her beauty, but I had the feeling I'd failed to impress.) Isa reached out a hand to stroke the little mico, and his head rose—following her movements as she moved toward him, then, as her fingers rested lightly on his head, he bit her, hard. She screamed. Sorry, I said and went to make us coffee.

When I returned to the living room, Isa was trying on several outfits she'd bought that day, trying to decide which to wear that night, modeling for us. Nel seemed distracted. She answered Isa in a bored flat tone as Isa held up one black dress, another brightly colored one, a skirt, a shirt.

—The black one, Nel said. Definitely more sophisticated.

—Are you sure, Isa asked. You think? Isa bit her lower lip. I have to look very good, she said. He says he's taking me to the Othon Palace for dinner.

The Othon Palace was the most expensive hotel in Salvador, set on a promontory in the same exclusive tony neighborhood as the American embassy. I'd only seen it from the street, in passing.

—I can see if he has a friend for you, Nel, Isa said. We could go together.

Nel frowned. I don't know, she said. For the first time Nel seemed indifferent to the offer. Anyway, I have a date. Focco is going to take me to a boite.

—Focco? Isa made a face.

Nel shrugged.

—That should be fun, I said. I'd love to go to a boite sometime. I had noticed them while walking home from the embassy a month ago, and while riding the bus back from school—discreet private clubs tucked into the lush greenery along the beach road. I knew that nightclubs were often for members only, and their exclusivity appealed to me.

—Let Elena go with Focco, Isa proposed. You can come with me.

—I don't know, Nel said.

—Who's Focco? I asked.

—You wouldn't like him, Elena, Nel said.

—He's rich, Isa said. He drives a red sports car.

—He's a fat and ugly old man, Nel said.

—Then why are you going? I asked.

Nel shrugged. Because Isa didn't want to go, she said.

—Focco's fine, Isa said. He's harmless. Come on, Nel, let Elena go. You can come with me.

—You don't even know if your date has a friend, Nel reasoned.

—I'll call and see, Isa said, and picked up my phone and dialed.

—I'd like to see a boite, I told Nel.

She didn't argue, but she looked a little sorry.

I'd rarely been out at night in Salvador and I was excited by the prospect. Salvador seemed a city of night, a place that revealed itself after sunset, that unfolded by dark; I felt that I was missing that life. In those days I often felt that life was happening somewhere else, at the next table, behind a closed door.

I dressed for the boite as if I were going to a Rotary luncheon, in an indigo silk dress and high heels that (unbeknownst to me) would set me towering ridiculously over the squat Focco. I aimed to look attractive but modest. I curled my eyelashes in a metal clamp, I brushed on mascara, powdered on rouge, rolled on lip gloss (never having got the hang of actual lipstick, I clung to the habits of seventh grade when shiny lips sufficed).

Egberto, the door man, gave me a worried look as I came down to meet Focco in the foyer. Focco was, as Nel had promised, both *feio e gordo*—fat and ugly. But I was impressed by Focco's ugliness, which given its extremity had the quality of an attainment. He was singularly the ugliest man I'd ever been out with. He had a head like a small keg, barrel shaped and bulbous, thickening at the cheeks. His faced had the unhealthy flush of high blood pressure. His lips were enormous, purplish and ichthyic, like a grouper's. His body was bulbous, held in by the gray suit he wore. I remember that he wore an expensive and beautiful slate-blue silk tie. He was the first person I'd ever met who made me pity his clothes, the waste of their beauty.

Egberto held the door open for us, nodded at Focco, wished me a good night.

Out on the street, Focco opened the car door for me, and—once I was seated—slammed it. It was, just as Isa had said, a lovely car. Small and round as Focco himself. But shiny and red. Focco said little as he drove. Perhaps he, like I, felt gypped. Perhaps he'd been led to believe I was a beautiful American, blond or busty, sophisticated, a woman of the world. It must've been obvious at a glance that I was not.

Probably he asked me what I was doing in Salvador. Probably he asked me what I was studying at the university. Perhaps he discovered quickly that

I did not speak his language well. I remember that we drove in silence and darkness to the nightclub along some beach.

The club was small, low-ceilinged, crowded. Mirrors lined the walls and a mirrored ball spun over the small dance floor. There was a lot of smoke. Small costly drinks. A leather banquette into which I was wedged between Focco and some others who did not appear to be his friends.

I felt sorry for Focco. He seemed stiff in his suit and hot. Sweat beaded on his brow and at his temples. He took off his suit coat and laid it over the back of the banquette; patches of sweat were evident beneath his arms. No one seemed to want to talk to him or me. We sat, mutually bored, ignored, waiting for the jet set to arrive. I kept yawning and then smiling in apology.

Somehow I had gotten it into my head, perhaps from some misguided guidebook, that the Brazilian musicians and artists for which Bahia was famous frequented clubs like this. I was under the impression that I might see Caetano Veloso or Gilberto Gil here, or perhaps an American or European celebrity, Sting or Jagger.

At around midnight, a scrawny, deeply tanned pair arrived, followed by a small phalanx of associates. The man and woman were both slender, hair bleached, streaked blond. They had great teeth and wore things that caught the light—gold watches and chains, black leather pants that clung to their narrow hips. This, alas, evidently, was the jet set, flown in like out-of-season fruit.

I had hoped for the famous—Michael Jackson or Maria Bethania—I had hoped that their glamour might be contagious, that I might catch it like a cold, but they turned out to be nothing really; they were merely rich, bearing cocaine, which Focco offered me and which I declined.

The couple invited us to join them for drinks at the Othon Palace. But I said I had to get home. I had classes the next morning.

—It's still early, Focco objected. It was only 1 a.m. What do you have to get home for?

The blond woman laughed. It's past her bedtime, she said.

I was aware that I was embarrassing the fish-lipped, rich Focco. But I didn't care. I was tired and I was bored and I was disappointed in all of us for not being more interesting.

—Take me home, please, I said.

His friends said they'd see him later at the hotel.

Focco drove me back to my apartment in silence, clearly annoyed. If we had still been speaking by then, we might have agreed that the evening had been a disaster. But we weren't speaking.

Nevertheless, it took me a solid five minutes to get out of the tiny red sports car, fighting off Focco's fishy kisses, his thick stubby fingers and fleshy hands. I felt I owed him, but I did not know how much, what was the right amount to tip in the economy of sex, what was the going rate of exchange.

Amazon Snapshot #8

I didn't see numbers' limitations then. I was comforted by their unvarying sameness, their reliability in any language. One remained one; two remained two, whether applied to a girl, a boy, a brick, a pile of lumber.

This is the appeal of cost-benefit analyses, free-market democracy: we can imagine that we are all equal before the disinterested dollar, that value can be clearly assigned without having to deal with messier considerations—assessments of the good, the beautiful, the virtuous and worthy. In economics' stark terms, an acre of land may be worth its yield in gold, corn, timber, or minerals, but what about its breathtaking beauty? The quiet it provides, the visual relief from cityscapes? Stripped of the messiness of ethics and morality, stripped of consideration of the public good (the beautiful, the virtuous, the worthy), such calculations can badly mislead us.

Economics, in the twentieth- and twenty-first centuries, has come to be associated with market predictions, with balancing supply and demand, a faith in the freedom to consume. Price, our principle standard; cost-benefit analyses, our debased logic. But it wasn't always so. Economics comes from the Greek *oikos*, meaning "house" (a root it shares with the word *ecology*) and *nemein*, "to manage." We often think of the two matters—ecology and economics—as being at a great remove from one other: nature on one hand, cold cash on the other. But etymology reminds us that the two are intimately linked, and that their original meaning—their original purpose or aim—was to address the human place in the world.

Higher Education

From the hilltop campus of the Federal University of Bahia, you could look out over the bay for which the city—Salvador da Bahia—was named and glimpse Itaparica. As Nel and I were walking home together from campus one afternoon, she told me that Isa had acquired a boyfriend there since I'd seen her last, a man named Marcos who had a house on the island. She rubbed her thumb and fingers together and raised an eyebrow to indicate that he had money. She shrugged. We will go sometime, Nel said. He has a nice house. He likes Americans.

I smiled. It seemed that we would go, that we'd do everything we planned.

But then in late March the university workers went on strike, shutting down classes and putting an end to Nelci's scholarship. Without money for rent, her options narrowed. Isa's new boyfriend Marcos offered to let her stay with him on the island for a while, but she needed to stay in the city to earn money. Nel and I had become friends, and it seemed natural that she should move in with me. I thought hard about inviting her to move in. At the time I flattered myself that I could do something to protect Nel from having to depend on some man, but it was no sacrifice for me. I wanted the company and I felt generous being able to offer help.

We were still in the infatuated stage of friendship. I was flattered that she spoke to me of serious things—politics, her ambitions, occasionally family; she was smart and I felt smarter in her company.

One night, not long after the strike was declared, we went for a walk through the port toward the lighthouse and then past that, out beyond the Barra Vento bar to a promontory with a grassy knoll on which a statue of Christ stood overlooking jagged black rocks and pale surf visible in the moonlight.

The sky was full of stars and a sliver of moon, and as we walked in and out of the shadow of streetlights, Nel told me about growing up in Feira de Santa, a small town in the interior. She said she'd been very close to her father. Now, they no longer spoke. When I asked why, she hesitated.

—I got pregnant, she said. I had an abortion.

I nodded. I knew that here, in a Catholic country, this was a very serious thing.

She said that she used to live in Amaralina, a suburb a few beaches east of us, just ahead several miles. She'd lived there with her best friend, Valeria, who was also a university student then. When Nel's father learned of the abortion, he cut her off.

—I had to move out, she said.

—Where's Valeria now?

She shrugged.

—We don't speak much anymore.

It made me like Nel, her sorrow and history. And I liked her for confiding in me. Here hardly anyone had deemed me worthy of confidences.

When we came to a public gym that marked the end of Barra and entry into another more elegant neighborhood, we stopped to lean on the railing and look out over the water, and I made up my mind.

—If you want, I said, you can live with me for a while, until you find a place of your own. I was glad to find the right words in Portuguese.

—Thanks, Elena, she said, but I have no money for rent. I couldn't afford to pay you.

—You wouldn't have to pay me, I said.

She looked at me as if trying to gauge my offer.

—I don't need money, I said. I have my *bolsa*.

—It's generous of you to offer, she said. I appreciate it.

—It would be nice to have the company, I said.

—I'll think about it, she said. But she sounded skeptical.

We began to walk again, turning back now toward home.

—It would only be temporary, until you find a job, I said.

—I hate the boarding house, said Nel.

—You can let me know.

—I will, Elena, she said. And we dropped the subject.

We walked home under the artificial lights, the faraway stars.

Salvador

A few days later, Nel stopped by my apartment, alone. She stood outside the door a little formally, grave, restrained. She offered me her cheek and we exchanged kisses.

—*Tudo bem*, Elena? she asked.

—*Tudo bom*, I said. *Entra, entra*, I urged her. C'mon in.

—Are you busy? she asked, looking around the unsociably tidy room. I don't mean to interrupt. I'm sorry for coming by like this.

—You're not interrupting, I said. Have a seat. I gestured toward the make-shift couch. *Quer cafezinho?* I asked. In the northeast I'd learned it was common to offer guests a cup of hot, strong, sugary coffee and a shower to fight off the enervation that the heat here inspired.

—*Quero,* she said, *obrigada.* Nel picked up the magazine on the end table and began to flip through it. I went to the kitchen and lit a burner and put on the red-enameled kettle to boil water for coffee that I'd later strain through a filter.

When I returned to the living room, Nel was seated on my makeshift couch with the magazine open on her lap, but she was looking around the room instead of at the pages, squinting, as if deep in thought. The monkey sat tethered in the window, his back to us, facing the forest across the street, occasionally letting out a shriek, calling to other monkeys there. She took the coffee I handed her and thanked me. I sat down next to her, legs crossed.

We talked awhile about Isa, who was on Itaparica for the weekend with her new boyfriend.

—She asked me to come with, Nel said, but I didn't feel like it.

I nodded and sipped. I couldn't tell if Nel missed Isa. Secretly I was glad to have her to myself; I was more at ease when we were alone.

—I've been thinking about what you said the other night, Nel said, addressing her coffee. Y'know, when we walked to the farol.

—Uh huh, I said.

—If it's still all right with you, I would like to move in.

—Oh, that's great, I said. I felt briefly that pinch of trepidation that accompanies an offer accepted, the vague fear that we were embarking on something complicated here, something that could go wrong. But I was too relieved by the prospect of company to care.

—That's great, I said again, smiling. I believed it would be.

—I won't stay for long, Nel said. Only until I can find a job and a place of my own.

—You're welcome to stay as long as you like.

—As soon as I get a job, I will pay you rent, she said.

—You don't need to. I'll be paying it anyway.

—I want to, she said. I don't want to be a burden.

—You won't be, I said. I'm happy to have you here.

It didn't occur to me that I was not the one Nel worried for. It didn't occur to me that she was protecting herself, or trying to. I felt magnanimous, as if I were doing something useful here: protecting Nel from the necessity of depending on some guy—the married dentist, or Focco—protecting her against exploitation.

—Do you really think two people can live here? she asked.

—Definitely, I said.

We talked about what we could do with the space to make it homier, more comfortable for two. I proposed we get another bed.

—Where would we put it? Nel asked. I can't afford one just now, and there isn't room.

—You can share the mattress with me, I said, feeling the smallness of the offer, the poverty of my furnishings suddenly a thing I noticed with embarrassment, as if I'd forgotten to dress.

—No, Elena, she said. I don't want to put you out.

—You wouldn't.

—It's not big enough for two, she said. You wouldn't be comfortable.

—I'd be fine.

—I'll sleep on the floor, Nel said, rubbing her palm over the stiff stubble of carpet. I'll be fine. It's sufficient.

This seemed a penitential proposal, and I wondered, briefly, if she expected me to propose that she take the bed, that I take the floor, but I didn't. I argued the point with her halfheartedly then I gave up and said, I can buy a hammock. I've been meaning to anyway. I can sleep in that, and you can take the mattress.

She shrugged. Maybe, she said.

I offered half the guardaropa for her use, but she said she didn't need closet space.

—I'll be fine, Elena, she said. I don't have much. I don't want to inconvenience you.

—You won't, I said.

—I'll try to stay out of the apartment during the day, she continued, resolutely, so that you can have your privacy.

—I'm happy to have you here, I said. And, at that moment, it was true, I was.

The next day, Nel arrived in the afternoon with a small clear-plastic beach bag decorated with yellow daisies and filled with clothes, and a paper sack containing toiletries, magazines, and shoes. Her worldly possessions in two sacks. She brought little with her, she had little to bring, but she brought know-how and superstitions.

Not long after she moved in, I noticed a glass of water under the coffee table and one in the corner of the room. When I asked her what these were, she told me it was a wives' tale, a superstition: a glass of water in the corner of a room will collect spirits so they do not haunt the inhabitants. I didn't ask if she felt haunted there, if she felt the need for protection. I thought it was a charming custom, a bit of local color.

The afternoon that Nel moved in, we left the door open to the hall to let a breeze from the windows blow through. I hadn't yet gotten around to putting up curtains over the enormous sliding glass windows that composed most of one wall facing the street, so the afternoon sun blazed in, filling the room with heat.

Zé, a Mexican-American guy from Texas who lived across the hall, passed our open door as Nel was moving in and seemed delighted. As a rule, Zé avoided speaking to me, embarrassed to be seen with a fellow American, as if I'd outed him, but he had something of a crush on Nel and seeing her, he stopped in the doorway. He smiled at me, as if I'd risen in his estimation. He stepped into the apartment and leaned against the wall, one leg bent, a tennis shoe placed against the wall behind him, and watched Nel unpack her few belongings.

—So, Nel, he asked, Where're you gonna sleep? Looks like you'll need another bed in here.

—I'm going to get a hammock, I said. So Nel can have the bed.

—I'll sleep on the floor, Nel said.

Zé laughed, as if this were a joke.

—You won't want to do *that* for long, he said.

And we laughed too.

If I could not save the forest, I would save Nel.

Lembrança do Senhor do Bonfim

As soon as Nel moved in, I began to feel more at home in Salvador. Nel arranged a laundress to pick up our clothes each week and wash them, so that we wouldn't have to bring them to the lavanderia in the port, which Nel said was overpriced and where they often stole the buttons off my clothes. Our first weekend together, we went sightseeing, my first time. Nel took me to the Igreja do Bonfim, the Church of Happy Endings, a church famous for its miraculous powers of healing.

Outside the church, in a *praça* quilted with white cobblestone, vendors sold colorful silk ribbons—sky blue, violet, emerald green, yellow, pink, orange, red *fitas*—printed with the slogan *Lembrança do Senhor do Bonfim da Bahia*. Nel bought us each a ribbon and tied one on my left wrist. Before tightening each knot, she told to make a wish.

—When the ribbon falls off, she said, your wishes will come true.

—Do I have to tell you what I wished for?

—No, she said. You shouldn't tell anyone or they won't come true.

I don't remember what I wished for, but I can guess: I would have wished for an internship at INPA, that Paulinho (who lived still in the city where we'd met) and I be reunited. Foremost among my wishes would have been the wish that I grow thin, thinner, that I lose more. I didn't know then that wishes often come to pass in a fashion other than intended.

Inside, the church was dark and it took a moment for my eyes to adjust to the light filtered through windows, to see the Virgin in blue standing to the left above the altar, the cherubim over our heads.

Nel guided me to the right, where a doorway opened onto a room softly lit by candlelight. The room was small, rectangular, perhaps 15 feet by 30. The room was white plaster, and in the candlelight the very walls seemed to glow from within; the ceiling was crossed by rough-hewn wooden beams and seemed close, low, though when I looked up I realized that the ceiling was not low but merely appeared so, because it was hung with pale arms and legs that dangled like stalactites over our heads. On the thick wooden tables that lined the edges of the room were hands, feet, heads—each a perfect life-sized wax replica of a body part, as if the body were a child's toy disassembled here. I walked around the room, looking at the severed heads and hands, the feet with their perfectly formed toes, the glass eyeballs staring blankly up.

I was horrified and fascinated both. I had never heard of a shrine like this. Nel had to explain to me that the wax effigies were offerings brought by pilgrims, left by the suffering hopeful who hoped these figures might bring healing to that part of the body. The faithful came and lit candles and left these votives and their prayers.

SENAC

After Nel moved in, I began to make plans. I still thought about heading to the Amazon, but I thought about it less and the idea of staying in Salvador a while grew more appealing.

I got up the nerve to go to Pelourinho and inquire about arranging an internship at SENAC, a cooking school that trained students in traditional Bahian cuisine. The school, it turned out, was not a Brazilian Cordon Bleu as I'd imagined, but a vocational training program for the poor who lacked formal education but scored well on an entrance exam. The course was free to those few who passed the exam and provided a certificate that enabled graduates to work in restaurants and hotels. It provided them with lunch each day, clean uniforms. Everyone enrolled was Bahian, smart, black, and poor.

To study cooking in Bahia is to apprentice yourself to history, to become a student of another people's palate, tastes accumulated over time; embedded in Bahian cuisine is the taste of yucca and yams, hot pepper and lime, palm oil and coconut milk, the flavor of a lost homeland. Salvador has been called the "soul of Brazil" and the African capital in the New World, in honor of its rich Afro-Brazilian culture; in four centuries of mid-Atlantic slave trade, the country imported more than 3 million African slaves, a third of all those trafficked, a violent legacy that lingers. It was the last nation in the Americas to renounce slavery in 1888, and its culture bears the traces yet.[2] Years later I'll wonder if we're tasting history's violent imprint in Bahia's haunting cuisine: if this is the flavor of heartbreak.

2. In 2007, the Brazilian government freed more than 1,000 workers from enslavement on a sugar-cane plantation, the largest anti-slavery raid in Brazil's modern history.

I arrived around 11 to inquire about enrolling in the school and spoke to a receptionist in a whitewashed, second-story room. I did not realize that I had come at an inopportune time, pre-lunch, approaching the restaurant's busiest hour. When I showed up, the head chef and program coordinator was called away from the kitchen to deal with me. He was built like a refrigerator, huge and commanding; he wore a white chef's hat above his broad black face; he was dressed in immaculate white pants, white shirt, a big white apron. He held a wooden spoon in one hand and looked sternly at me as he told me firmly that they could not accommodate a foreign student.

—You cannot enroll without having passed the entrance exam, he said, an exam that had already been administered for the year. You cannot earn a certificate.

—I'd be happy to audit, I said.

—You cannot audit, he said, firmly. He seemed to consider the subject closed.

—I am very interested in learning about Bahian cuisine, I said. I think how we eat tells us a lot about a culture and its people. I will work very hard.

He told me that he was sorry, but that he could not help me. He had to get back to the kitchen now.

—Please, I said. I will work hard.

He turned to the woman seated behind the desk, evidently done speaking with me, and said, Have her fill out the forms.

The woman looked surprised.

It took me a moment to realize that he had said yes.

—I can participate? I asked.

—Come back on Monday, he said, at 8 a.m. Do not be late.

I thanked him profusely. You won't regret it, I said.

—He laughed a huge round laugh and said, Oh, I will.

On my way home, buoyant with success, I stopped in a stationery store—a *papelaria*—and bought myself a small portable typewriter, a manual Olivetti 440X made of molded plastic, the gold of mangoes, charmed by the Portuguese keyboard's diacritics. At home, I opened its pale orange case and sat down at the coffee table and slowly, one finger at a time, typed a letter of inquiry to INPA.

At the cooking school the following Monday, I was directed upstairs with the other students to the attic—a cramped space already hot from the morning sun. The university term had been canceled due to the strike, and I was relieved to have somewhere to go each day. But it was more than relief that I felt.

Entering the old baroque building from the cobblestone square of Pelour–inho, it seemed as if I'd slipped inside Salvador by some secret door. I, who, till then, had felt so often on the outside even of my own life, looking in, felt like an insider now. The air smelled of burnt sugar and coconut milk, onion and *dendê* and sun-warmed floorboards—a heavy sweet smell that made me hungry. As I waited on the stairs with the others on our way up to the attic, a magnificently handsome man with a face like a Giotto madonna—with almond-shaped eyes—color of cacao, smiled at me as he went past.

In the low-ceilinged attic, we were split into lines: girls to the left, boys to the right. Everyone was about my age, in their late teens, early twenties. I was not surprised to find that I was a curiosity, being pale-skinned and foreign. As we waited in line, people around me elbowed one another to point me out and whisper.

A beautiful woman, tall, model gaunt, with fabulous cheekbones and white square teeth, her head like a Masai sculpture, long and smooth, turned to me and introduced herself as Yvette.

—You are from the United States, she said.

—Yes, I said.

—Why are you here? It was not a hostile inquiry. She appeared neither impressed nor unimpressed. Merely curious.

I told her of my plans for Amazonian study and how they had gone awry. A few other girls leaned close to listen until Yvette glared at them, and they backed off.

She rolled her eyes.

—Don't mind them, she said. They don't mean to be rude. Yvette slapped the nearest girl. Introduce yourself, she said. She treated the others like younger sisters, with affectionate disdain, and I wondered if they'd known each other long. I envied them their intimacy.

Slowly, giggling, the other girls introduced themselves, giving names that, in my nervousness, I'd forget almost immediately. One stocky tough girl held out a limp hand to me, as if to shake, with joking formality. But in the blur of faces, Yvette's was the only one I would recall clearly, Yvette's and that of the Giotto madonna who'd smiled at me on the stairs.

When we reached the front of the line, we were sized up by a plump matron seated beside a huge white bag of clothes who, on a guess, issued us a size. We stood in the middle of the low-ceilinged attic room and tried on our uniforms.

The boys were on the other side of a curtain and occasionally someone peeked or threatened to and there was much screaming and laughter. Great hilarity. Girls flopped around like marionettes with sleeves too long. Others —tall girls like me and Yvette—found ourselves in pants that fit like capris, in shirts tight as sailor suits with sleeves that did not even reach our wrists. Yvette clasped a hand to her waist, shoved one hip out and a hand in the air, modeling her elegant attire. People fell over laughing.

Our first day was spent dressing and undressing and getting a tour of the kitchen. The chef and head instructor did not treat me differently from the others and I was grateful for this, that here I was just another student, one of them.

We were each issued a mimeographed recipe book, but mostly we would learn by taste. On that first day, we were introduced to the head cooks in each section and were told what we would study with each one. Then we were taken on a tour through the kitchen, where half a dozen giant steel ranges divided the space into sections. There were ovens where crème caramel was being made in a bain-marie. There were enormous ranges topped by huge aluminum pots, large enough to bathe a child, in which simmered okra and golden *vatapá*, in which *acarajé* boiled in palm oil.

The head chef walked us through each section of the massive kitchen, sampling the pots we passed: first brushing the fragrance under his nose, he then borrowed a spoon and tested on the heel of his palm—like a mother testing the temperature of formula on a wrist—the flavor of this dish or that. He approved, praised, suggested. Here, in the coming weeks, we would learn how to chop an onion with our fingers curled, so the blade could race through the white flesh without taking a fingertip. We would learn how to blend into a magnificent paste the ingredients of *vatapá*—cashew and onion, tomato and palm oil, garlic and small dried shrimp. How to mix and boil *acarajé*—bean balls made of black-eyed peas. How to flavor a *moqueca*, a Bahian stew of palm oil and coconut milk, cilantro and lime, thinly sliced tomato and sweet onion, in which are poached shrimp, fish, chicken or eggs.

We were shown the door that led into the dining room where tourists would come to eat each day, and for whom we would be preparing our food.

No one talked about calories; no one even mentioned them: instead they talked about flavor—*sabor*.

Probably this is where my conversion began—though I didn't know it then, would not recognize the shift for years, until at twenty-five my life had changed, become a marvelous feast—there in that industrial-sized kitchen, where cooking was raised to the level of a calling and the body's sustenance was not a matter of clinical calculation but of taste. In the coming weeks, I would arrive each morning at 8 and work till 4 to help prepare the daily offerings; I would immerse myself in flavors, textures, heat, scent, sweet, and spice.

The Economy of Beauty

As I grew more at ease in Salvador, Nelci seemed less. We talked less and less about her plans, as if they had blown off like morning haze. In the hard bright heat of the apartment, she would lie on her back and read. When I went out, she rarely came with. Her only request was that I bring back tiny sanitary pads from the pharmacy; she was not bleeding, but she liked to wear them anyway, to mask her own scent. When I arranged for a manicurist to come by to give us pedicures, a special treat to cheer her up, the woman inadvertently cut Nel's cuticle too close and Nelci screamed at her and threw her out. She told me later that her grandmother had died from such a cut. More and more Nelci's unhappiness felt like an accusation. A sign that I, too, had failed her.

Isa was spending more and more time on the island and we saw her less and less. Sometimes Nel brought home another friend, but these girls struck me as incongruous companions for her. One, in particular, alarmed me. She was nice enough, young, tomboyish, with a compact, plush muscly little body, well tanned, with a mop of short hair bleached blond. *Po*—a crude slang, comparable to *fuck* (literally "sperm")—ornamented her every phrase, the way certain kids in the States used "like." She spoke in a slang so idiomatic that I often could not make out what she'd said.

But I could not mistake this: she said the man in the apartment across the street was an admirer of mine; he'd watched me—in the days I lived alone— parade naked around my place; he'd dubbed me *mulherona*, big woman. I felt queasy at the news. It was not just that I'd been watched, observed in the one place I'd imagined myself free of observation, but something in the way Nel's friend delivered the news made me wonder who the man was to her. From the way she spoke it was clear he was no relative, no boyfriend, no friend. Just a guy she knew.

I kept my clothes on after that, undressing only in the bathroom, safely behind closed doors.

On Saturday, after capoeira, several of us hung around in the hall to chat. Barbara was there and several of the best capoeiristas. The handsome lanky blue-eyed Paulista, the prettiest man in class, who had never so much as given me a smile, flirted with me; he said we should go out some night. Why not? I replied, as if such invitations were commonplace.

On the way home, I felt pretty and hopeful. But Barbara seemed annoyed, and when I mentioned the Paulista's invitation, she said that he was mean to lead me on like that. He was just trying to make her jealous because she'd re-fused to go out with him. I wanted to believe that she was jealous, but I knew that she was right. Of course he wouldn't be interested in me. Of course not.

—I knew that, I said, as if I had.

At twenty-one, I was not plain, but I was in possession of that handsome Anglo-American beauty that does not translate well. Five feet nine and lanky, I was not considered beautiful in Salvador, a city—like Rio—known for its beautiful women: delicately voluptuous, dark-eyed, black-haired, cinnamon-skinned.

Everywhere I went, I was conscious of this one fact, the fact that I was unbeautiful, unwanted by men whose wanting, I believed disastrously then, was my measure.

Walking with Barbara in the street, I heard men call out to her, sweetly, entreatingly: *fofinha*, fluffy. At me, they shouted *tesão*, erection. After a while, I grew accustomed to being treated differently—as I supposed the poor must grow accustomed to being treated less well than the rich—but I never really got used to it. And when, later, I grew nut brown and easy in my body and vendors in the street called out to me *fofinha*, I would hate them and hate myself for feeling grateful.

Of all of us, Barbara was the one I would have guessed might eventually make money from her looks. But I was wrong about that.

As we walked home from capoeira, our talk turned to movies. We began discussing Lina Wertmuller's *Swept Away*, a film about an aristocratic woman stranded on an island with her boat's captain, who for a time becomes her sexual master. I was trying to claim that the film was feminist in its portrayal of fierce female desire. Barbara was having none of it; she knew better.

Barbara said her responses to movies were often perverse: she often laughed in very serious movies, cried at what others found funny.

I told her that I was usually trying to figure out how I was supposed to respond.

—I never do anything I don't want to do, Barbara said.

It hadn't occurred to me that this might be an option.

—*Really?* I asked, incredulous.

—Really, she smiled.

Nel's presence encouraged me to go out more. On the days I did not have to go to the cooking school, I found other reasons to go out. Partly to have solitude, partly to give her time alone, some scrap of privacy, I began to go to the beach in the mornings in hope of developing a tan. I knew now what to bring and what to leave behind—I knew not to carry money or a passport, to bring only a towel and tanning oil, maybe a book to read. I was often bored at the beach and self-conscious, but my absence from the apartment gave Nel time to sleep on the mattress, which she would not do when I was there. So I went.

I was at the beach, laying face down on my towel, when I felt a hand on my back. When I looked up, it was the guy I'd met in the street weeks ago. Chequinho.

—Where have you been, *boneca*? he asked, squatting beside me. I've been looking for you.

—I've been busy, I said, pleased to be remembered and to be busy. I'm in cooking school now.

—You still *joga capoeira*? he asked.

—Of course, I said.

As we chatted, I wondered if he noticed my pale skin, my fleshy thighs, my too-small breasts, my soft belly.

He said he'd missed me and though I knew this was not true, it was flattering nonetheless to have someone go to the trouble of lying.

—Come take a swim, he said.

—I think I'll stay here, I said, afraid to get up and expose still more of my body.

—C'mon, he said. A quick swim, to cool you off.

—Okay, I said, suspecting that he would not go until I did. Pushing up from my towel, I hoped my thighs wouldn't wobble. I didn't realize that at 5 feet 9 inches, 135 pounds, I was not fat. Not at all. At the time, I had no idea what I was. I was waiting to find out. I was waiting for someone—anyone—to tell me.

We waded out into the water, the lukewarm, bottle-green waves. I waded up to my chest, the water around his shoulders; he told me I looked beautiful, that he had been hoping to see me here. I told him I'd been busy. For a while we stood in the water talking, then he cupped my chin and kissed me, a not unpleasant taste of cigarettes and salt water, the brush of stubble. He drew me to him and held me in his arms. I leaned back, held up by him, the water stretching out to Africa, the sun a bright disk over head.

I was not attracted to Chequinho, but I was flattered. Someone wanted me after all. His hands moved over my back, my ass, inside the back of my swim suit, and I let this happen because I thought being wanted was the most important thing, and besides it was not unpleasant. And I did not want to seem a prude.

I told myself there was nothing to fear. We were not in so deep as to be in danger; we were not alone, there were people everywhere; there was nothing to fear in this, nothing to fear.

Not until I felt his hand pull the crotch of my swim suit aside and press his hips to mine did I say, No.

—No one can see us in the water.

—No, I said again, and then, more gently, Not here, as if location were the problem. I did not want to seem undesiring, reticent as girls are said to be. I was more ashamed of my lack of desire, of being found without desire, than to be subject to the desires of some man I did not want. In truth, I was beginning to doubt that I desired anything at all, and this, above all else, frightened me. The Buddhists have it wrong, I will think years later: desire is not the source of all suffering; its lack is what torments us.

On the beach, Chequinho asked if he could walk me home.

—I'm going to stay here awhile, I said, though the sun was too hot now for tanning.

—Some other time, he said.

—Some other time.

When he left the beach, I was glad that he did not know where I lived.

When I got back to the apartment, Isa was there with Nel. They were seated on the couch, talking.

—*Tudo bem*, Elena, Isa said, standing and coming over to give me a kiss.

—*Tá um pouco mais preto*, Nel said, appraisingly. You are a tiny bit darker. She held out her arm. I can't go the beach, she said. I become black as an African.

I asked them if they wanted a *suco* and went to make one for myself from the *maracujá* in the fridge. When I came back into the living room, I sat on the coffee table and told them about meeting Chequinho at the beach. I told them he was cute, that he called me *boneca* (they laughed at this), that he'd tried to take me in the water.

—What, Nel asked. In the water?

—With people around?

—They couldn't see, I said. We were under the water.

—Oh, Elena, Isa said, admiring and disapproving both.

—Be careful, Nel said, gravely.

—Where did you meet him? Isa asked.

—In the street, I said. In Avenida Isabella coming home from capoeira.

They howled with laughter, as if this were the punch line to a very very big joke.

Another word for territory

Probably it was while I was swimming at the beach that I picked up conjunctivitis. By Friday, my eye was swollen shut and I called the cooking school and left a message for the head chef that I would be out sick. I spent the day on the mattress, wearing sunglasses against the glare of light, rinsing my eyes with chilled saline I kept in the fridge. My eyes itched and I lay there waiting to see clearly again. The apartment was small for two people and I felt the edgy annoyance of constant company, though Nel and I tried to approximate solitude and spaciousness by not speaking to each other most of the morning, pretending we were each alone. When the afternoon heat grew intense in the uncurtained room, I went down to the garage and lay on the low cement wall that edged the open-air room, because it was cooler there and because I desperately needed some privacy.

I was lying there on the cement wall, saline at my side and my sunglasses on, when I heard footsteps approaching and sat up.

—Hey, doll, Chequinho said, coming toward me across the garage. Your doorman said I'd find you here.

For a moment I was startled. How did he know where I lived? But I said, instead, Stay back. I'm sick.

—You don't look sick, he said, smiling, imagining—I suppose—that this was some coquettish game.

—It's my eyes, I said.

—Your eyes? You have beautiful eyes.

He leaned down to kiss me, but I pulled back. I shifted away from him and removed my sunglasses. When he saw my red and rheumy eyes, he drew back.

—What is it? he asked.

—Conjunctivitis, I said. It's highly contagious.

He took a step back. I'll come by another time, he said, when you feel better. How long will it last? he asked.

—How should I know? I said.

—You look beautiful, he said, recovering himself a bit, and I understood then, though only dimly, that he hated me, this little man. Only someone who hated a woman would lie like this. Only a man who hated women would attend to them this way. With such obvious insincerity.

—No, I said, coldly, I don't.

—I'll come back, he said. His tone was not friendly. I'll come by another time.

—Do what you want, I said, hoping I didn't sound afraid.

But he did come back, a week or so later, when you and Nel were in the apartment one afternoon. When he comes in the open door, you introduce him to Nel and she recognizes his name from your story of the beach, and trying to be helpful, she chats with you for a moment, then contrives to go across the hall to have some of Zé's famous rice.

After Nel leaves, you two sit on the mattress that serves as a couch and talk. You try to make this ordinary, a visit by a friend, an expected thing. When he leans over to kiss you, you stand up, and offer him a *cafezinho*—the sugary local coffee brewed strong as tar—and a shower, because this is the Bahian way, the normal thing to do. It is polite to offer coffee and a shower to your guest.

—*Quero*, he says, accepting both.

You point him to the bathroom and you go to the kitchen and start the water boiling on the red enameled stove in the red enameled pot. And when it's ready, you knock on the bathroom door.

—Come in, he says.

You crack the door and shout over the water, Your coffee's ready. I'll leave it here.

—C'mon in, he says.

—I've showered already, you say, as if his were an ordinary invitation.

—C'mon, he says. It is not a question.

And because you do not want to seem a prude, because you want to be polite, to please your guest, because you are curious, because showering seems clean, not really dangerous, not like accepting an invitation to go to bed (you have not yet heard that most accidents happen in the bath), because you find yourself committed to a course, the momentum of your trajectory built on small decisions that made sense at the time somehow carrying you forward and it seems harder to change direction, to stop the unfolding of events that you see unfolding, and maybe anyway, you hope, it won't turn out so bad after all, how bad can it be really—a world warmed, a forest felled, a shower —and you wouldn't know how to stop this anyway, not now, and besides you do not want to look ridiculous, alarmist, silly, naïve, so you do as he asks and strip outside the shower stall, saying, I'll take one when you're done, but when he emerges from the shower, you do not have a chance to get in before he grasps you, turning you away from him, his chest to your back, his hips to your soft ass, your face to the bathroom door where a full-length mirror hangs. You do not see what he is doing but you feel him behind you pulling apart the fleshy cheeks of your ass, trying to shove his cock into the narrow opening of your sphincter, and you say, *No*, and you say, *I don't want this*, *No*, but he is not saying anything at all, and the only face you're looking into is your own, in the bit of mirror before you, its length engulfed in steam; your eyes are the last thing you look into before he forces your head forward, bent over, your torso soft and floppy as a rag doll's, and you try to relax, to give way, to accommodate what he wants to do to you, hoping that it will not hurt too much if you let him do what he wants to do. And pretty much that is all you remember.

Except this:

When he is done fucking you up the ass, he tells you to clean yourself, he'll wait outside, and you get in the shower that is still running and scrub. Your soft ass. Your face.

When you come out, he is gone. You are not sorry.

Only later will you discover that a small gold necklace is missing from your closet, and understand as one does in retrospect that he has taken it, as if in payment for services rendered.

Across the hall Zé is making his famous rice, and Nelci is there. When there is a knock on the door, some minutes later, I think it is Nel, locked out and returning from Zé's, but it is Linda instead, an American journalist from Maine. I invite her in, offer her juice and coffee, a shower, a seat.

—How are you? she asks, taking a seat. What's up?

—Have you ever had anal sex? I ask.

—Why do you ask? she says. Linda is matter-of-fact, a little affectless and flat, and our conversations often have this strained and effortful quality. But she is older, twenty-seven or twenty-eight, a professional, a woman who has known a lot of men, and I feel I can confide in her, figure out how to feel about this new fact.

I tell her what has happened. I tell her that I just have. I try to sound sporting, to sound game and hip. I do not want Linda to think I am unsophisticated about sex. That I am naïve.

—Oh, Ellen, Linda says, her voice gentle with pity, her face strained. That's what they do to animals.

It is her tone that makes me choke up. I do not know what to say.

—Are you okay?

I shrug.

She is sitting on the couch and I am seated on the floor, my back propped against the low coffee table. She comes to crouch beside me and pets my hair over and over.

—Oh, honey, she says. Oh, honey.

Her voice has never sounded so gentle, and I begin to cry. I feel stupid all over again. Crying, I let her rock me back and forth; I listen to her coo into my hair.

—It's gonna be okay, she says. You're gonna be okay.

When Nel comes in, Linda takes her aside and tells her what has happened and after that Nel treats me carefully, gently, the rest of the afternoon. She asks if I'd like her to get me a *suco* in the port, if I need anything. She suggests we go to the island that weekend. I tell her that I'd like that. And after that we don't mention it again.

And is it rape if you let it happen, if you simply fail to identify with the girl in the mirror, if you believe that being wanted by any man, even a man who hates a girl like you, your rapist, is more important than what you want, the only thing that gives you value, his wanting you? Is it rape if you do not know that your body is lovely—developed or undeveloped—that it does not require improvements, slash and burn, aerobics, diuretics, laxatives, calisthenics, tightening, tucking, silicone? Is it rape if you think of this, the way boys want to touch you, as a part of growing up, of getting on with it, if your sister has told you that sex with a man is what distinguishes a woman from a girl, the only sure way to prove that you're grown up, so you let boys touch you any way they want? Is it rape if you think that some man's wanting is the only way to lay claim to the vast tracts of skin that are you, but that still, even at twenty-one, don't seem yours? Is it rape if you say only No, Don't, and try not to cry when a man whose last name you will never know shoves his cock past the delicate pink ring of your sphincter, forcing you forward, like a rag doll, bent in half, floppy and numb, your body numb? Is it rape if *you* feel guilty?

Is it—*was* it—rape, or was it simply a failure to identify, a failure of heart, a failure of education, a failure to muster the necessary courage, a failure to master the rudiments of Western philosophy that led you to misconstrue that Cartesian formulation and believe that because you are female *cogito ergo sum* does not apply to you, that philosophy is differently formulated for girls like you, that for you, it's not *cogito ergo sum* but more like *desiderabile ergo sum*: I am desired therefore I am.

Is it—*was it*—rape?

It doesn't really matter, does it? Definitions change after all with the times. And rape, not so very long ago, was merely a term for an administrative district in Sussex, a certain amount of land, a jurisdiction, just another name for territory.

Itaparica

For those who lived in Salvador, the island of Itaparica was a defining presence; romantic and promising, it informed our days the way remarkable buildings do great cities—the Tour Eiffel or the Empire State. It was something your eyes went to in the white heat of midday, when the new high rises and the body in the cardboard box on the sidewalk and dark shop windows and beggar boys left you drained. You could see, most any hour of the day, tourists and locals alike leaning on a balustrade facing out to sea, looking out toward the disk of land in the shimmering bay.

It was easy enough to get to Itaparica, but somehow I'd never gone. There were always errands to run, groceries to buy, calories to walk off, dinner to make, all those tasks on which we spend our days. And in truth, I was reticent to visit the island, afraid I'd be disappointed. It was the idea of it that I loved, the possibility of paradise that I wanted to preserve. I liked to imagine its fishing huts and thatched roofs, uncut forests, sweet springs, open beaches —I needed to believe that it was out there, waiting for us: a place I could imagine was better than this, than where I was, we were.

That weekend, Isa invited us to spend a few days on the island of Itaparica at the house of her boyfriend, Marcos. On Saturday morning, the three of us caught a ferry in the lower town and rode out to the island, watching the city grow small behind us.

At the ferry launch on the island, we caught a bus that took us deeper into the island. From where the bus stopped and let us off, it was about a mile walk along a beach to Marco's house. The beach was a parenthesis of sand, parallel to the mainland, terminating at the far end in a murky band of river. We walked along the cream-colored beach for a mile or so before we came to a narrow, deep stream, which we must wade through to reach the road to Marco's house. The water, a current of dubious origin and considerable stench—some twenty feet wide—smelled of raw sewage and dead fish and Isa complained that it would make us sick, going through this. I trained my eyes on the road that ran up from the beach on the other side of the water, trying to keep my imagination in check as I slipped one foot in front of the other, tentatively testing with the ball of my bare foot the soft indeterminate mass beneath it.

Once on the other bank, we walked up the gravel road, away from the beach. Walled houses rose on either side of us. When we reached a wooden door set in the side of a high cement wall, Isa pulled out a key and opened the lock. The wall we passed through was ten feet high, at least, and its rim was capped with the jagged stubs of broken bottles in brown and green, like tiny crowns or teeth. On the other side was an enclosed garden. Marcos stood at the grill, at the far end of a flagstone path that dotted the lawn from the gate to the back of the house. He was dressed in blue shorts and a white knit Izod sports shirt, turning the meat when we arrived.

As soon as we were inside the wall, Isa began to swing her sack impatiently. She crossed the lawn, her chin raised, with an air of studied indifference.

—Mar-cos, she called plaintively, in a bored sing-song. We're here. He turned from the grill to face us.

—Hey, he called. Isa draped her arms around his neck and kissed him briefly. Then she let her arms fall away and began to murmur petulant complaints about having had to cross the river, which she was sure was full of sewage, in order to get to his house. She told him that he should build a bridge. He told her that they would talk about it later. His tone was quiet but warning. And Isa fell silent. She frowned but said nothing.

—Welcome, Marcos said, extending a hand to me. I'm Marcos.

—Elena, I returned.

—Elena, he repeated, shaking my hand. That's fine.

He was older than I expected, maybe thirty-five, and plain. I was surprised that he was neither tall nor handsome, but a small man with a mop of straight brown hair like an overturned bowl. I'd have put him at about five feet six; though trim, he gave an impression of stockiness. He seemed gentle and serious in that moment. And it seemed to me that he was the first grown-up I'd met in Bahia. I liked him and found myself pitying him a little. He nodded to Nelci and began to joke with her when Isa cut in. She said she was tired and wanted to shower. She went in and we followed.

The house was two-story, large and modern, white stucco. João, Marco's friend, opened the sliding door for us and invited us in. He was good looking, with a DA haircut, a tan, taut face. He was small and wiry and reminded me of guys from the fifties, innocent hoods. He joked wildly with us, grinned a lot. Moving quickly, always in motion, like a monkey. He will spend the weekend making obscene jokes about chickens and cooing at Nel, *Te amo,*

Te amo, I love you, I love you, and making kissing sounds as she passes by. He was wild and wired and a little scary, but I liked him, his antic desperate humor.

—Do you like to eat chicken? he asked me, grinning, as later we all stood around the grill watching Marcos work his magic on the meat.

—Sure, I said.

He burst out laughing. Did you hear that Marcos? he said. She likes to *eat* chicken.

—*Para,* Isa said. Cut it out, Marcos.

Nel frowned and rolled her eyes. He means, Elena, do you like to fuck them. "Eat" is a colloquial term for fuck.

I turned to João and said, Ha ha. Very funny.

João laughed and laughed, thrilled now that I got the joke.

—Fool, Nelci said. *Bobo.*

João turned to Nel and made kissing sounds. *Te amo,* he said, *Te amo.* Why do you scorn my love?

Marcos looked at João, and João laughed, then he looked at the sky and whistled.

At night, alone in our room, I asked Nel, Does he really fuck chickens?

—He does, Nel said. Really. Guys like him will screw anything.

The next morning, Marcos showed us around his store. Furniture modeled on suburban ranch homes from the sixties. He had gotten rich from this. Rooms full of things no one was using. Marcos was not a bad man, but he did not seem to care for what lies beyond his walled garden. Isa came to him, rarely the reverse. He wanted her to move in with him here, but she said she would go crazy, with nothing to do, no one to see.

The store had all the elements necessary to make a home, but it wasn't one. I looked around in the dusty gloom and felt sad for all of us. For Isa, Marcos, Nel, João. I could not imagine anyone making a home from this.

When we returned from the island, I did not hear from Chequinho again and I didn't expect to. If he had called I would have hung up. But I would have liked to have had the chance to hang up. I concentrated on errands, on cooking classes. I tended to the little monkey, though he rarely let me pet him now; he glared at me, like an enraged tenant confronting a lousy landlord. I shopped. I bought a broad cotton hammock in the *praça* where I had bought the monkey, one day on my way home from cooking class. I made lists of things I needed. Weight goals. Calories eaten and burned.

I went out in the late afternoon each day to buy groceries, needing an excuse to go for a walk. I bought manioc root, fat plums, and yogurt in squat, plastic, half-cup buckets. It felt good to be out in the street. It felt good to walk the dimly lit aisles of the grocery. To give my money and receive the brown paper bag, to hold this to my chest, my arms bowed out as if in an embrace.

The bag was loaded with a tin of guava paste, a tenderloin roast wrapped in white paper, a plastic sack of bleached rice, water crackers in cellophane, tomatoes, pale green grapes. Returning from the market, I wondered if the boy had been careful. I lowered my arms, peered over the lip of the sack, saw only crackers and yogurt, and worried that the fruit was squashed. Shadows of trees twitched in the breeze.

At home, I unpacked the bag into the fridge and even before I was done putting away the groceries I opened a container of yogurt, and began to spoon it into my mouth. I was tired and hot and sad and lonely; Nel was out somewhere or maybe at Zé's, and I thought this food might revive me. Cheer me up. It was something to do anyway for the next five minutes.

I squirted diet sweetener into the plain yogurt and a measured tablespoon of *guaraná*, a powerfully caffeinated seed from the Amazon. My latest diet scheme. High protein, high caffeine, low calorie. Then I walked to the living room and stretched out in the hammock.

I had just settled back into the broad cotton cloth, carefully holding my yogurt aloft so as not to spill it, and was leaning back—exhausted, dispirited, the room stale and too bright, barren, lacking personality because (I'd begun to suspect) I did. I thought of Barbara's rooms with their pale blue light, their rattan, the mandolin, woodcuts and Levi-Strauss, and I was lifting the first spoonful of yogurt to my mouth when the mico sprang from the far end of the hammock into the small plastic container of yogurt in an act of remarkable acrobatic hubris.

Without thinking, I screamed and grabbed him in my fist and flung him, hard, hard, against the floor, pissed off. When I looked down, he was just lying there, perfectly still beside the hammock. His little gray tufted body deflated, flat.

—Oh my God, I said. Oh my God.

I was afraid to get out of the hammock and crouch down to look. I could already see that he was dead, crushed because he wanted to eat. Poor stunted thing. He never grew, as the monkey vendor said he would. And it occurred to me that maybe he didn't eat the fruit I had given him because he wasn't weaned, craved milk, needed another kind of nourishment than what I offered.

I kneeled down and stroked his still body. He looked so sweet. Alive his eyes had seemed accusing. I felt sick. It wasn't the monkey I wanted to kill after all, but the girl. The girl who'd checked into a too-expensive hotel, who was no good at repartee in any language, who had not mastered Portuguese, who was pale, overweight, too self-conscious to lie on a beach; the girl who desired nothing except to be less than she was, to lose.

I wanted to be rid of the girl who went shopping nearly every day for food so that she could stick to a pointless Hilton Head diet, that diet book being one of the few books she had brought with her from the States. I wanted to kill that girl I once was, the girl it seemed then I would always be.

And then it began to rain. Drops spattered my hands and the stretch of carpet beneath the open window. Drops fell on the furry unmoving side of the mico. I looked out at the sky, which was pale and cloudless, and realized that the drops were tears.

When the monkey stirred, groggy, he roses unsteadily to his four paws and crawled away from me, leaving me alone, crying in a little patch of sunlight for everything.

Ilhas

I'm surprised by how little I recall now, as I wade back into the middle of that year, how memory grows less and less clear after Chequinho's visit to my apartment. What I remember are islands, bright patches of memory, reminding me of the island conservation scheme in the Amazon, the studies done to see whether small isolated patches of forest could sustain life in the midst of development's ravages. Of course, they could not. Can't. My own self-development schemes were beginning to take their toll as well; in memory, my days grow patchy, islands of brightness in a sea of unremembered hours. Strange, radiant.

This much I remember:

I remember meeting Rogeirio—another Rotary scholar, a Bahian ten years older than I, who was slated to leave for the U.S. in a few months' time—in the port at Barra at an ice cream café I had passed often on my walk to the beach but never entered. A Rotarian had proposed I meet Rogeirio after I gave a speech to their club in Salvador ("speech" a lofty word for my modest recitation, which I had memorized word for word and repeated like a parrot).

The café had its usual Saturday crowd when I walked in, but Rogeirio was easy to pick out. He had a diffident elegance, an inwardness that was rare here and apparent in the way he watched the crowd and smoked slowly, deliberately. He was tall, slender, willowy, with hair cut close to his head like black stubble around a balding pate. His hair looked felty, like the nubble on a blanket well worn. He had enormous eyes that bulged slightly, chocolate brown irises, the sclera slightly yellow. His lashes were long and black. He had a tender face, smooth save for a black mustache, with deep, kindly grooves at either side of his mouth from smiling.

I remember being surprised that he was black, because the Rotary Club was—from all I'd seen—exclusively white. (The myth of racial equality in

Brazil, championed by Gilberto Freyre in the 1930s, was clearly a myth in Salvador. Freyre had argued that a history of miscegenation had tempered racial divisions in Brazil, that race was an economic category here, not a matter of skin color. But this was only partly true. The prestigious Clube Bahiano excluded black members, I'd been told, and you didn't need to be a statistician to see who was rich and who was poor in Salvador. Years later I'd hear an eminent historian, Emilia Viotta da Costa, say that Brazil's myth of racial equality was akin to America's myth of the self-made man: a story intended to convince the disenfracnshised that their exclusion was a *personal* failure, not a societal one, so as to discourage organization along economic or racial lines. But by the time I arrived in Salvador, the only people I spoke to who believed Brazil was race-blind were white.)

I remember that Rogeirio wore faded jeans and a sport shirt and that he had a camera at his left side suspended by a strap from his shoulder. I remember that he was someone who set me at ease; he seemed peaceful, gentle, at home in the world, and I relaxed a little with him. In a month or two he would leave for the United States for a year's study at Texas A&M on a Rotary fellowship. He seemed very much older than I, though in truth he was perhaps thirty, thirty-one. He'd studied engineering in Brazil but a year's study in the States would offer new information and connections. He was excited to hear about Texas, but I worried for him there, as a black man, unaccustomed to the intricacies of American racism.

I remember that he proposed that we walk together in the port and that we did. It was afternoon and the light was long and angled at that hour, good for the black and white photographs he shot. We strolled along the promenade, past the Bahianas in their lace skirts and turbans, the smell of *dendê* and onion and sea salt and exhaust around us. He took pictures and chatted with the people he photographed and we walked and talked casually, as if we knew each other well. I told him that I liked to take photos as well, that I'd spent a lot of hours in darkrooms at college, developing and printing images. Seeing him onto a bus in the port, I said I was glad to have met him. I wished him luck in Texas.

—I'll call you sometime, he said, and we can go shoot photos. All right?

—I'd like that, I said.

The sunlight glinted off the small, white tiles of a *praça* in front of the Igreja do Bonfim, where we went to take photographs a few weeks later. I remember that we went to the Ribeirão, an old quiet port down the hill from Bonfim. I remember descending together through the steep and narrow cobblestone street that led from the church down to the waterfront, a cool shadowy passage between two-story stucco houses painted pink and green and lavender. There, as we descended from the church to the waterfront, Rogeirio took my hand. And for a while we walked like that, to the water's edge, until our hands got sticky with sweat and we let go.

Pelourinho

Portuguese is a deceptive language with its rolled Rs and sensual susurrus. Everything you say in Portuguese sounds like you are talking about sex. *Meu bem, como vai?* The open mouth, the sliding tongue, words roll out like an overturned basket of *goiaba* fruit, tumbling, rolling.

It was a Saturday afternoon, a few weeks after we'd started seeing each other, when Rogeirio proposed we have lunch at a restaurant in Pelourinho that a friend of his ran. He wanted me to try *sarapatel*, a stew that was, he said, a specialty of Salvador.

We caught a bus from the port at Barra to the ladeira—the enormous elevator that connected the two cities, upper and lower—and from there we walked the few blocks north to Pelourinho. As we descended a cobblestone street between old buildings, Rogeirio pointed to a door on our right, a small discreet door I'd never noticed before. He said this was the headquarters of Ile Aiyé, the carnival group to which he belonged, which insisted on an exclusively black membership in response to the exclusively "white" bloco International. Ile Aiyé had been among the first to openly challenge the racism in Salvador, their formation an early salvo in what had become only recently a black civil rights movement in Brazil. All that behind a door I'd never noticed.

The restaurant, farther down the street on the left, was not yet open, so we strolled into the cobblestone square of Pelourinho, which I loved, loving too that shift from the shadowy street into the bright open light of the square. Pelourinho, the heart of the old city, was touristy, but I loved it in those days, as tourists did.

High up on the cliff that overlooked the *cidade baixa*—the modern lower city—Pelourinho is a steeply sloping square of black cobblestone (stones rubbed smooth by human traffic, feet, and time) that falls away steeply, like a rug hung out a window in a breeze, or like a thing out of nightmare, a dream in which the world tips too far and you cannot help but fall. One leans back descending into the *praça* (which narrows like a funnel at its lower end to a single, cobbled street) as one would lean back descending a steep mountainside, or a path into hell; it is a disorienting vantage: one looks down on rooftops and at the same time up at church spires, a confusing latitude, where it seems space bends, one stands in a fold where past is present tense.

At the high end of the plaza is the former customs house; facing the square are baroque buildings, two and three stories tall, gaunt and brightly colored with shuttered windows trimmed in white and ornate ironwork balconies, where shops selling leather goods and jewelry cater to a foreign crowd, and where in the evenings in the 1980s, prostitutes stood on the balconies and in the narrow streets soliciting another kind of tourist. I'd bought a leather purse there and a money belt to replace the one stolen at the beach, huarache sandals. I liked to go there to sketch, but I couldn't get the hang of perspective; it always seemed my buildings were in danger of toppling into the square.

We were holding hands as we entered Pelourinho, Rogeirio's hand smooth and soft in mine. He squeezed my hand gently and said, "*Sabe*, y'know, a hundred years ago, less than a hundred, we couldn't have walked hand in hand like this. A hundred years ago, if I'd come here, I'd have come here in chains."

Pelourinho. The diminutive makes the word sound endearing, like a child's name. I have come down these streets often by myself, thin ribbons of cobblestone and shadow and sudden shafts of light from between the high walls on either side. I'd never considered the meaning of the name—Pelourinho, little pillory—and that this cobbled square, my favorite place in a city praised for its beauty, was a place meant for public humiliation.

In the restaurant, we took a table in the middle of the room. On the wall behind me, a black velvet oil painting of a clipper ship in a storm, another of a guitar player leaning against a palm tree in the moonlight. A slow fan turned overhead.

—*Cara, como vai?* Hey, man, how's it going? A small, round, shiny-faced man clapped Rogeirio on the shoulder.

Rogeirio stood. They embraced.

I smiled and watched them, listening to their exchange, still finding these formalities captivating in a foreign tongue, their staccato rhythm, savoring my new understanding of these words.

Rogeirio had wanted to bring me for weeks but we had been lazy, spending our afternoons in bed, long afternoons of cloying heat, sheets sticking to our thighs and backs and knees. After sex I was often restless. I showered alone, brushed my teeth, tried to retrieve my own salty scent, wet scent of the ocean, the sharp odor of onion and skunk, an acrid smell that I secretly loved because it was mine. I did not desire Rogeirio, but I liked him. He was kind, and I still believed that sex was the proper thing to offer a man I was dating; like serving coffee, it was more a matter of etiquette than taste.

Rogeirio was smoking now, as he did after sex, blue smoke in soft tendrils from his nostrils and lips as he talked to his friend. He said my name, introducing me to the owner, his friend.

—*Prazer*, we said, smiling, taking each other's measure.

I was conscious of my pale skin, my sun-bleached hair. Outside this cool whitewashed room, the street was bleached under the overbearing sun that erased shadow at this hour, everything bared like the teeth.

—Are you hungry? Rogeirio asked.

—A little, I said.

—Only a little?

Rogeirio was teasing, flirting with me in front of his friend.

—You have to eat, he said, playing on the double entendre of "eat" and "fuck" in Portuguese.

I knew that he was showing me off, but it didn't matter. We were both ornamental for the other. I was proud that he was tall, lanky, well spoken, Bahian. He was, I suppose, glad that I was fair, American. What I felt for Rogeirio was not love or desire but a gratitude that approximated both. He was kind to me, knew the town, was a decent man.

I smiled and said, "I'll eat."

It was for this after all that we had come: to eat sarapatel, a thick Bahian stew, a dish no one mentioned at the cooking school. Rogeirio promised that his friend made the best there was.

When the food arrived, Rogeirio dished up rice for each of us, heaped it on our plates and then ladled over this the thick, brown sarapatel. The stew was delicious, salty and thick, the color of black beans and fragrant with spices—cumin, pepper, cinnamon, clove, bits of meat or noodle. I couldn't tell which.

—Wonderful, I said. What is it?

Rogeirio smiled. Blood stew, he said.

It seemed a fitting food for us in a place where a bloody past still bled into the present, and where I often felt just beneath the surface of our affair something painful, a wound, though whether it was his or mine or both I couldn't say. He might have been describing the city itself, whose horrific past seemed to flavor the present; he might have been describing the sad, violent blending of bodies that I was learning about that year, which for a long time I would mistakenly believe was all that could exist between a woman and a man.

Filha de Iañsa

Though I would live in Bahia for most of six months, I never visited a *terreiro*, the house of a *mãe de santo*, a saintly mother, in which is practiced the Afro-Brazilian religion of *candomblé*, a syncretized blend of African deities and Catholic saints. But living in Salvador, you could not remain ignorant of its gods and goddesses.

Their names were among the lyrics of Bahian pop singers, their images were everywhere, painted on murals, on T-shirts, carved in wood. Their saints' days were celebrated with verve. In January, there had been a celebration of Yemanjá, the beautiful mermaid goddess, whose day was celebrated with a flotilla of boats and wreaths of flowers cast onto the waves at dawn.

Devotees of *candomblé* were said not to be practitioners but sons and daughters of their gods; in the midst of worship, one became possessed by the spirit of the god, became that figure, danced his or her dance in the circle of the devout. I had been to a small museum of Afro-Brazilian art at the edge of Pelourinho and was fascinated by the garb and the natures of these gods. Each one had a personality, traits that their followers were said to share: Yemanjá was beautiful and vain; Xango was the warrior; Exu, the trickster; Iañsa, the fierce, blade-wielding Amazon. As with my passing acquaintance with astrology and the Myers-Briggs, I wondered vaguely what I was, of which god was I a daughter?

Barbara had told me that she wanted to be a filha de Iañsa, daughter of the goddess of storms and thunderbolts, who was associated with the Catholic Saint Barbara. Iañsa's color was red, she carried a machete; she was a force to be reckoned with. I was surprised that Barbara would identify with Iañsa. I thought she must be a filha de Yemanjá, the beautiful, self-regarding mermaid, depicted always with a mirror in one hand.

It was Boa Gente who settled the matter.

In one of the last classes I took with him (opting, at the end of the eight-week sequence, not to pay tuition for the coming term though Barbara would continue on), Boa Gente brought up the subject. He was, as usual, touring the room as we struck positions. He was adjusting our poses, commenting, correcting, praising, when he came to me.

I never knew what it was that he saw in my posture that day, but as he watched me press my foot into midair, he stopped and looked me dead in the eye, eschewing commentary on my pose to comment instead on me.

—*Você*, he said, frowning with concern. You are too competitive; you must not be so competitive. So angry.

I smiled, trying to joke it off.

—I like to compete, I said. I'm not angry. I smiled but I felt exposed, summed up, and blushed.

—You think too much about what the others are doing, he continued. You must think about what you are doing, not them.

I nodded, hoping he'd let me go. But he held my foot in midair, cupped the heel in his palm. I couldn't say what I wanted: that I wouldn't know what to do if I didn't watch the others. I wouldn't know what to want if I didn't compete with them, if I didn't want what they did.

—You are a child of Iañsa, he said. Do you understand?

I did not.

—Iañsa is the goddess of storms and thunderbolts, he said. *Você e a filha de Iañsa.* He let my foot go.

I knew that this was neither a judgment nor a curse, but a statement about my nature, plain and simple. He saw, I think, that I was at war with my own nature and that this was what made me clumsy. He wanted to help me to recognize and lay claim to what I was. I was embarrassed that he had watched me so closely, seen so much in me. But I understood that there was also a benediction in this, his observation. He saw what I could not: that I was, despite my clumsiness, fierce, kin to divinity, child of a god, a warrior.

News

When I got the envelope from INPA, it was thin and I was nervous, anticipating rejection. I had, after all, no real credentials to offer. Nothing but hope. I was just another student who had read their work, not one of them. I sat on the mattress and leaned against the wall. Outside, monkeys screamed in the trees. The wind rustled among the dead flowers in the window boxes, rattling like bones. I sat on the mattress with the monkey sleeping beside me. I tore off the end of the envelope and pulled out a single sheet of letterhead.

The letter said they would be delighted to have me join them, that while it might be difficult, given my brief stay, to integrate me into an ongoing project, they'd be happy to make available whatever I needed to pursue my own research. I recall that my bibliography was praised. I know for sure that I was asked to phone as soon as possible to discuss project options and dates. The letter was signed by my hero, Philip Fearnside.

Territory

I did not want to notice, as the weeks passed, how Nel grew listless and despairing. How she left the apartment less and less. How she stopped talking of jobs. She spent her days cleaning up the small studio apartment, reading books, sleeping on a mattress on the floor, chatting with our neighbors. She kept her few belongings in the clear plastic beach bag that was patterned with yellow daisies. Often I found her arranging her sack, taking out and refolding her few shirts and underthings into neat stacks. Maintaining perfect order in the small realm that was hers.

We talked about her getting her own apartment when I left for the Amazon; sometimes we went out apartment hunting. The university had closed for the year, so she had all day to search. But like the jobs she searched for, which always seemed to pay too little or ask too much—for qualifications she didn't have, or sexual favors for the boss—she never found one.

What We Talk about When We Don't Talk about Love

Nel and I were downtown, near the city center, in a part of town we did not usually visit—perhaps we had come to a doctor's office, perhaps we had come for something else—and were crossing into a cobbled *praça*, when a navy blue Mercedes pulled up in the street beside us.

Nelci screamed, a little sharp intake of breath, and I thought at first that the car had clipped her. But instead of drawing back, she leaned in the car window and hugged the woman behind the driver's wheel.

I could see that the woman was pretty and young, that she had the confident poise, the calm beauty, that wealth often confers. She had long dark hair, dark eyes, a wonderful smile. Her glance, it seemed to me, was sharp, intelligent. She was clearly rich.

The woman spoke animatedly to Nelci, but Nel—after recovering from her initial surprise—appeared calm now, standing aloof from the car, erect so that the woman had to hang her head out the window to converse. Nel addressed her with the formality that we reserve for those we do not like and those we have once loved and love no longer, those we once knew well but do not now.

I could not make out most of their conversation; I tried to appear engaged in surveying the *praça*, to look uncurious.

—Are you still in Amaralina? Nel asked.

—Oh, no, I left there months ago, the woman said. I live over there, she gestured across the *praça* with a little wave. She had an elegant hand, long slender fingers, smooth skin. Where are you now? she asked Nel.

—I'm living in Barra, Nel said.

—Not bad, said her friend.

—Not bad. Nel did not sound convinced.

Nel opened a hand toward me and introduced us.

—This is my friend Elena, she said. Elena, this is Valeria. We used to live together in Amaralina.

We shook hands, lightly.

Nel spoke as if she had never mentioned Valeria to me, and I wondered if she could have forgotten. But I didn't ask her until later, when, after a minute or two, after another series of hurried hugs, the girl in the car drove off.

For a moment Nel stood quietly watching the car go. Then we walked into the *praça*. She was quiet for what seemed a long time.

—I have to apologize to you, Elena, she said. I thought she was going to say something about our bickering, her criticisms of me, but she did not. I lied to you.

—About what?

—There wasn't an abortion, she said.

It seemed a strange thing to invent. I waited for her to say more.

—Valeria and I were lovers, she said. Do you understand? Here they call them *sapatonas*, big shoes. Lesbians. Understand?

I nodded.

—My father found out. He threatened to cut me off if I didn't move out. I refused.

—What happened with you and Valeria?

She shrugged.

—It didn't work out. I couldn't afford to stay after a while. When I met Isa, I moved into the boarding house.

Though I'd never met a lesbian before as far as I knew, it did not surprise me to learn this. It was as if Nel were telling me something I'd known all along; all along this possibility had been there with us. I was impressed that she'd had the courage to love her friend, another woman. How, I wondered, had it begun between them? Who had initiated it? How did it start? Were people born knowing who to love?

The irony did not strike me then; only later would it occur to me that Nel had confessed to an abortion rather than tell the truth about love. Love was more difficult to admit to than loss.

But perhaps I misremember this.

Perhaps I only want love to be the secret that Nelci finally revealed. I know, for certain, that we met Valeria in a *praça* in those last days together. I know that Nel addressed her in a formal manner, curt, the way one is sometimes with an ex. I know it was Valeria we met that day and that Nel was affected by the meeting.

But my mother, when I speak of Nelci now, recalls another story. She says that I told her then that Nel was estranged from her father because he'd taken a mistress of Nelci's age. She recalls that Nel was outraged, protective of her mother, maybe jealous.

We each have a different story. And our stories are telling, whether or not they tell the truth. My mother (who was betrayed by my father) recalls a mother betrayed. I (who will fall in love with a woman at twenty-five) recall a secret Sapphic love affair.

Our stories differ but they have this in common: in both my mother's memory and mine, love's a dirty secret, a thing we try to hide.

In June, people began to leave. Barbara returned to the United States to complete a PhD at Yale. Rogeirio departed for Texas. Linda went, as did her friend Michael. In less than a month, I would leave for the Amazon at last.

My days were occupied with farewell parties and classes at the cooking school. After Rogeirio left for the States, I became enamored of the handsome young man at the cooking school, the one who resembled the Giotto madonna. Yvette made fun of me for mooning over him. She reminded me that he was married. She said that he was just a pretty face. But I wanted that beauty he had, as if his calm radiance might be transferred to me by touch.

When, eventually, we went to bed together, I did not think about his wife. As we made love, I thought only of his face, beautiful as a madonna's, over mine. The color of cacao. At his cheekbones, the skin was brighter, almost gold. He had a face you wanted to touch, a smooth carved head. Seemingly permanent by virtue of its beauty. I did not take pleasure in this. I did not think about his wife. I failed to make the connection between us.

Help

Nel was getting up later and later. She packed and unpacked her plastic bag. Napped in the afternoon on the mattress. Read *Manchete* or *Veja* if she could borrow them from Zé. She left the apartment only rarely. When I come home from shopping, she woke.

—I'm sorry to be sleeping on your bed, Elena, she said, as if apology were necessary. She drew herself up to rest an elbow on the giant yellow pillow I'd sewn. I don't sleep too well on the floor, she said. It's so hard. And you weren't here . . .

—Don't worry about it, I said, but I knew my voice sounded annoyed. Lately, we had had this conversation too often. At other times I had said, You're welcome to sleep there, Nel. I have the hammock, but I was tired of repeating myself.

Her apology, I suspected, was an accusation. Her apology let me know that I had offered help but hadn't helped her. Perhaps it was because I knew this was true that I was angry.

I brushed through the room to the kitchen. I set the bag on the stove top, next to a pot of something thickened and unidentifiable.

I glanced into the pot.

—You can try it, Nel said, stroking her stomach as she stood.

—What is it? I asked, suspicious.

—It's farofa with salt and a little oil. It doesn't have much flavor, but it's filling and it's cheap. I bought two pounds of farofa today for mil cruzeiros (50 cents). Not bad, eh? She dabbed a finger in the congealed paste and popped it in her mouth.

—Nel, I said, we *have* food. I opened the fridge. Look.

She leaned a hand on the red stove corner but looked at the floor, not to the fridge. She raised one shoulder in a tense shrug.

—I know, Elena, but I don't like to eat that. That's your food. I need to have food of my own. I don't like always taking from you.

She shook her head, slowly, from side to side.

—Besides, she said, looking up at me, I need my own money. I went out with Isa on Saturday to the port and I couldn't even afford a *suco*.

Nel's face was taut, and I thought she might cry, but her voice was strong as ever.

She walked into the living room, leaving me to unload my sack of groceries.

—It's horrible, she said. She spread her arms out like braces against the windowsill and leaned out over the withered flower box. The sound of a Rede Globo announcer came from the neighboring apartment, and from the street came the screams of monkeys in the trees.

I set a bunch of bananas on top of the fridge and took a couple of water crackers from the box I'd just bought. I went into the living room and sat on the edge of the mattress to eat my cracker.

—Have some, I said, holding out a cracker to her. I got the kind you like.

Nel glanced at me, but shook her head before turning away. She rested her forearms on the windowsill, leaning farther out.

—Maybe we could work something out, I said.

—Like what, she said, turning to face me.

—I don't know. I mean, I could pay you to clean up the apartment. I don't know how much, but it'd be something.

I could see her jaw working, as if she were chewing on the thought, her chin jutting out as it did when she was thinking hard. I watched Nel for a moment then I read the name printed on the pale toasted cracker. I liked its neat holes, its toasted blisters.

After a while, Nel began to nod, slowly.

—What would you want done, Elena? she asked, almost whispering.

—I don't know, I shrugged. It's just an idea.

Something had gone wrong, I knew, but I didn't know what.

—I could scrub the bathroom, Nel said. It's disgusting. And polish the stove and fridge. Sweep the kitchen.

I found it hard to swallow the wad of cracker in my mouth. I got up to get some water to wash it down. I had a sudden fear of choking.

—I'll do it, Nel said.

When I turned to face her, her eyes were dark, hard with something I did not want to name.

As the date of my departure approached, we could hardly stand to be in the apartment together. Its single room shrank precipitously with our mutual disenchantment. We passed through it with elaborate unspoken choreography. Each morning Nel emerged from the bathroom at a later hour—her toilette taking longer each day, prompting me to speculate that she lingered there expressly to annoy me, waiting for me to ask her to come out so that she could once more, patiently submit to my outrages, my selfishness.

I refused to knock. Instead, I lay each morning in the hammock tightening my buttocks to stay the urging of my bladder until after 40 minutes or so she appeared and—without glancing at me (for my part, I posed as if absorbed in a magazine)—padded to the kitchen to prepare her coffee. Filaments of tension wrapped us round so that each turn of a page, each cough registered like the pressure of a fly on a web.

• • •

By the time I left for the Amazon, Nel and I were weary of sharing quarters. Nel rarely left the apartment and we hardly spoke except to exchange criticisms. She complained that I was spendthrift and that I left my underwear on the bathroom floor after I showered. She criticized my familiarity with our laundress, whom Nelci said should not be encouraged. I complained of Nelci's constant presence, of her lethargy and dependence. She gossiped to our neighbors, and began to treat me with the disdain the needy lavish on those they need.

I was glad to leave the apartment when I left, but I wanted Nel to pay the rent if she wanted to remain there. I told myself that I could not afford to pay for my housing in Manaus and maintain the apartment for Nelci in Salvador. My fellowship was ample, but it would not easily cover two residences. I decided I had to give up the apartment we shared. Nelci would have to fend for herself, return to the boarding house, get a job. Had I economized, I could have kept the two apartments, supported Nelci, but I was not feeling generous by then. But to my surprise, Nelci said she would stay on and pay the rent on the apartment. So I left it to her, in her care.

A few days before I departed for Manaus, I brought the monkey to the house of the man beautiful as a madonna. It occurred to me to be embarrassed meeting his wife, but this was fleeting. Mostly I was grateful, deeply grateful that he would take this creature I could not care for and nurse it back to health. The monkey crawled onto his shoulder and perched there, as if it has found its place.

—Don't worry. We'll take good care of him.

—He likes yogurt, I said.

—Yogurt? He laughed.

—Yeah, and he's not big on fruit.

—Okay, he said. Yogurt it is.

We shook hands and then kissed each other on the cheek, three times, and I left, not wanting anyone to see—as if caring were a kind of weakness—that I was crying.

PART III

AMAZONS

The Amazon

Some halfway up the Amazon River in the tropical moist forests of the Brazilian Amazon is the capitol city of Manaus. It has been more than twenty years since I lived there, and a great deal has changed, but then as now Manaus was a kind of urban mirage. A construct of myth as much as of stone, a fantasy of a city. An imperial dream. Manaus was as close to a mirage as a city could be, because it was a projection of urbanity as much as an embodiment of it. Many of its most prominent buildings had been built in the cities of Europe and then dismantled, brick by brick, to be brought whole from England or France. The fish market beside the river was designed by Eiffel; the customs house was English, each yellow sandstone block numbered so it might be disassembled to be reassembled here.

When I think of the Amazon now, what I recall is not the forest or the cry of howler monkeys, not the figures I once knew by heart nor the hours spent mapping loss at a small desk in the corner of an office on the grounds of the National Institute of Amazonian Research; I recall strange disconnected images. A bus ride through back streets of the city, and how—stopped for a moment in traffic—I glanced up and met the eyes of a man whose face had been ravaged by leprosy or leishmaniasis, a gape where his nose should have been. How I watched a mob of workers on the grounds of the National Institute of Amazonian Research slowly beat to death with sticks the dazzled figure of a three-toed sloth because its slow and unhurried movements had amused or annoyed them. I recall conversations with scientists from Australia, England, the U.S., who spoke over beers and plates of fish about the discoveries they had made of species, few of which were expected to last the decade, exciting nevertheless in a technical and professional way. An American man who invited me to join his team in catching bats in a valley that was to be flooded by a new dam, the construction of which had been funded by banks from our country. A drawer full of taxidermied birds.

I recall how little it seemed any of us could do to prevent this loss.

I arrived in Belem at the mouth of the Amazon River at dawn on Friday the thirteenth of July, having traveled thirty-six hours by bus from Salvador. There were only two viable ways to get to Manaus in those days: boat or plane. I had originally planned to go by boat, considering it a romantic mode of travel. I'd read in *Fodor's* that one might catch a ride on a supply steamer in the waterfront at Belem and travel cheaply the 930 miles upriver to Manaus that way. Many of the local peasants—*caboclos*—traveled like this. So, for that matter, did all the livestock and much of the dry goods destined for Manaus.

In Salvador, where I'd lived for the last six months, I'd met a couple from Indiana who'd made the trip by boat. During the day, they'd told me, you squeezed on deck and squinted at the green thread of shoreline in the distance and prayed for a breeze. At night, you went below with the cargo and strung your hammock between beams. With hardly any space between the hammocks, you slept with your arms tight to your sides, swaying into your neighbor with each rock of the boat, the smell of chickens and pigs and humans constant through the long night. I found the prospect of the five-day trip romantic; it sounded wonderful.

But in July, as I prepared to leave Salvador for the Amazon, several supply steamers sank on their way from Belem to Manaus, overloaded with cargo and passengers, and I bought a plane ticket.

What I remember of Belem is the airport: a cement, two-story terminal with a runway edged by billows of forest, dense as cumulus clouds, a seemingly impenetrable green. On the airport's upper terrace, I stood leaning on a railing, staring out across the runway where a few small planes were parked. American pop music from the 1970s came over a loudspeaker in another part of the building.

After all I had imagined, the Amazon was disappointing. Smaller. Shorter. Just a forest, after all, at the edge of a runway.

I had not had breakfast. I had not slept. I had approximately ten hours before my flight. So I went downstairs to the snack bar and bought a sweet roll, doughy and sticky (literally a sweetened roll), and came back upstairs to wait. I returned to the railing that overlooked the runway and chewed. To my left and right were row on row of plastic chairs. In the distance, the Bee Gees sang. Tired of chewing, I dropped my roll onto the runway. A young boy, maybe five or six, in a tattered shirt and shorts ran out and grabbed it and stuffed it inside his shirt. He looked up at me and I looked down at him and then he casually walked away.

By evening, the terminal that had been empty hours before was filled with the unsteady glow of fluorescent lights and reverberant with voices. I went to the café where I'd spent a solitary hour that morning and found the place mobbed with travelers.

I bought a bottle of water at the concession, made my way to an empty table in the back, and sat down to wait for my flight. I pulled out my book, a novel by Doris Lessing as I recall (which, as I recall, I never finished), but I couldn't get my eyes to focus; I sat staring at the black lines trying to look absorbed.

When a hand came to rest on the chair next to me, I looked up.

—May we join you?

The man who asked was handsome, well-dressed, middle-aged. He had a carefully trimmed moustache and dark hair flecked with silver; his face was deeply tanned. Beside him stood a square-jawed, Teutonic guy of perhaps thirty; blond and blocky, he held a shopping bag and a small wicker case. I closed my book.

The men were part of a veterinary congress from Curitiba, São Paulo, which had been touring the Amazon to get a feel for the region's fauna. The older man told me about what he called the civilized south and urged me to visit him there. He pressed a business card into my hand. I could stay at his ranch, he said, where he raised thoroughbred horses and cows.

—Have you ever tasted fresh milk, still warm from the udder? he asked.

The younger man sat back in his chair and watched me over the rim of his drink. I was leaning forward onto the table, my arms folded before me. I could feel his eyes move over my neck, my shoulders, my brown arms. He clicked his tongue, and I looked up. He smiled.

—Come here, the blond said. He reached out and took my hand. I want to show you something.

There was an excitement in his eyes that made me hesitate, but the older man nodded at me and frowned. I got up and went to stand by the blond.

—Look in the bag, he said. I leaned over the bag and looked in.

—Oh, it's great, I said.

—Shhh. He held a finger to his lips. It's our secret.

—May I touch it? I asked.

He winked and nodded.

The contraband three-toed sloth lay on its back in the shopping bag, grinning—so it seemed—oblivious of any malice in the world. I knelt down and stroked its belly.

—What's in that one? I asked, glancing at the wicker case.

—Parrot, he winked.

Now, of course, I wonder why I didn't do something. Why I played along. I might have alerted someone; I might have had the contraband creatures confiscated and freed. I might have saved their lives. No doubt they didn't last long in São Paulo, on the pampas, 3,000 miles from their forest home. But I didn't. I was in on it, after all. I was more afraid of the poor opinion of strangers than of what might be lost. I played along, still believing then that if I went along with the plans of men like these—knowledgeable, reasonable, professional men—that I would be, we would all of us be, all right.

INPA

Two guards were posted at the entrance to the National Institute of Amazonian Research when my cab pulled up the next morning. The guards leaned against the guardhouse, trying—it appeared—to stay out of the dusty morning glare. They wore khaki uniforms; pistols hung in holsters at their hips. They watched a truck thunder past. Even this early in the day, curtains of heat rose from the asphalt. On the other side of the two-lane highway, a trampled patch of brown grass served as a bus stop. The guards called out flirtatiously to two young women who waited there. The girls ignored them. The guards laughed, waved us through.

Past the guardhouse, the road meandered back through the INPA campus. Here shade replaced glare: the sunlight was filtered by a canopy of trees, the road kaleidoscopic with shadows. Instead of sidewalks, wide paths of hexagonal tiles wound through the manicured, well-maintained grounds. Trees on either side of the walkway were identified by green nameplates that jutted up from the soil on steel spikes: *Paullinia cupana* (guarana); *Hevea brasiliensis* (rubber); *Theobroma cacao* (cacao). Every detail conspired to give an impression of order and control, of a forest on good terms with the people who moved through it.

Set back from the road, veiled by leaves, were clusters of single-story buildings. Oblong structures of red brick with large picture windows indistinguishable from one another save for the wooden sign nailed over each door, which identified some as classrooms, others as laboratories. Ichthyology. Ornithology. Morphology. One was a medical facility. Others were classrooms.

At the far end of the loop formed by the road, grouped in a semicircle like a wagon train, were the *alojamentos* where visiting researchers were housed. There were two wooden lodges, each comprising six apartments, each of these with its own patio deck and sunken living room.

I was assigned to an apartment with a Brazilian ichthyologist named Ayda. In her early forties, Ayda wore the uniform of a grad student: jeans, tennis shoes, a baggy sweatshirt. Her jowls sagged a bit and lines scored her pale face. Her silver hair was shorn in an androgynous cut. She offered me prune juice when I arrived, then sat on my bed to tell me about herself.

Ayda had come to INPA at the urging of a professor of hers, having begun her doctoral thesis on the suggestion of a friend who felt, after Ayda's divorce, that she needed a project. Her two children had been living with her sister in another state for over a year. Her bookshelves in our shared apartment were stocked with pills and self-help books: *The Power of the Subconscious, Psychosomatic Illness*, a Brazilian version of *Cosmo* with articles on improving your sex life and weight-loss tips. She confided that she'd had the cellulite surgically removed from her thighs. At the time Ayda seemed to me a slightly ridiculous figure, but now I am amazed by the courage it must have taken for a middle-aged mother to leave her children to come save some part of a forest.

That afternoon, after Ayda left for the lab, I phoned Fearnside's office to arrange a time to meet and discuss what I might do here. I expected to reach a secretary, but I got Fearnside himself. He suggested that I stop by that afternoon. He asked that I bring a copy of the research paper whose bibliography I had sent with my letter of inquiry, a bibliography that had evidently helped secure me a place here. I told him I'd be happy to.

Fearnside's office was about a half mile's walk from the main campus and my apartment, in a collection of brick buildings at the end of a dirt drive that branched off from the highway. I found him in an office on the second floor of a brick building of white offices and labs. He looked like Ichabod Crane, tall and gaunt and ghostly pale, his pallor enhanced by his dark hair and walrus-like mustache. He was stiff and formal, but not unfriendly.

He greeted me with a handshake, offered to have someone show me the labs after our talk. He said the labs were at my disposal, then asked what it was I planned to do here, what precisely my project would be.

It was a perfectly reasonable question, but it was a question for which I was perfectly unprepared: I had no answer.

When I'd determined to get myself to INPA, I hadn't thought about what I'd do once there. I had imagined that I'd tag along on someone else's project, that I'd fit in to someone else's plans. I knew the outline of my desires—that I wanted to help save this forest through sound development—but, as in love, the specifics confounded me.

I told Fearnside I wasn't sure yet.

After showing me around his office, Fearnside turned me over to an assistant who would show me the facilities. We shook hands and I gave Fearnside my paper. We agreed to meet the next day for lunch to discuss my work and what I might do there. As I left, I felt buoyant. The paper I had given him was one that I'd presented in a graduate-level seminar at Yale; the seminar professor—an exigent visiting prof from Columbia—had praised my work and kept a copy for his reference, proof (I thought) that I was well versed in the subject, one of them.

Amazon Snapshot #9

Graham Greene famously said that it's hard to write happiness; joy lacks the compelling texture of sorrow, the distinction that Tolstoy rightly noted every unhappy family has. The same can be said, I suppose, of writing about a rain forest and nature, the world's magnificent wild places—how is one to make its value visible to those who do not see it? Like Cordelia, it seems unwise to heave one's heart into one's mouth—to try to name or (worse yet) enumerate the things I love. To argue for nature's value is to allow for argument against it. I want to say now of the rain forest, as I did of that sunset glimpsed in childhood, *Beautiful, beautiful,* but I fear the reader, like my childhood friend, may scoff, think, *Jeez. It's just trees.*

When writers write of the Amazon, they often speak grandiloquently of its beauty, its marvelous diversity (the poet Pablo Neruda spoke of it as "the endless secret of fertility"), as if it were an Eden, reclaimed.

In truth, the forest smells like a bog, of moist decay, leaves, black tea, and dirt.

There are said to be 200 kinds of mosquitoes there.

There is a fish (the candirú) that swims up the human urethra, where it grows large, and lodges until its host dies of renal failure or hemorrhage.

There are, famously, piranha and poison dart frogs.

In truth, the rain forest is a tedious green.

The novelist Andrew Holleran, after a recent trip to the Amazon, said he found it uniform; I believe he said he found it dull. Green and dull.

The Amazon has been a story as much a place. Accounts of its exploration often conform to certain forms and tones: part documentary, part breathless adventure story, the stories emphasize physical hardship, natural wonders, the ruthless (or magnificent) "primitive" juxtaposed with the supposedly "civilized" writer. (Titles like Sebastian Snow's *My Amazon Adventure* (1951) are unfortunately typical.) In his book *The Rivers Amazon* (1978), Alex Shoumatoff of the *New York Times* self-consciously harkens "back to the great nineteenth-century naturalist explorers of the Amazon, Spruce, Wallace, and Bates . . . Forging into unknown territory, these men were intrigued by everything." Like many others, Shoumatoff compares the forest to a woman: "I reached down and ran my fingers along the midribs of a little plant called

Mimosa pudica. *The leaves folded up like a woman shrinking from someone's advances"* (italics mine).

What Africa was to a nineteenth-century imperial European imagination, the Amazon arguably has been to the United States' and Brazil's. We have seen in it what we've longed for and feared: a verdant frontier, an answer to overpopulation, the ultimate wilderness against which to test our civilized selves, a gold mine, a spiritual restorative, a pharmaceutical cornucopia, a threat to national sovereignty, a base for popular guerrilla insurgency, the promise of paradise, a paradise in the process of being lost.

By and large, the Amazon's explorers have been men; travel narratives by men of many nations abound. If women have gone there, they've generally not gone on about it. (The once-famous Isabela Godin des Odonais—toast of French society in the 1770s for having been the first woman to descend the Amazon—did not record her story; her husband did.)

Accounts of Amazonian adventures inspired generations of would-be explorers. Mark Twain was "fired with a longing to ascend the Amazon" after reading Lieutenant William Hernadon's *Exploration of the Valley of the Amazon* (1851–1852). When he found $50 in the streets of Cincinnati, he set off for New Orleans to find a boat to Pará (now the city of Belem) at the mouth of the Amazon; unable to find passage, his money running out, Twain met a river pilot whom he begged to teach him the Mississippi. John Muir, the American naturalist whose efforts would lead to the creation of the national park system and conservation movement, was ambitious of going to the Amazon when a lung condition prevented him, so he went to Yosemite Valley instead.

It can be hard to see the forest for all the words.

Fast

When Fearnside and I met the next day for lunch I could tell that something was wrong. He seemed cooler toward me than he had the day before, and when he proposed that we drive into town for lunch, I had the feeling he'd rather not go at all.

I wondered, briefly, if it was my outift: I had dressed like a Bahiana, in a thin, sleeveless indigo blue shirt with a plunging neckline and jeans that hugged my hips, realizing only now—as I waited for Fearnside—that none of the few women at INPA dressed like this. (They wore T-shirts, sweatshirts, oversized khakis and jeans, practical clothes, the sort I'd worn at college.) I was aiming to look pretty by Bahian standards but those standards didn't apply here.

Despite my nervousness, I was eager to lunch with Fearnside. Even meeting him was a thrill, this man whose articles I had read for years, who was fighting to save this forest, charting its loss so that its absence became a presence. He asked if I'd been in town yet, and when I said I hadn't, he suggested that we go to a Chinese restaurant in the heart of Manaus, so we got in his car and drove there.

Fearnside was in his late thirties then, perhaps fifteen years older than I, but he seemed to me infinitely old; he was an ecologist whose work addressed, as one biographer put it, some of the most controversial issues in the Amazon region, from challenging official Brazilian government estimates of the greenhouse emissions from deforested tracts to revealing the true sources of deforestation.

The restaurant, as I recall, was on stilts, off a dry dusty street, a huge, square, two-story bamboo structure. The main dining room of the restaurant seemed dim after the brightness of the street, and empty of customers save for us. I felt the pleasant thrill of anticipation, both eager and afraid to hear Fearnside's opinion of my paper.

We sat down at a table in the large, bamboo dining room where fans turned slowly overhead, and Fearnside ordered tea for two. Then he told me that he'd read my paper and that I had it wrong.

I don't remember precisely what his criticisms were, but the gist of it was this: my paper was marred by errors, principal among which was a confusion of silviculture with cattle ranching. Silviculture, of course, is tree farming; cattle ranching involves cows. I *knew* the difference; I had written research papers on both, but in this—my longest and most comprehensive—I'd evidently conflated the stats somehow, writing as if they were the same thing. I didn't know how it happened, but I could guess: I must have transposed the terms at some point during some late-night all-night revision and once confused kept going, misapplying statistics on the damage done by one to refer to damage done by the other.

I had come thousands of miles to learn that I had not been paying attention.

My face was hot and blushing. I wanted to explain that I *knew* the difference, that these errors were *not* errors of *understanding* but more like typos. But instead I nodded, mute, afraid that if I opened my mouth I might cry, as he cataloged in a tired and disappointed tone my mistakes and offered simplistic advice on each point as if I required such simplicity.

Perhaps memory makes matters worse: perhaps my humiliation magnifies the moment. Looking at the paper now, I see that the errors are actually few and minor, but I didn't know that then. I scanned the menu with a lump in my throat.

When the waitress returned, I said, I'll just have tea.

—You're not going to *eat*? Fearnside asked.

—I'm not very hungry, I said.

—Eat *some*thing, he said. I don't want to eat alone.

—Tea, I said, I'll have green tea. That's all I want, I lied.

In truth I wanted so much more. But if I could not have what I wanted—which was to be one of them, one of those who could make a difference here, to be like Barbara, who knew how to dress, how to speak, what to say, what she wanted and how to get it, who seemed unafraid to take her place, to take action and the consequences—then I would practice not wanting. My fast, my penance, at least, was mine.

Moths

That night, while Ayda was out working in the ichthyology lab, I stood in the doorway of our apartment. I leaned on the doorframe and watched the lights click on in the other apartments. I was lonely and discouraged after my meeting with Fearnside; I felt nervous, self-conscious as I often did then, as if straining to hear some call or tone just beyond my perception.

Moths drew near the light that emptied from our doorway onto the cement porch. They fluttered around my face, then battered past me into the apartment where they'd likely die, disoriented by the artificial light. Researchers came too. An affable and inebriated Nicaraguan was the first to arrive, coming over from a neighboring apartment to offer me a drink from his private stash of rum (a powerful brew he claimed to have smuggled past Customs). Another Nicaraguan showed up. Then a tall American, who gave his name as Ron and who had thin nervous lips under a rust-colored beard. Ron said he was a professor of zoology. He named the small private college where he taught. I nodded, smiled, sipped my rum. I'd never heard of it.

When Ayda returned with a friend from her lab, she served coffee. We stood around on the narrow strip of cement that served as a porch, talking and drinking, until a dark-haired Australian showed up. He had a black beard and moustache, aquamarine eyes; he entered our circle with the complacent self-regard of the handsome, the showy laconic indifference of the alpha male. He introduced himself to me as William Magnusson and said to call him Bill. I didn't know if it was a general dislike for Bill or the lateness of the hour that ended our party, but soon after he arrived, the others left and so did he and we each of us went to our beds alone. I fell asleep listening to the papery sound of moths battering the windowpanes.

Mating Rituals

The following night Bill and Ron knocked on my door and asked if I wanted to join some of the other researchers for dinner in town. There was a fish restaurant they said was great, and some of the guys were going, did I want to come along?

I pocketed a few thousand cruzeiros—enough for bus fare and a drink, not enough for a meal so I wouldn't blow my diet—and stepped out onto the sidewalk between the two men. They were old enough to be my professors, those guys, and that comforted me. I felt protected by their presence, grateful they had thought to invite me along.

As we walked through the campus toward the bus stop, I listened to them talk, keeping my mouth shut, hoping to appear intelligent, as if silence were somehow smart.

When blue-eyed Bill asked what my project would be here, I admitted that I didn't have one.

—You could assist me at Tucuruí, red-haired Ron said.

Tucuruí was a valley northwest of Manaus, where a hydroelectric plant was being constructed and a river dammed. Ron was heading up a team to rescue—for taxonomic purposes—fauna in the area to be flooded.

—It will mostly be catching bats, he said. He described the massive nets used, the painstaking process of extraction.

—I'd love to, I said. And I meant it.

I turned to red-haired Ron, grateful for the offer to assist him and amazed at my good luck. But he was not looking at me. He was looking at his feet. In the light of the street lamp we passed under, I could see that he was smiling a compressed, timid smile.

—Of course, he said, you realize that in order to get clearance to enter the site—as, uh, Bill here has pointed out to me—you'll have to go as my wife.

He looked at me for the first time. Or mistress, he added. He had a high laugh.

I might have suggested that I go as his daughter instead (I was young enough), had I had my wits about me. But at the time I didn't have much wit. I was witless, straight man to every joke. I looked at handsome Bill, who stared blankly back at us, his face unreadable as a Rorschach.

—I'll think about it, I said. Thanks.

I had known from our first evening on the porch that there was a bidding war of sorts going on over me among the researchers, most of whom were male. And I knew that Ron was a part of this, but I recall the sense too that he was trying to protect me, trying to offer an honorable escape. A way out of here, a way into the forest, a chance to be part of a team, not a pair or a ménage.

Even at the time, it was obvious to me that I was not the object of their attentions so much as another opportunity for the cheerful exercise of masculine rivalry, the territory they fought and bonded over. Theirs was a sporting noncommittal game to see who could bed me. The fight was the thing they cared for, not me.

On the bus into town, I sat across the aisle from Ron. Handsome Bill sat behind me. As we rode, Bill leaned forward across the back of my seat and proposed that I work with him on a project at INPA's Reserve Duque, a 10,000 hectare ecological preserve about 35 kilometers from Manaus. I would collect tadpoles and fish to study which of the former were palatable to the latter and which were not, then speculate about why. It wasn't nearly as exciting a prospect as gathering monkeys, bats, and parrots at Tucuruí, but I thanked him for the offer.

—You wouldn't be a technician at Duque, Bill said. You'd be a researcher.

—Of course, I said, as if the distinction were clear to me. Beyond my window, the outskirts of Manaus ran like a watercolor.

—The difference between a technician and researcher, Bill continued, is courage. The courage to continue your work with uncertainty of success and the courage to succeed.

I'd read a little Ayn Rand by then and should have recognized in Bill's rhetoric something of her fervor—a weird eco-survivalist hybrid that flourished at outposts like this, where geeky researchers could fancy themselves Crusoes, scientific cowboys, John-fucking-Wayne. But I didn't realize that he was right: that what we need *is* courage.

The restaurant where we met the others was on the edge of town, a simple tent roadside that served beer and fish fresh from the river and *farofa*—manioc meal salted and dried. The air smelled of roasting meat, a salty charcoal smell, oily and rich.

I hadn't brought much money, so when the waitress came by, I ordered only a beer and settled back to listen to the others talk.

—What? A guy seated next to me asked. You're not eating?

—I'm not hungry.

—Don't tell me you're on a diet, he said.

—No, I said. I'm just not hungry.

—You have to eat. This place has the best pirarucú anywhere. She'll have pirarucú, he yelled to the waitress.

—*Um outro?* the waitress asked, looking at me. One more?

—*Não, obrigada,* I said. No, thanks. I'm really not hungry, I told the guy, embarrassed to admit that I couldn't afford it.

—*Um outro,* he said to the waitress. He said to me, We'll split it, okay? Then he laughed a good-natured laugh.

The waitress looked to me.

I shrugged and hoped they'd take a check.

At dinner, I was audience to the conversations of men. Ron, the red-haired zoologist, led off with an informal lecture on the mating habits of possum— perverse polymorphs of the animal kingdom. He informed us that there were over seventy-five species of possum in the Americas. Some fluoresced if you stuck them under ultraviolet light, glowing all the colors of a rainbow: purple, green, orange.

After a couple of beers, Ron got around to describing his favorite, a Venezuelan breed, which he called a sexual kamikaze. (I don't remember if he told us, or if it was later that I learned, that some possum have forked penises, that others are born without an assigned sex, becoming whatever sex the group needs them to be—male, female, a matter of social necessity.) The Venezuelan possum that Ron described has protruding tusks and grows to be twice the size of the tusk-less female. When it's time to mate, the male's genitalia swell to the point of dragging and change color. After mating, the male dies. The female lives long enough to suckle her litter; when they're weaned, she too dies.

The specifics of Ron's research escape me now, but the moral of his story that night was clear: reproduction is the possum's raison d'être. They have their mating rituals; this, alas, was one of ours.

When the check came after dinner, I pulled out my checkbook but the waitress said they only took cash. I hadn't enough money for my share, so I asked if someone could lend me 10,000 cruzeiros—about $5 bucks—till we got back to INPA.

—I left my cash at home, I said.

—*Ahhh*, said the guy who insisted I eat. She expected us to buy her dinner. She's one of those.

—I didn't expect to *eat*, I said.

Mine was assumed to be a coquettish gesture. But they missed the point entirely. I didn't want their help; I simply wanted to control my losses.

Back at INPA, as we walked from the bus stop to the *alojamentos*, along the neat mosaic-tiled paths of INPA, the conversation shifted from possums to my preference for working with handsome Bill or red-haired Ron. I knew the subject had never really changed. Sex had been our subject all along. I wanted to be taken seriously. I wanted to be of use here. I wanted a way into the forest, to be part of a team, not a couple or ménage, but I'd take what I could get.

Probably I would have joined Ron's team to trap bats had I not feared for my diet. That calculation was my priority, at the expense of everything else. I was like the researchers in this way, though the absurdity of my regimen was more obvious, if perhaps not wholly more absurd. We were all absorbed in calculating loss, in hopes of controlling it, mistaking control for security, its ironic opposite.

—I'd rather have a project of my own, I said. At Duque Reserve.

Handsome Bill nodded, as if indifferent to this outcome.

Ron, miffed, stalked off into the darkness alone.

Bill walked me back to my apartment. He offered to take me on a motor-cycle tour of INPA's grounds the following afternoon; he said we'd go to Duque Reserve over the weekend, go in on Friday, come out Sunday night. He'd make all the necessary arrangements.

I knew what he was saying. I understood that we would spend the night together, the weekend. This was the price I'd pay for his help. But I didn't really mind; he was handsome and I couldn't afford to mind. I needed his help, or thought I did.

I didn't realize then that there was another option, that there had been all along, there beside me—like the shimmering island of Itaparica in the Bay of all Saints—another possibility: I didn't realize that I didn't need someone else to make a place for me, I didn't need permission. I didn't realize that the choices were mine to make, simply waiting for me to make them.

The following Friday, Bill and I took a jeep into Duque Reserve in the early afternoon. We were to camp on a sandy bank of a tributary at a site deep within the 10,000 hectare reserve, which meant a long drive to the ranger's station and then, from there, an hour's hike in.

The road we took was slick with mud and deeply rutted from jeeps that had passed over it. Rainwater from an earlier storm had run off and pooled in milky patches that teemed with larvae and water skimmers. When we reached the ranger's station, Bill went inside to speak to the ranger and I sat under a metal awning that covered several picnic tables, like a camping site in a public park. When Bill returned, he tried to get me to take off my tennis shoes and leave them at the station.

—You won't be needing protection against the world in there, he said. There are no big animals left this close to Manaus. There aren't even mosquitoes to bother you. He explained that without human settlements to attract them, significant pest populations didn't exist in the Amazon. People, in his view, were the problem, the pest.

—What about leishmaniasis? I asked, eying a milky pool outside the ranger's house. I knew from my reading that pools like this, left by human activity, were breeding grounds for mosquitoes, which carried the disease, which produced chronic subcutaneous ulcers and disintegrated—in advanced stages —the nose and palate.

Bill shook his head and started down the path without me.

As we walked in along the wide, muddy road, Bill proposed projects I might pursue, a study of frogs I might undertake. He posed this as a series of questions, reeling off facts about the frog and inviting me to answer, a sphinx offering me a chance to enter the city for the price of a clever answer. But these days I couldn't make things fit together, add up.

I grabbed fistfuls of branches, trying to steady myself as I made my way along the thin ridge of solid ground that separated the soft trail from the tangle of forest. Bill walked ahead of me, splashing through puddles, his bare feet sinking into the soft earth.

I tripped over roots as I struggled to keep up with him.

He turned to look at me.

—It would be a lot easier, Ellen, if you'd just take off those shoes.

Leaning against the damp bark of a tree, I slipped off my shoes. There was a hum of what sounded like crickets in the trees and the whir of a bird behind me, chirps and rattlings. The sun was a white blur, flaring through the canopy. The leaves, silver and green, seemed less like something organic than like green vinyl cut to form. Tall, thin skeletal trees, their elongated, white bodies reminiscent of ganglia, branched into twigs and leaves. Gigantic and still.

It was growing dark by the time we rounded a bend and caught sight of our camp, where a lean-to of untrimmed logs, with a khaki tarpaulin stretched over it, stood in the center of a clearing. Enormous Morpho butterflies, iridescent blue, flitted around the clearing's edge.

Beyond this, the forest pressed on all sides.

We slipped down the embankment to the clearing and began readying ourselves for night. Bill unpacked our gear: beakers, lanterns, plastic bags, tackle boxes full of measuring tapes and balances. I strung up our hammocks under the tarpaulin and walked into the forest to gather wood for a fire.

The afternoon shadows swelled and deepened, leaving the trees gray. I was down at the water's edge, gathering kindling from the underbrush when the light dimmed. Sunset comes suddenly in the forest, the dense canopy blocking out the light long before the sun reaches the horizon. I made my way back to our camp, squinting at every tree root that rose above the soil, fearing snakes.

Bill had already started a fire and skewered a slab of beef and begun roasting it; the meat dripped into the flames as it cooked, sending up sparks and making the flames hiss. I piled the wood I'd gathered next to the cooking pots and sat down on the ground in front of the fire. I tore open a pack of saltines at my side. Around us the forest was dark, an indistinguishable darkness. (I'm certain there must have been sounds—the forest at night is full of racket—birds, frogs, bugs, cries and chirs and barks, but I don't remember these.)

It's when I stopped moving that I first noticed that I was feeling bad, weary and feverish and a little disoriented. Uncoordinated, edgy, and tired. I chalked it up to stress. I wanted nothing more than to stay there in camp and rest.

—We can't waste the whole night here, Bill said.

I could not understand why not. Wasting an evening by a fire would have suited me just fine. I was feeling ill and needed rest.

—We'll lose our chance, he said. If we don't go soon.

It occurred to me to argue with him, to ask if we couldn't gather specimens in the morning. It didn't occur to me that this might be a test. An impractical joke. In any case, I did not want to appear weak, a sissy, a girl, so I crumpled the cracker package closed and stood up, wiping the dirt from my palms on my pants.

Bill riffled through the supply pack and pulled out two miner's lamps, plastic belts with a lamp midway round. He handed one to me.

—You put it on like this, he said, taking my head in his hands to show me how to fit the band around my brow so that the lamp sat securely on my forehead.

Then we stepped out into the forest.

Bill led the way down the sandy path that ran from our camp to the river. The beam from his lamp illuminated a small circle of light ahead of him, mine lit one behind his feet. When we reached the river's edge, he walked in and sank up to his chest in black water. I stood on the sand above.

—Well, c'mon, he shouted, his lamp bobbing midstream. Don't tell me you're afraid of getting your feet wet.

I placed a foot at the edge of the river, holding onto a branch to steady myself. When at last I stepped off, the river rose to my armpits. The riverbed was slick under the soles of my feet. Plants and mud oozed up between my toes as I waded to the other side, holding my arms above my head, trying to keep my head above water. I tried not to think about electric eels, piranha, crocodiles. Reaching the other bank, I grabbed at roots and vines and hauled myself up onto the fragrant peaty earth.

Bill was waiting for me on the path and waved for me to join him, scooping his hand in the air. As I approached, he raised a finger to his lips. He pointed at the ground at our feet. In the beam of light from his lantern there was an enormous megalomorph spider, big as my fist. Two inches tall, five inches wide, it crouched beside a broad tree trunk. Bill pointed out its burrow among the tree roots. He pointed out the downy black fur across its back, which he claimed was a set of poison quills that could be fired at will (a claim I doubted, even as I feared it might be true).

We walked on. Barefoot along the path. Bill had insisted that it was safer to go barefoot out here. If you stepped on a snake, he had told me earlier, you'd feel it—maybe before it bit. It didn't occur to me that he might be joking. He went barefoot; so did I. Soon my head ached from squinting into the shadows of roots, trying to avoid stepping on spiders or snakes; we crossed roots, waded through streams. My mouth tasted sour and dry.

I was relieved when, maybe fifteen or twenty minutes later, we reached the pools we had come for: broad shallow stretches of water where the tributary's current had slowed. Bill walked downstream while I walked up among the fallen trees and mats of leaves that decomposed in the still, shallow pools. These were the best places, Bill had said, to catch the little fish and tadpoles that he suggested I study.

I approached the inlets stealthily, my net extended in front of me, poised to catch the small fish, the soft gelatinous eggs, the sperm-like tadpoles. Two snakes coursed by, skimming past in search of bigger fish. I pointed them out to Bill, finding them beautiful. Bill said they were poisonous and to avoid them. We gathered fish and roe from the water's edge, glistening and globate; they darted and quivered in the baggies we would carry back to camp.

On the way back to camp, Bill insisted that I take the lead. I tried to show no fear, but I was relieved when we reached the river bank across from our camp. I stepped into the water, sinking straight away up to my armpits. I was halfway across, too far to turn back, when Bill shouted that there were crocodiles. Turning was slow and difficult in the current, but I managed to twist my head in time to see the red retinas of a freshwater crocodile, some three yards downstream from where I was, illuminated by Bill's lamp.

The battery for my lamp had been growing weak as we'd walked, thinning out, and the beam was now too faint to see me across to the other side.

—My light is going, I shouted. Can you shine a path over here?

Bill did not respond; possibly he did not hear me. There was a splash of water downstream, and I watched as Bill's lamp illuminated the current beyond me in a weird orange glow.

My lamp went out. Around me the water was dark as oil. The pressure of the current seemed increased by this absence of light. I had to fight to stand upright. My feet sank into mud; I worried with every brush of a pebble or weed against my feet about piranhas.

—Bill, I shouted.

He did not answer. Then I saw him downstream, in the center of a tannic glow—a strange illuminated underwater scene—embracing the crocodile. It occurred to me dimly that this might all be for show, a calculated adventure, his idea of an aphrodisiac, but there was nothing I could do about it. Right or wrong. There was nothing to do but go on alone. I put my hands out in front of me, as in a game of blind man's bluff, and began to feel my way toward the other shore.

After changing into dry clothes, I went to bed while Bill stayed up by the fire to eat and make notes, whether on the croc, the tadpoles, or me, I was not sure. When he entered the lean-to for bed, I pretended to be asleep, wrapped in an alpaca blanket in my hammock. But I did not sleep. I felt terribly chilled and nervous, my skin itched as if I had been bitten by ants.

Bill seemed to fall into sleep quickly, his breath slowing and deepening. I lay awake, listening to the constant patter of rain on the canvas overhead. I found the deep silence beneath the sound of rain disquieting. I felt strange and disconnected from the world, unreal to myself. I felt like maybe I was going crazy. I had the panicked sense of unreality that sometimes overtook me as a child, as if the world were a scrim I might force my hand through. I looked over at Bill who lay in his hammock on the other side of the lean-to. Real or unreal, he was snoring softly.

Danger Signs

The next morning when I woke, the world appeared weird and glassy, and despite the heat, I was shivering. Bill asked if I'd ever had the measles, because—he said—it looked like I had them now. I was covered in red spots. I couldn't recall if I had or hadn't. I thought I'd had those shots, those illnesses, hadn't everyone?

Back at INPA, he dropped me off at the medical center, a modest, one-story, wooden building, reminiscent of counselors' quarters at summer camp. There, a kindly lady doctor examineed me—she looked in my eyes, down

my throat, took my temperature—and announced that I was having an allergic reaction. A severe one. My throat and tongue were beginning to swell.
I had a very high fever. My body, I could see for myself, was covered in red
bumps: hives.

She asked what I had eaten, had to drink lately, where I had been, whether
I was on any medication. I told her I was only taking Fanzidar, an antima-
larial medication I'd been given in the States. I did not mention the herbal
laxative teas I drank by the quart.

She said, We have to stop the swelling immediately. I'm going to give you
a shot of cortisone, okay? To reduce the inflammation. And you are to stop
taking Fanzidar.

—Is that necessary? I asked. The cortisone? (I hated shots and didn't want
to take it.)

—You are in grave danger, she said.

—What about side effects? I asked, stalling. Cortisone damages the kidneys
or liver, doesn't it?

—If we don't reduce the swelling, your throat could close, she said. You
could die. It is already swelling.

It was true that I was having trouble swallowing, that my tongue was
thick. But I was afraid of shots, afraid of this doctor whom I did not know.
What if she was wrong? What if the shot didn't help? What if the drug ex-
acerbated the problem? (The mind fastens on minor threats in the face of
serious danger.)

—You are having an allergic reaction to Fanzidar, she explained, which
she believed had built up in my blood, triggering the allergy. If we don't treat
this immediately, you could go into anaphylactic shock. Do you understand?
You probably have an allergy to sulfa drugs; many people do. Understand?

I nodded. I sat on the examining table, looking out through a small rectangular window above my head, at the pattern of leaves, the green and gray
shadows, flickering against the screen.

—Okay, I said.

As she prepared the syringe, she told me about a researcher who had recently died while researching malaria at INPA. The drugs he was taking,
perhaps Fanzidar itself, had only masked the malarial symptoms. By the
time he realized he was sick, it was too late.

—The cure, she said, is sometimes worse than the illness. Illness at least
you can cure.

As she rubbed alcohol on my arm, she said, You're a very lucky young
woman, you know. You could have died out there. An allergy to sulfa can be
fatal. Next time, it probably will be.

I nodded and braced myself for necessary pain.

· · ·

On the bus I took to town the following day, people stepped away from me, clearing a path as if I were contagious. I could not explain that I was not really ill: that my symptoms were merely a reaction to a drug that had built up in my blood, that my effort to protect myself had become the thing I needed protection from, the thing I needed to fear.

The bus route was familiar now. I had come this way several times since Fearnside first took me into the city more than a week ago; I had come on my usual errand, in search of diuretics and laxative teas. These errands that gave my days a semblance of purpose.

INPA was on the outskirts of town, a twenty-minute bus ride from the city center. On the way to town, the bus crossed a bridge. At the far end of the bridge was the governor's palace: a baroque confection in yellow with pillars at the entrance, ornamental urns, sculpted shrubs. Below the bridge, on either side of the river, were the makeshift houses of the poor—os favelados—which rose on stilts along the river bank. The houses were small and boxy, built of corrugated tin and weathered planks. One shack had a sign nailed to its side, facing the bridge: No Dumping. It struck me as a surprisingly dignified declaration, though it should not have come as a surprise; it is only natural to protect the place you live. It is unreasonable, unnatural, not to.

Amazon Snapshot #10

Jews, I've recently learned, are not supposed to care about nature. In an article published in *Tikkun* magazine a few years back, Professor Andrew Furman argues that Jews have traditionally been antagonistic toward the natural world. (There are, he notes, few Yiddish terms for specific varieties of birds, flowers, trees.) While American literature as a whole has been marked by a celebration of wilderness, Jewish American writers have largely written "city scriptures," Furman claims; "Jewish American writers" he says, ". . . have, by and large, created a literature that either ignores, misrepresents, or . . . vilifies the natural world."

This emphasis on text over terrain—he maintains—reflects the Mitnagged tradition, Jewish rationalism that reached its peak in eighteenth-century Lithuania and Russia and that emphasized a "text-centered mode of Jewish life." The ethic was pragmatic as much as principled. Jews did not own the land, so they'd better not rely on it. The word—Torah—would always be theirs.

We're not supposed to be attached to the land, but on my father's side (the Jews), we're marked by where we've lived. My grandmother's family name—Bialtzokovsky—was taken from the land they left (or were driven from), a small town outside Chernobyl in the Ukraine known as White Church; a common practice then.

In this way, perhaps, destination and destiny—*destino*—are linked: the places we live mark us, shape us, whether through the isotopes we ingest that record where we have been or through a name taken on departing a town or through the subtler shaping of sensibility that comes of a life spent in a forest, a city, or on high desert.

"Landscape is culture," landscape architect Peter Latz told the *Times Magazine* in May 2004. "Landscape is not the opposite of the town." Latz designed the Duisburg-Nord, a landscape park in northern Germany, built on a former industrial site; instead of trying to recover the "natural" terrain, he left the industrial structures—slag heaps, blast furnaces, a transformer station. This, our landscape now.

Latz means, I suppose, that humanscapes have become first nature for many of us in the industrialized West, but I think another meaning applies as well, that he is right in an altogether different way—that we are where we live: Landscape shapes us and thus our culture, as much as we shape it. I wonder how what we are doing to the natural world now will shape our future, reshaping perhaps the civilizations we have built.

It became our habit in the West at the close of the twentieth century to imagine that the personal is projected out onto the world, made global by grandiosity. The world is not out there to be encountered but invented, a complex of cultural, historical, semiotic, economic, and personal projections writ large. And yet, what if the world were projecting onto us? Might the grief and fear I felt on behalf of the Amazon at twenty-one be a kind of world-sorrow that I absorbed like sunlight? Is that possible? What if the recent increase in the incidence of so-called panic disorders is not merely the consequence of more stressful lives but a signal from the natural world, a tremor we feel the way horses scare before a storm. Its fear, ours. Its sorrows, our own.

The poet Jane Hirschfield notes that the elegy was more and more the mode of literature at the close of the twentieth century because our age is marked by a pervasive sense of loss, by wars and extinctions of species, a sense of ecological fragility. We like to call ourselves the Information Age. It sounds so optimistic. But I imagine we will be called other names by those who look back and wonder how we let this come to pass.

The Cartographer of Loss

In the wake of my failed outing to the forest, I returned once more to Fearnside's office and asked if I might assist him in some way. I offered myself up as a flunky, willing to do anything. At first, he could find nothing for me. He was working on an article for publication about his effort to map deforestation rates using LANDSAT images from space. He hadn't the time to supervise me on a project. Eventually, however, he said he could use my help mapping coordinates—translating the LANDSAT coordinates to localized maps. Cartography, he called it: it was the first time I'd heard the word. Map making.

I thanked Fearnside and left his office to begin the long hot walk back to INPA. As I walked the shoulder of the asphalt road, dodging rocks thrown up by passing truck wheels, squinting at the pale sky hazy with dust, I was grateful for my new job. I was glad to have something to do here, to be—at last—of use.

For the next six weeks I would map absence; I would be a cartographer of loss.

As a child, I could never manage to keep straight north from south, east from west; though we would live for years in the same modest, white-brick ranch house in a suburb on the outskirts of Minneapolis, Minnesota, I never got it down. Even now, returning to my childhood home, I have to remind myself where New York City is (east, beyond Saint Paul) to get and keep my bearings.

In childhood directions seemed reversed, as if glimpsed through a mirror. Perhaps I was distracted, too much immersed in my own thoughts to note the cardinal directions; perhaps I was absorbed elsewhere, observing my beautiful brilliant mother, whose despair held my attention like a work of art. Whatever the source, I was not aware of my body in space: I was aware of my mother's sorrow.

It is only in the wake of my stint in the Amazon that I will begin slowly to orient myself; and in discovering desire, laying claim to the intimate territory of the body at twenty-five, I will finally get my bearings and begin at last to chart by the truth north of desire.

At INPA, I settled easily into my routine. Rote, comforting. Each morning, after Ayda left for her lab, I would go into the bathroom, lock the door, and run in place, jogging in front of the bathroom mirror, flapping my hands over my head as if jumping jacks, in a parody of activity, going nowhere fast.

Each morning, on my way to Fearnside's office, I stopped at the canteen for a cup of sweet *café com leite* and a hot-dog-bun-sized roll that was split down the center and heavily slathered with shiny white salty butter. I sat at a picnic table alone and listened to the leaves rustle, observing the mangoes' gradual ripening as the weeks passed and the growth of the small red bananas, the palmettos, and the red-orange palm nuts clustered among the fronds of the trees from which *dendê* comes. I batted away flies. I chewed, almost happy.

Then I walked the gravel path among the buildings to a white office in which I sat at a white drafting table and annotated maps as if the forest were not a place but a set of shifting coordinates, an abstraction, a series of neat transparent squares to be filled in.

On free afternoons, on Saturdays and Sundays, I took the bus into town to buy laxative teas, walking the city streets for hours in the hope of burning off calories. A purposeless exertion. At the time, the irony did not strike me: my public effort to stem loss, my private campaign to lose. My days revolved around these calculations.

Looking at photos of myself from the time, I realize that I was pretty then and slim and might in time be beautiful. Whatever it was that I was trying to lose is not evident in the photos; whatever that was doesn't register on film.

In truth, I don't remember much of what I did there those months at INPA.

I had set a course and simply followed it unquestioningly to its illogical conclusion, as the Brazilian government seems intent to do, and ours, even after it has become plain that by destroying the Amazon, we are destroying a global treasure, that greenhouse gases—of which the U.S. produces nearly 25 percent—are warming the world, that we are risking massive extinction on a scale unseen since the last Ice Age, that there are options and better ones. I stayed my faulty, fruitless course because I'd set it, and it seemed more frightening to diverge from the path I'd set—to reconsider—than to continue on.

I never again saw red-haired Ron. When I saw handsome, blue-eyed Bill with his Japanese girlfriend, he was cool, remote. Ayda finished her research and went home to her kids, leaving our room to me. I don't remember much else. What I have are these few notes, taken shortly after my return.

I remember a study of raindrops. Touching, really. Almost a child's meditation. The scientists were British, as I recall. The project was no doubt scientifically sound, this hydrological study, given the complexity of water distribution in the rain forest, but it seemed whimsical in the extreme (to study raindrops). I wanted something more heroic. I didn't realize that heroism is often composed of such small gestures (a woman sitting down on a bus or a man taking a seat at a lunch counter, or a study of rain).

Amazon Snapshot #11

Twenty years after my first visit to the Amazon, I will return to Manaus to see Dr. Fearnside at his office at the National Institute for Amazonian Research. He will be just as I remember him—a tall, gaunt man, with the clichéd physical awkwardness of the scientist; his neatly trimmed hair is going gray, as is his walrus-like mustache; his bright blue eyes visible through gold-rimmed glasses.

In his office on the campus of the National Institute for Amazonian Research, there is no sign of the forest he has dedicated his life to protecting, not even a poster of trees. The only suggestion of the subject of his thirty years of study is a single, desiccated leaf in a small glass jar on one of the high shelves that line his office walls to the ceiling. His office is heaped with papers, gray file cabinets; boxes of manuscripts are stacked on chairs; in the entryway we pass through to enter his office, several sets of hanging folders are filled with copies of his articles.

In a recent editorial, Fearnside had written of the *valor de existência*—a value that transcends monetary measures. I ask him repeatedly what he means by this. What *is* the value of its existence? I ask. Why should people care about the rain forest? Why does *he*?

I suppose I want him to say what I have not yet been able to: to explain why this forest matters so very much to me, even now, even after I've turned my back on it.

But he has no answer. Or rather, he refuses to answer. He speaks instead of the environmental services the rain forest provides (hydrological cycles, biodiversity, carbon sink); he talks about how he'd planned to be somewhere else, serendipity of a sort having kept him here in the Amazon for twenty-eight years. I'm annoyed, but I get it. Like Shakespeare's Cordelia, he won't heave his heart into his mouth. He says, finally, Once you start talking about the beauty of the forest, they dismiss you as a poet, a romantic. He would calculate an answer, a figure cold as cash, translatable as currency.

Amazon Snapshot #12

On a cool, tiled veranda overlooking a plantation surrounded by rain forest deep in the Brazilian Amazon, Senhor Gabriel—the agricultural engineer who is my host this afternoon on my return trip to Manaus—slams his palm on the table between us and shouts, What *use* is the rain forest?

He means, of course, what use is it undeveloped?

Our conversation has been drifting all day into the dangerous terrain of religion—my host insists God gave us the earth to use; he quotes Christ as saying, "If the fig tree does not bear fruit, cut it down." A secular Jew, I'm in no position to argue, especially not in my pidgin Portuguese, having lost the fluency I'd gained twenty years before. But Senhor Gabriel rants eloquently on. He believes that we are on earth to work, to better ourselves and the world; he believes "man can improve on the creation."

It's an argument he made repeatedly that morning as he drove me here from Manaus. Careening along Highway 110, through what once was dense jungle but is no more, dodging tire-sized potholes, passing bulldozed patches of red and white earth, land skinned and raw, ribbed with erosion, from which here and there plumes of gray-white smoke rose (from once-forested lands now cleared by fire) but few trees, I had asked Senhor Gabriel what he thought of the sight. He said he thought it beautiful.

Now, after our lunch of chicken, rice and peas, shredded cabbage, he wants to know what value *I* think the forest has, what use it is. And I feel acutely my lack of language, how inadequate my vocabulary is to say what needs to be said here.

What use is *love*? I say, finally.

Senhor Gabriel sits back, red faced, and stares at me, whether with admiration or contempt I cannot tell. Beyond the terrace, enormous clouds scud by. Beyond us, the rain forest—what remains—thrums with life.

Amazon Snapshot #13

When I return to the rain forest that second time, I will find it beautiful—heartbreakingly beautiful—as I failed to when I was twenty-one. The variety of trees, the tea and coffee smell of it, the marvelous animals and the birds. On my first day back in Manaus, I go for a walk in INPA's urban forest preserve, a little island of forest habitat in what has come to be the suburbs of an expanding city; strolling among the trees, I see a toucan with a blue beak, squirrel monkeys, red macaws, peixe boi, marvelous yellow-hooded blackbirds.

Later I will travel up river to a preserve where I will canoe through flooded forest, past trees ringed with three-inch spines long as sewing needles; past the massive trunks of kapok trees like poured concrete curtains; past dolphins pink as bubble gum and rare, red-faced *uacarí* monkeys in their white fur coats; through the marvelous symphonic night.

Even the city of Manaus will delight me. The strange enjambment of new and old, human and wild, charms me now. The great vital mess of it all—the crowds down by the docks; even the jarringly mechanical jingles blaring from advertising trucks, the trees in front of the police station cacophonous with birds.

I will love all of it; even the weird, surreal, obscenely misplaced Taj Mahal, that five-star hotel in the middle of the city where none was before, where I will lie beside a turquoise pool in the morning and watch the chlorinated water pucker and lap under fierce Amazonian winds as towers of gray-white cumulous clouds scud by close overhead (like having mountains pass you by while you stretch in a chaise lounge), nineteenth-century church bells tolling the hours.

And I will wonder, do I love this place now—this forest, this city—because I love now? In the years since I was last here, I have discovered joy, desire, sex, the nature of my own heart, a deep guiding pleasure that I could not have imagined then, and with it trust in myself, a strength I did not know I had. Was the ugliness I perceived in Manaus years ago my own? Its lack my own? Is the change in the forest or in me? And when we see only lumber when we look at trees, when we see only oil when we stand on a tundra or look out to sea, what poverty of vision is that? What exactly are we looking at?

Landlords

I spoke to Nelci only once by phone when I was in Manaus, just long enough for her to tell me that she was moving out and would be gone by the time I returned to Salvador.

True to her word, the September night I returned to Salvador, Nelci was gone. She left no message, no forwarding address; she did not call. Instead I received phone calls in the middle of the night from strangers asking for Marcy, men with accents I could not place. My doorman gave me long looks.

A week after my return, my landlord called to notify me that he wanted me out.

—You will have to move out by month's end, he said, a full two-and-a-half months before my lease was up. Nel had been paying the rent, or had paid me to pay it—so I knew that I was not behind on that. When I asked why he wanted to break the lease, my landlord said only that he needed the apartment.

—But I can't possibly move now, I said. I explained that I was recently back from the Amazon, that my parents were arriving soon to travel with me through Brazil, after which I was scheduled to visit half a dozen Rotary Clubs across the country to give talks and present them with tiny flags of friendship between nations. I have plans, I explained. Moving out is not among them.

—You must be out by month's end, he said, then he hung up.

Maybe it was because the stakes were small and the territory comprehensible, 400 square feet at most, not millions of hectares; maybe it was because I'd had my fill of loss, of getting along and going along; whatever it was, whyever it was, that time I made another choice. I decided to fight for this little bit of territory.

That afternoon, I went to my landlord's apartment, not understanding why he wanted to evict me, not understanding what the trouble was. He was not home, but his wife—my landlady—was. She told me at the door that he was out. I said I'd wait. She seemed reticent to let me in, but did.

We sat together in her dim lace-filled dining room, amidst her carefully polished table and sideboard and crystal, and she said again and again that she could not tell me why her husband wanted me out.

—It is for my husband to tell you, she said. It is his business, not mine.

After a while, she offered me a cafezinho and I accepted. And when she came back with the hot sweet demitasse, she stood by the couch where I sat and said, with feeling, I am sorry. I like you, but my husband said that he needed the apartment.

—I signed a lease, I said. Without cause, he has no right to evict me. I have nowhere else to go.

I told her that I had plans to leave town in a week, that my family was about to arrive from the United States for a visit; I was going to fly with them to Rio and travel in the south. I had a ticket. I could not move. I wouldn't.

When she began to cry, I was dumbfounded.

—I'm afraid he has a mistress, she said, wiping her eyes with a handkerchief from her pocket. She pulled out a chair from the lace-covered highly polished table and said that she was afraid that he wanted to install a mistress there. She rested her hand on the table like a discarded glove. She cried.

—I don't know what to do, she said.

I comforted her as best I could, patting her back and making sympathetic sounds. I waited for one full hour, reassuring her that her husband loved her, which I hoped he did, then I got up to go. At the door, before I left, she told me that she'd talk to him.

—It is not right for him to put you out, she said. You are a good girl, a good girl.

I thanked her then and left.

And because I was near the offices of *A Tarde*, because I was out this way and was agitated and had no friends and nowhere to go and no one I wanted to see and had something to prove, I went to see Pinheiro.

I told myself that it was only polite to let him know what I was doing. I would stop by his office to let him know that I was back from the Amazon and would be heading south soon to tour for a few weeks. Say good-bye. But in truth, I wanted to show him. I wanted to show him that I knew now how to speak, how to dress, how to make my way around, that I was *bem Bahiana* now.

When you are shown into Pinheiro's office, he smiles hugely at you; he looks surprised (you are gratified to see this); he says, in fact, what a surprise it is, his eyebrows raised a little, admiringly, as he stands and leans across the desk to extend his hand to offer you a seat, which you take.

When he sits again, he leans back in his chair, interested, it seems, in this new development, this twist. He comments admiringly on your clothes (indigo blue nylon shirt that drops in a loose cowl to show the tanned curve of your breasts, fashionably flared jeans that hug your belly like a corset—fastening with metal clasps—then flare at the hips like harem pants, huaraches), your speech, your tan.

—*Você e bem Bahiana*, he smiles. You are—it's true—very Bahian now.

On the street, you are taken for Brazilian, you tell him, though people take you for a Paulista, like being taken for a New Yorker in the States. Sometimes they do not believe you are American at all; they make you say things in English to prove it, then they laugh.

Pinheiro asks how you are. You ask how he is, then you tell him that you will be leaving soon to travel a bit with your family.

—I just wanted to stop by and extend my thanks for all you've done, you say, standing to go. It has been an education.

He stands and you shake on it, as if you've struck some deal.

In the street, on my way to the bus stop, I bought a pack of Chiclets from a newspaper vendor just for the pleasure of buying something I did not need, and I decided, *Fuck the bus*, I'll walk. I was not afraid to ride the bus anymore. I just needed air. No doubt, I wondered, as I often did then, how many calories this would burn: a walk from Rio Vermelho to Barra. Could I even get there from here, from the place I was to the place I wanted to be?

I crossed the street and walked along the sidewalk until I came to a narrow pathway that descended to the right through a favela carved into the side of the hill. The path was a narrow precipitous walkway—built of chunks of discarded cement, pieces of board, and stones someone had dragged here—no wider than my shoulders; the path wended between walls of cardboard and wood and tin, boards lashed together with wire and rope, past rusty corrugated tin roofs. It was the most direct route, the fastest; if I'd tried to avoid this, walk around, I'd likely have gotten lost, spent hours on circuitous paved routes.

I made my way down through this neighborhood that smelled of piss and sweat and shit and rotting things—there was no running water here—and partway down the path, it occurred to me that if someone were to come out from behind or in front of me now and pull a razor blade or a knife, I'd have nowhere to go, but no one did. I heard voices from somewhere in the clutter of makeshift houses, people maybe or a radio or TV, if someone had found a way to tap an electric line.

What I had been told to fear was not what was dangerous, I realized: the real danger lies in feeling safe and in trying to be, in all we'll sacrifice for the sake of safety and comfort; the danger is the lie we tell ourselves when we take for granted all we have, believing that things will turn out okay if we just go along and get along, that we are safe and can afford to ignore the consequences. We can't afford it.

When I got to the bottom of the narrow walkway, I was on a shady expensive street and though I didn't know where I was, I kept walking; I turned in the direction that I felt was right, going on instinct now, on hunches, and began to make my way from here home.

I didn't realize then what seems obvious now: that the doorman must have told my landlord that Nel was turning tricks in the apartment. The landlady's line about the mistress may have been a ruse. But why, then, was the landlady crying? She seemed sincere, her tears did. I wonder, was she crying because I was so dumb, so innocent of the score? Or perhaps my ignorance was painful because it reminded her of her own? Perhaps there really was a mistress. It's remarkable how little I understood then of what was transpiring around me. It's remarkable how little I know now, in fact, of what really happened then.

In the end I was not evicted. Whether this was due to my landlady's intervention or my own stubbornness I will never know, but my landlord relented.

A few days before I was to leave for Rio to travel with my family, Nelci finally called and explained that the strange callers I'd been hearing from were her clients. She'd had to get a job in my absence, she said, to pay the rent, and this was the most lucrative she could find. She had left a few things at the apartment, which she promised to come by and get, but she never came.

Pão de Açucar

When my family arrived, I showed them around Salvador for two days before we flew to Rio. We planned to tour the sites then fly south to the Falls of Iguaçu at the southern tip of the country. My family were excited to play tourists. But all of it made me sad. Pão de Açucar—Sugar Loaf—Rio's famous pinnacle, 396 meters tall, was just a hunk of rock after all, not sugar, not sweet, but hard.

My mother and I were shopping in Rio one morning while my father and brother remained in the hotel, when I suggested that we catch a bus instead of hailing a cab; I was used to public transportation by then and cabs were a rip-off, too expensive. The previous night a cabbie had charged my father half again the fare posted on the meter and I'd had to argue with him in my most colorful Portuguese.

As we started across the street to the bus stop, a motorcyclist ran a red just as my mother stepped off the curb, nearly clipping her. I stood in the street cursing a blue streak at the cyclist, fluent now in epithets.

—Thank you, my mother said, disconcerted. Thank you, honey. I didn't see him at all.

—The fucker, I said, taking her arm as we crossed.

Around the corner from our hotel, my mother and I stood in line on the sidewalk to enter at the back of a bus. The line was long: a man stood in front of me, my mother stood behind me, behind her were two other men, and then a woman. Two giant steps, with rubberized mats, led up into the bus, where a cashier would take our money and let us through a turnstile to take our seats.

The guy in front of me got on first; then I stepped up onto the bus. My mother followed; I turned to see her standing on the second stair; behind her, on the first step, were two men. One small, one big. They were standing very close to my mother and for a moment something looked wrong, like a painting hung at a slant. I looked at the two men, and the smaller man gave me a sort of smile and held up the pen in his hand, tipping it to his brow, as if in salute; a manila envelope was clasped under his right arm, the way my mother's purse was tucked under hers. He looked like a courier of some kind. But something did not look right.

I told my mother to hold onto her purse, to hold it in front of her.

—Don't worry, she said. I have a good grip on it.

—Hold it in front of you, Mom, I said.

—It's fine, Ellen, she says. Really, I've got a very tight hold on it.

Indeed the purse looked thoroughly wedged under her arm. Still, I stared at the two guys pressed too close to my Mom. The small one smiling, holding his pen.

When I stepped up to the turnstile to pay our fares, the guy in front of me spilled his change as he pushed through the turnstile and coins rolled everywhere; the cashier bent to help him, and my mother craned forward to see what had happened, as did I, and then suddenly, like catching a scent in the air, I understood that this was a setup, and though I didn't know how it worked, I knew what to do:

—Mom, I said, loudly. Watch your purse.

I grabbed my mother's purse from out of her hands and pressed her ahead of me in line, wedging my body between her and the two men behind us—the guy with the pen and the big guy behind him—and said under my breath, like a curse, *Não vai robar-la*, You will not rob her. My mother took her purse back as I told the cashier that I would pay for the two of us and handed him a 500-cruzeiro note and we pushed through the turnstile and took our seats, my mother clasping her purse now tightly to her chest.

—Make sure your wallet is there, I said, as we sat.

—It's fine, Ellen, she said, annoyed at my having seized her purse. Really. You needn't have worried. I had a good grip on it. It's sweet of you to be concerned but—

—*Please*, I said. Is your wallet there?

—It's *here*, Ellen, she said, but she checked anyway, while the guy with the pen and the big guy took seats up the aisle from us. I stared at them hard.

It was while she was unzipping her purse that my mother first noticed that the zipper's teeth had been worked open from the back, unlaced perhaps an inch and a half. Open. The wallet was still inside, but the zipper had been torn apart.

—Oh my God, she said. You were right, Ellen. Look.

I looked over at the hole in her purse and then I stared at the men across the aisle. The small one stared back at me, unsmiling now, then looked away.

—Thief, I said, quietly, in Portuguese, taking a chance by calling this what it was. But it felt good to call this by its rightful name.

That night in my hotel room, which cost per night twice what I paid each month in rent, I stood in front of a mirror with the lights out so that I was illuminated only by the dim glow of the city below my window. I studied myself, my unfamiliar image, dressed in ridiculous colors—chartreuse sweater, sky blue jeans—a parrot's bright plumage, trying to be something I was not, when I heard a knock on the door and went to join my family.

At dinner, my mother told again the story of how I had saved her twice that day (from the motorcyclist and thieves): to hear her tell it, I was a hero.

—Thank heavens you caught it, my mother said. I had all our money in that wallet. Traveler's checks, all our cash. We would have lost everything.

Only later, at dinner, would I piece together the scheme: how, after working open the teeth of the purse with the nose of the pen, the small man would remove the wallet while the tourist was distracted by the spilled change. Once he had the wallet, he'd drop it into the manila envelope under his arm, which the big guy behind him would take, stepping backwards off the bus into the crowd, while the small man with the pen paid his fare, took a seat, rode innocently on.

If the theft were discovered once the tourist took her seat, it would be too late. There would be no one to blame, no wallet on board, no one to accuse. It would disappear. Without the culprit in sight.

Amazon Snapshot #14

There was a time when I wondered if my interest in the Amazon were sublimation of a sort, transference or translation to the forest of feelings I'd had for Paulinho.

I think now perhaps it was—though not in the way I once imagined. It seems to me now that in loving that boy, I was trying to love the world, reaching for something larger than all of us, than any of it, him or me, reaching toward some sort of transcendence, which only years later I will understand.

Nearly a decade after I leave the Amazon, I will drive with a lover through the mountains of northern New Mexico. Moved by the beauty of the sky, the sage, the mountains capped with snow, I will reach out and press her hand and say, *I love you*, and in that moment know that I am lying; that what I really mean is, *I love all of this*. And that to try to compress that larger love into a single figure is a distortion of sorts, a misapplication of what is best in our selves—our ability to love the world.

The Greeks had many words for love—agape, eros, philos—but none to describe the ardor we feel for and in wilderness, even in tame nature, the exultation that attends something as simple as walking down a country lane, or listening (as I am now, here in the hills of Austerlitz, New York), to wind rustling in treetops, the calls of birds, watching the feathery heads of timothy grass bending to the breeze. These things marvelous and not of our making.

Rapture originally referred to seizure by force, especially sexual seizure, a meaning now grown obsolete (and one I find hard to reconcile with my own experience). Later it became synonymous with transport, with the carrying of a person to another place or sphere of existence, and it is perhaps through this latter definition that its theological significance took hold. To be raptured—an adjective dating from the last quarter of the seventeenth century—is a theological term that refers to religious ecstasy as a result of one's faith.

I was rapturous in my study of the Amazon at college, as I had been in amateur horticulture as a child. Mine was the monk's and the missionary's impulse merged: a passion to learn, married to an ambition to save. It didn't occur to me then that missionaries were often part of the martial retinue, they arrived with or followed on the heels of the conquistadors who brought with them priests and seed gatherers.

Perhaps the Germans have a word for the fervent passion for wild places, the longing that wide open spaces can inspire, the thrill we feel in wilderness, on remote lakes where the only sound you hear are bird calls and wind in leaves and a paddle pushing through water, or in red rock canyons whose walls recall hundreds of millions of years of change, the poignancy of waves breaking, the magnificent indifference of a blue whale or a flock of wild parakeets or an African elephant, the urgent profound passion to save all these from destruction, a passion that is close kin I imagine to the Enlightenment's love of justice, ideas, liberty, and learning.

Perhaps we've not needed words for this sort of ardor—our love of the natural world—until recently, until we became estranged from it.

We treat such ardor as anomalous, a little ridiculous, certainly odd ("tree huggers," we say; "nature boy"). "Nature is in bad taste," essayist Emily Fox Gordon said, at age nine, to amuse her urbane mom. My friend Suzi liked to say that her idea of nature was a potted plant. We seem to say with our dismissive declarations, *We are no mere mammals.* But the fact is we are.

E. O. Wilson has coined the term biophilia to speak of our feeling for the natural world, but it seems to me far too clinical a term. I crave a phrase more capacious, meet, to describe the heartbreak I feel sometimes on hearing something as ordinary as a cardinal's call, or seeing a coyote dart across a field, or the golden newt I saw today making his way (seemingly swimming) across a gravel road, compelled by atavistic dictates, or when I walk a country lane among eighty-foot trees or past an unmown field lush with clover, daisies, Indian paintbrush, lupine, black-eyed Susans, and a dozen kinds of grass, or feel in the dirt beneath my feet the pounding hoofbeats of hundreds of zebras as they race across the plains of Ngorogoro crater or witness at dawn 20,000 snow geese rise into the air over the Bosque del Apache like a single living thing, a river of white wings.

The *wonder* this world is. I want a word for that.

Saudades

If this were a novel, there'd be an epiphany round about now, a moment when I recognized the error of my ways, realized that calculation alone cannot save us, a moment when I woke up and made a change, a choice. But change in life is often slower than that; like destruction, it often happens gradually.

It's true that I often thought of Barbara's claim that she never did anything she didn't want to do and that I puzzled over this like a koan, aspiring to live by that same code, to act from desire not fear. But I recall no epiphany in Salvador (though such a moment would come later, sudden as luck, life-changing). There was no neat progression or straight line or course like those I'd run with Paulinho years before.

But there was this: in time, loss piled on loss until absence became at last a kind of presence in my life, inescapable, and I had to turn and stand my ground. The emptiness I'd fled all my life became a sort of presence; it grew in me like *saudades*.

Every language has its untranslatable words; in Portuguese, it's *saudades*. Saudades is the pride of Brazilians. "Homesick" is a crude and inapt translation; the word—like the feeling—is more capacious than that. Saudades is closer kin to longing, but it is a kind of supreme longing, longing raised to the level of a calling—to an epic, an heroic, an operatic scale. (Orpheus, one might assume, was motivated by saudades when he went to Hades for Eurydice.) *Tenho saudades de você*, distant friends write to one another and to family. *Tenho saudades*. Saudades is an almost existential longing, and it is a measure of one's capacity to love, to maintain ardor in the face of absence.

Significantly the word is not a verb but a noun. My *Pequeno Dictionario Michaelis* beside me tells me that saudades is a feminine noun, meaning "longing, yearning, ardent desire; homesickness, nostalgia." Saudades is more than mere feeling; it is the capacity to feel, an ability to keep alive and present in our lives what is at risk of slipping from our grip, to keep the beloved with us by means of fierce feeling.

In December, I flew to Porto Alegre to visit the Simões, the host family with whom I had lived when I was eighteen, and to see Paulinho, whom I'd been in love with then. I had imagined our reunion for years, longed for it, even bought a dress in Salvador for the occasion, hoping—I see now—that by reviving our old love affair I might revive myself, restore my faith in a creed I'd once shared with Paulinho but could no longer credit (faith in order and progress, in conventional notions of failure and success). I was delighted when my former host sister, Luciene, told me that Paulinho would meet me at the airport.

By the time I saw Paulinho again, a lot had happened: I had been to the Amazon; I had been raped; my good friend had become a prostitute. I was fluent in Portuguese now. I could scare muggers off with my mouth.

The airport terminal in Porto Alegre was large and the room where I collected my bags was crowded and confusing on that late December afternoon, and I worried, as I looked out toward the lobby where crowds awaited the new arrivals, that I would not recognize Paulinho. But he was a standout even in that crowd. He looked as he always had. Handsome, compact, tanned, still dressed in white, as if four years hadn't passed. I had to push through strangers to reach him. As I got closer, I could see that he had aged; he was only twenty-four, still young, but he looked older and weary. He looked the same but was somehow no longer beautiful.

Language should have made it easier between us but it did not. We were more awkward for it. We embraced formally and awkwardly.

—Thanks for meeting me, I said. It's kind of you.

—It's nothing, Paulinho said. Then he laughed, and added, *Você canta bem bahiana.* You sing like a real Bahian. It was not a compliment; my regional accent marked me as a hick, and suddenly I was self-conscious. I had not realized that I had an accent, a northern drawl akin to a southern drawl in the States.

I smiled and shrugged. *Sou bem Bahiana mesmo,* I said. I am very Bahian.

He took my bag; I took his arm. I wanted this to go well. I wanted to retrieve the love I'd lost, the girl I'd been. The hope I'd had, the desire I no longer felt for anything. Like Orpheus in the underworld, I sensed that a great deal depended on love's revival.

In the car, we lapsed into English. Partly because my vocabulary in Portuguese was limited. The subjunctive especially—that lovely, neglected tense, which allows one to express hope and desire, to speak of the possible that may or may not come to pass—tripped me up, slowed me down. But we used English, too, because what I said in Portuguese, I sensed, alarmed Paulinho, my speech peppered with epithet and street slang, hard sorrow. It was best if we did not understand each other too well.

—So I hear you're engaged, I said, repeating what Luciene—my former host sister—had told me by phone a week or two before.

—Not really, he said. No.

—Not really? I said, laughing.

—No, he said.

—Oh, I said.

He told me that he was finishing his law degree and that he had taken an apartment of his own in town. When I asked how his parents were, he told me that they separated a few years back.

—I'm sorry, I said. And I was. I remembered dining with his parents years before: his beautiful mother, who had lent me her mink to wear home, his handsome father, built like a boulder, presiding at dinner like a kindly judge. I did not ask what happened.

Instead I asked if he saw the Simões much and he said he didn't; after his family sold the apartment, he'd stopped attending the old church. He hadn't seen Luciene in a year or more; he hadn't spoken to her in months until she called to tell him that I was arriving.

I was pleased when—instead of taking me to the Simões where I was to spend the week—Paulinho asked if I'd like to get a drink.

—Sure, I said. Years ago we'd frequented nice restaurants. Quiet well-lit places that smelled of roasting meat, where we held hands and talked across a linen tablecloth.

Now he drove us to a disco. The sort of place we'd never have gone before. Never in a million years. Disco was long dead. The place seemed sad or maybe it was just us. I don't recall there being any other customers. It was still a bright summer afternoon outside, but inside it was dim as dusk. We were too old for this, I thought, as we took a table near the illuminated floor above which spun a mirrored ball. I felt infinitely old; worse, I felt middle-aged.

The lights, the music, were too loud. We couldn't talk and soon we gave up trying. When a slow dance came on, Paulinho stood and offered me his hand. We moved a little stiffly into one another's arms. We were not so much dancing as leaning on one each other, as if holding each other up. We seemed to me already thwarted at twenty-two, at twenty-four. We were still young, but we were already disappointed. I was filled with sadness because I felt nothing in his arms.

When he drove up to the Simões, we sat in the car a moment before going in. Paulinho told me that he was leaving town the day after next, going to Florianopolis—a coastal vacation area—with some friends to celebrate the new year and to see his grandparents, who lived there and were ailing. His grandfather might not last long.

Before he got out of the car, I said, Will I see you before you go?

—I'd like that, he said, with evident feeling. My sister would like to see you. We'll go out tomorrow night. Okay? I'll call you.

—Okay.

And then together, like old times, we went in to see the others.

Years before, when I'd first discovered the pleasures of the body with Paulinho, on my last night in Brazil at the end of my summer stay in Porto

Alegre, he and I had been alone in his family's apartment; we'd been out to dinner and had been talking about seeing a movie but had ended up instead on the floor of the living room, sweaty and breathing fast with our clothes in disarray.

—Do you want to go there? Paulinho had asked, his breath moist in my ear. Do you want to go there? Over and over he'd asked me this, speaking into my hair, his teeth on the tendons of my neck, his hands moving over my breasts, between my legs, as we lay in a tangle of clothes on his family's living room floor. He'd meant, did I want to go to his room and make love, on this my last night in his country (to enter the territory of desire with him, *to go there*, as if desire were a place, another landscape).

It was clear he'd know how to make love (he may even have told me he'd been reading up; it would have been his *style* to read up), and I wanted terribly to go with him, but I declined, thinking I might get it wrong, thinking about what nice girls did and didn't do—morality the thing one clings to in the absence of grace.

His older sister had come home soon after and we'd scrambled up from the floor pulling up and down various bits of clothing and then we sat on the couch awhile, talking to her as she smirked at us. Paulinho had walked me out and offered to walk me home, but I declined, knowing I wouldn't manage to say no again. Instead I ran away from him, and from desire, all the way home through empty streets, breathless.

I supposed that neighborhood gossip had conveyed the story to Xande, my former host brother, who seemed to know now what had happened then, on that night—or rather, what had *not* happened.

It was from Xande that I learned that Paulinho had remained chaste since I'd declined to sleep with him three years before, our responses to that one evening sending each of us—in our different ways—away from desire. Paulinho had become celibate; I had become profligate, squandering desire where I felt none.

I told Xande, as we sat chatting in the Simões' living room, that I'd be happy to help Paulinho now.

—It's not too late, I said, trying to sound smart and worldly, like one of the boys.

Xande reminded me that Paulinho was engaged to be married.

I told him that Paulinho had said he was not.

Xande raised his eyebrows at this and repeated it to Luciene as she passed through the room.

Luciene shrugged and rolled her eyes, flashing the international sign of the older sister, a beleaguered frown.

I made a show of my desire, but what I felt was not desire but its surrogate, its poor cousin—greed. I wanted to acquire Paulinho, to wrest from him some token of affection—a scrap of our old faith in order and progress and love—to replace all I'd lost.

That afternoon at the Simões', I imagined that if only Paulinho and I could retrace our steps to that one point of divergence, we might recover passion, for each other, ourselves.

I tried to be offhand when Paulinho called late the next afternoon to break our date. He said he'd try to stop by later, if he could.

—He's afraid of you, Xande said, when I got off the phone.

—Maybe, I said.

I tried to take comfort in Xande's hypothesis. But I did not feel for Paulinho what I once had. Desire was gone between us and perhaps he knew this too. His life was here in southern Brazil, running in a park, practicing law, having children with Sylvana; my life lay elsewhere, among people I'd not yet met. But I felt a shaky emptiness inside, panicked.

I couldn't imagine then what kind of life I might lead if I left this one behind; I couldn't conceive of a passion more intense than what I'd known with him, that powerful present-tense, a relief from relentless teleology. With Paulinho the world had seemed intelligible, reduced to a few clear rules—like the Air Force calisthenics he'd given me back then.

I was surprised when Paulinho came by around 10:30 that night. We sat out talking by his car. The metal would have been hot from the heat of the day and we would have leaned against it and looked up into night and stars, into the cool blue of a summer evening. He was supposed to leave the next morning for Florianopolis. We would not see each other again.

—I'm sorry to be going, he said. I don't want to go, but I feel I should, for my grandparents' sake.

—Of course, I said. I just wish we had more time.

—Me too, he said.

—I've never been to Florianopolis, I said. Can I come? I was joking and not joking.

—Would you want to come? he asked.

—Yes, I said. I would.

—What about your flight?

—I can change it, I said. Do you want me to come?

He looked me in the eye and said, Yes. I'd like that.

—Then I'll come, I said.

But the more we talked, the more complicated it became. He must consult with his friends, the others were not bringing girls, it would only be guys and me; maybe it was not such a good idea. I wanted to argue, but there was nothing to say.

—No, he said. It won't work.

I was heartbroken. I could not figure out why this hurt so much. Why I felt as if this romance had never ended, though it had ended years ago.

Probably I cried. I was crying a lot by then. Not really knowing why or what for.

Perhaps out of pity, he proposed to take me out on my last night in Porto Alegre, even though it meant he would miss going to Florianopolis, since his friends would be leaving for that trip before I was scheduled to leave there. Probably, I should have declined the offer, but I didn't. I wanted a chance with him. One last night.

I spent the next day, my last in Porto Alegre, playing chess with Xande at the dining room table. I dressed in a soft sherbet green dress I'd bought in Salvador a few weeks before especially for this occasion. Xande told me that I looked beautiful and that Paulinho wouldn't be able to resist me; we laughed and I felt hopeful.

Luciene and I had hardly seen each other since I'd arrived. I declined to go out with her and her friends on my last night for fear of missing Paulinho's call, for fear of looking dumb with people I did not know. I preferred to look dumb among intimates.

I waited all day for Paulinho to come by, only to have him call at 6 to say that he wouldn't be coming. I was scheduled to leave the next morning and it was our last chance. He apologized, said he had plans he couldn't break, said he'd call later when he got back, if it wasn't too late.

I waited all night, but he never showed. I called his apartment and let the phone ring until the operator disconnected the line. I wrote letters to him that I rewrote.

A little before 2 in the morning, I reached Paulinho. He had just arrived home.

—I didn't come by because it's so late, he said. His words were a little fuzzy, soft; he was drunk.

—You could've called, I said softly.

—I didn't call because, because . . . he seems to lose his train of thought. You're right, Ellen. I was wrong.

—I don't want to be right, I said. I want to see you.

—You can come over now, he said, almost whispering. You can come now. To talk. No one's here.

I hesitated. It was not exactly how I'd imagined it would be, but then, almost nothing was.

—Will you come get me? I said. I'll wait outside.

—I drank too much at the churrasco, he said. I can't go driving around the city in this condition. You can call a cab.

—I'm not going to call a cab, I said.

—Fine, he said.

—Fine, I said. When I hung up, I was numb except for the swell of grief in my throat, which made it hard to swallow.

Mãe came in the bedroom in her quilted robe and scolded me for making a fuss and a fool of myself in the middle of the night and waking the others up.

—It is too late to be on the phone, she said, arms crossed in evident annoyance.

And she was right. It was too late.

I apologized and took off my dress and went to bed.

I lay on the bed listening to the sound of traffic passing in the street. Hoping he'd come for me. The neighbor's air conditioner hummed. The sherbet green dress that I'd bought with Paulinho in mind, knowing it cost too much, hung by its collar on the closet door. A street lamp outside the window threw figures on the wall, grotesque and yellow. There was a screech of breaks and honking. Could it be that he ran a light at the corner? Years ago there was no stoplight there. He used to tear through that intersection without hesitating.

At 9 a.m., the following morning, when I was scheduled to be on my way back to Salvador, in midair, Paulinho called, regretting his refusal to see me the night before, knowing that I'd already gone to the airport.

He was shocked to find I was still there.

I told him that I'd changed my flight; I told him that I'd overstayed my welcome at the Simões'; I asked if I might stay the night at his apartment. My flight was the day after tomorrow. What could he do but agree?

I remember a car ride through the city at night. I remember picking his sister up at work. That she and I sat in the back seat, while Paulinho drove. In truth, it is she who interested me now. Quick and dry and beautiful as Paulinho once was, with a spark, a sensuality he used to have, and a smartness that I liked; together we argued with Paulinho as he drove, about politics and international banks. She looked like him but was shorter, slighter of build, in a trim black suit; her long glossy hair fell straight to the middle of her back; her skin was brown and smooth. She seemed to like me and I liked her. Paulinho seemed vaguely to disapprove of us both.

After we dropped his sister at home, Paulinho took me to his apartment and showed me around. It was spacious and modern and seemed grown-up, with a study, a nice kitchen, a dining room with glass doors that opened onto a balcony, a bedroom. He told me I could sleep in his bedroom. He'd sleep in the study across the hall.

I told him we could share the bed.

He shook his head, no.

—Why not? I asked.

—What happens if you get pregnant? he said.

—I'll have an abortion, I said, shocking him into silence.

We were standing on the balcony, overlooking a street. He leaned his arms on the railing and looked out. For a while, we were quiet together.

He told me he'd thought of me a lot during these last years, he'd admired that I had refused to sleep with him years ago.

—I was stupid, I said. I was wrong.

—No, he said. You were right. I respected you.

I noted his use of the past tense. I knew he meant he did not respect me now.

—I don't want respect, I said. I put my hand on his arm. Make love to me, I said quietly.

—I can't.

—It's no big deal, I said. Sex.

—It wouldn't be just sex, he said.

—Because of Sylvana? I said, dropping my hand from his arm, as I mentioned the girlfriend he never did.

—Not only that.

—Not only that? I said. I imagined that he meant that I was undesirable now, that my desire precluded his. That I was no longer beautiful, as he'd once thought I was. If we slept together, I thought, it would mean I was beautiful, desirable, all right.

I argued with him for a while. I made an idiot of myself trying to convince this man I'd once declined to sleep with to sleep with me.

I was exhausted and went to bed early. When I was in bed, Paulinho came into my room and tucked me in. He kissed me on the forehead. Then he went across the hall to his study with a highlighter.

If Jane Austen were writing Paulinho she might write of his good but conventional turn of mind. His faith in *ordem e progresso*. His lack of imagination. That he was a young man made old by an unexamined sense of right and wrong. Propriety took the place of ethical considerations. He languished in the shade of convention that protected him from the bracing light of experience. But he was kind and good and wished to do right and one could hardly fault him for such virtues. But I did: they made him dull. Nevertheless I spent my days in Porto Alegre wooing him.

In the morning, we did not speak much; we did not discuss the previous evening. We passed the morning reading together in his apartment. He read the newspaper with a yellow highlighter, highlighting the main points, and I pretended to read the book I was pretending to read in those days, a book on the mid-Atlantic slave trade. When he turned on the TV and started to watch cartoons, I went for a walk. When I got home, he was readying himself to play tennis at the club, a military club where I'd watched him train years ago.

—Can I come and watch? I asked.

—You can't, he said. Sylvana never goes, so you can't either.

His tone took me aback. His coldness. I did not like the idea of being left alone in this apartment in a part of town I did not know on my last day here; I wanted to be with him, even if I couldn't watch him train.

—I could go for a walk near the club, I said, or sit in the sun and wait for you. I'd rather do that than stay here alone.

I pressed and in the end he took me along, and there I found Sylvana, waiting for him. It seemed they met there every Sunday at this time.

Paulinho introduced her as his *namorada*—his girlfriend—the word he used to apply to me. (He did not say "my fiancé," and I tried to take some comfort from this.) Sylvana had long straight mouse-brown hair that she pulled up into a ponytail. She had an American build: five feet seven, slender but busty, sturdy, what they called *forte* in Bahia. She was pretty in a perfectly conventional way.

Paulinho suggested that Sylvana train on another court, that I sit by the pool and read, but we defied his plans for us and decided to sit together and talk.

For a while, we sat by the court and watched Paulinho hit a ball back and forth with another guy and Sylvana told me about how she'd met Paulinho. She had been dating the same guy for four years, she said, from the time she was sixteen until she turned twenty, her first boyfriend.

—I never did anything, she said. I just sat at home. I didn't even like him so much. I just got used to it. Then Paulinho started courting me. He asked me to try gymnastics. I was resistant at first, but he enrolled me in a class. He paid for my lessons.

She told me that he had paid for driving lessons, too, and for lessons with a tennis pro. He had bought her a tennis outfit, shoes, a racket, even little matching socks. She told me about the wonders of gymnastics, how they'd go to class together in the afternoon, have dinner, and then go to the university to study at night.

—Never a moment free to think, I said, more to myself than to her.

Sylvana looked hurt and I realized how rude I'd been. I admired that she showed her hurt. Vulnerability is its own kind of courage.

—No, I said. It's admirable. But sometimes, when I'm working like that, I feel I'm filling up my life with activities, not living, y'know?

—I love gymnastics, she said. Before I just sat at home, I never did anything.

—Of course, I said. I nodded and watched the men play tennis. When Paulinho looked over, I wondered if he was looking at me or her.

She told me Paulinho gave her vocabulary words. He was helping her to be *better*.

I asked her if she wanted these things, the lessons and words, if she *liked* these things.

She said not really, not always.

—He wants me to run with him, she confided. But I don't like it. It's so *boring*.

I laughed.

—You want to go to the pool? she asked.

—Sure, I said, almost liking her.

As we walked across the grass, I told her about my studies, the grant that had brought me here, INPA, the Amazon. We were almost exactly the same age, but I felt infinitely older. Used up.

At the pool, we spread out on lawn chairs and faced the sun. She in her tennis minidress; me in my khaki shorts. Both of us tall, tan, slender girls, pretty and young, with long brown hair, sun bleached.

—I used to have fat thighs, she said, touching her long bare legs. My poor mother-in-law must've been horrified when Paulinho first presented me. Oh, what a fat thing.

In truth, she was beautiful and I might have told her so, that she was beautiful with her long firm thighs, but that was not the kind of thing that girls told girls or so I thought then. Instead I lied.

—I used to feel that way, I said, but now I think appearance is less important. I am who I am, whether I weigh 57 or 67 kilos.

—I suppose, she said.

Neither one of us believed me.

It was around that point in our conversation that Sylvana began referring to Paulinho's mother as *minha sogra*, my mother-in-law. *Minha sogra sempre diz*, My mother-in-law always says . . . *Minha sogra sugeriu este perfume*, My mother-in-law suggested this perfume.

She told me that Paulinho lunched at her parents' house every Sunday, with the family—a fact he had failed to mention. He told me that he practiced tennis and volleyball on Sundays. She said they were almost always together; he said he hardly saw her. She said they were engaged; he said they weren't. I tried to figure out whose story was true. I knew that he had lied to me before: he'd told me that I couldn't come to this club because Sylvana never came, that I couldn't get in as a nonmember. But here I was and here she was.

—We're already buying things for our house, she said.

—Really? I said.

—Didn't Paulo tell you that we're getting married? she asked.

—No. I'd heard that from friends, but he'd denied it. He said he isn't engaged.

—Well, no, she said, pulling at the hem of her tennis skirt. It's not official yet, but we're buying things for our house.

—Funny. He said he was buying things for his apartment.

She got up and stretched, drawing a palm over her flat stomach.

—Is this yours? she picked up the thick beige book.

—Yeah, I said. I intend to write a thesis next year on why West African cultural practices were diluted in the United States in the wake of the slave trade while they flourished here in Brazil.

—Do you like that stuff? she asked.

—Love it, I said.

—No you don't, she said. Look, you've hardly read any of it.

She was right, of course. It was, as she evidently suspected, a prop. The textual equivalent of a cigarette, which I hoped would make me appear sophisticated. It was something to hold onto, to clutch, to read, in case I was left alone, had no one to talk to, was dumped.

I looked out across the pool to the brown hills of Porto Alegre.

—I'll never marry, I said, quoting a line Barbara had said to me just before she'd left Bahia, trying to sound as she had—sophisticated, above such conventional arrangements—but I heard how it sounded from my mouth: merely sad.

—Why *not?* Sylvana asked, like I was crazy.

I shrugged.

—Paulinho and I talked about getting married once, I said. We thought that I'd return here, or he'd come to the States. He tried to come there but couldn't. We're too different now. You'll be great for him. I did not realize how patronizing this sounded, or maybe I did.

—I'm sorry I'm not very intellectual, she said, putting down the book, as if she were the one who had something to apologize for here.

As we walked back toward the tennis courts to meet up with Paulinho, I tried to sound smart and tough. She said that I was cynical and I wished I were, but in truth I was only young and in pain and ashamed of being in pain. I believed that I must take things in stride, that I must remain cheerful. I believed it was weak to care too much or show it, except perhaps in regard to a forest, a political cause, human rights and wrongs. I shocked her, I think, which was not hard. She was young and sheltered and not especially smart. But she was honest, sincere, as I was not.

When we joined Paulinho and his friends for a drink on the patio, Sylvana sat quietly at Paulinho's side, patiently waiting as he drank a beer and talked with his friends. They asked me questions and I answered, joking with them. Sylvana raised a hand to her mouth and chewed her cuticles nervously. Without taking his eyes from the circle of his friends, Paulinho batted her hand from her mouth.

I wanted to slug him.

Paulinho's friend Koy was pretty as a girl and a flirt. At the tennis club, he invited himself along with us to dinner. So that night, we four went out— Sylvana, Paulinho, Koy, and I. During dinner, Koy whispered to me and told me jokes and fed me spoonfuls of chocolate mousse. He was charming; I was charmed.

Paulinho watched us from across the table; occasionally, he tossed little comments in between us. Koy and I dismissed him: *Bobagens, meu filho, bobagens*, Koy and I said in unison, Foolishness, my child, foolishness, quoting a lyric by Caetano Veloso about seizing the moment and desire; then we laughed.

We made jokes and puns that Paulinho had to explain to Sylvana. I watched his face as he spoke to her to see if he looked at her the way he looked at me. Sylvana looked on as both men vied for my attention, the handsome blue-eyed friend who was my date, and Paulinho who was hers. In the course of dinner, Paulinho grew sullen.

He protested when Koy offered to take me home; Paulinho insisted on taking me with him and that Koy drive Sylvana.

Koy shrugged and said, It was a pleasure to meet you.

—It was a pleasure, I said.

Koy kissed me on the cheek three times before departing. As he bent to embrace me the last time, he said, into my ear, Paulinho is still in love with you. I wanted him to see for himself.

On the way home, Paulinho was quiet.

—Koy thinks that I'm jealous, he said.

—Are you? I asked.

He didn't answer.

At home in his apartment, both a little drunk, I leaned in the doorway between the kitchen and the living room, while Paulinho took off his shirt. He stood facing me. His bare chest so near that I could feel its warmth.

—Would I ruin your night if I kissed you? I asked. I was trying to sound like Lauren Bacall, like a heroine from a noir flick, like somebody, anybody, else. But from my mouth, the line sounded less like a seduction than an apology.

Paulinho looked into my eyes a moment, then dropped his glance and brushed past me into the living room.

I leaned my head against the wood doorframe. I could hear him in his room. I listened for a while before I rolled off the doorframe and went to bed alone.

What I thought his kiss could cure, I did not know then. But I think now I wanted nothing less than for him to turn back time, like a fairy tale told in reverse: seeking a kiss that would not wake but send me back to sleep, so that all that had happened in that one year might be undone.

I thought Paulinho's desire might orient me, in the absence of my own. I was terrified then that I belonged nowhere, to no one.

I stretched out on the cool sheets of the bed. Through the doorway, a band of light from his study fell across the bedroom carpet, making a sharp angled form on the rug.

—Do you want me to shut off your light? I said.

—Is it disturbing you? He sounded tired.

—No, I said. I just thought maybe you were sleepy. I'd do it for you, if you wanted.

He made no response.

And so I fell asleep like that, waiting for an answer that never came.

On the way to the airport the next morning, Paulinho told me that it wasn't for lack of desire that he didn't make love to me last night.

—I didn't want to create a seed of hope, he said.

—For you there isn't hope anymore, I said, letting my eyes drift over the city beyond the windshield.

He turned to me, watching my profile as he spoke.

—There's still hope, he said. But like this it's not greater than myself. It would've been, had we made love last night.

I smiled as if this were merely an interesting line. We were saying lines out of movies, unable to come up with any of our own, afraid, perhaps, of saying what we meant.

The last time I saw Paulinho, he was a speck of blue seen through a scratchy airplane windowpane, a bit of blue among the concrete and airport crowds, like a piece of fallen sky.

Last Days

The last time I saw Nelci she was in the dim interior of the brothel, a few streets over from the apartment we had shared. She had phoned me to say she'd like to meet. So about a month after my return from Manaus, I visited her there. It was an elegant apartment in a fashionable neighborhood, made grim only by the heavy curtains that were drawn at midday, and by the lugubrious madam who answered the door with an air of absentminded dolor.

The madam had a huge, pallid, moon-like face. She was enormously fat and short and dressed in something flowing and dark. She seemed an unlikely doyenne of the demimonde. Nelci emerged from the gloom of the interior and stepped out with me into the hall. I was surprised how unchanged she was—how ordinary she looked, like any young student. Her dress and hair unaltered from months before, only her expression was sadder, stiller, than it had been then. I think she wore a modest denim skirt, a T-shirt. She did not talk about politics or what she'd read in *Veja* or what she might yet do. She moved slowly, calmly, as if drugged or old.

We walked through the streets together, past familiar houses. There was not much to say. She apologized for having turned my apartment into a brothel. And I apologized too.

She asked me to tell her about the Amazon, and then asked me whether I was doing all right. I asked the same of her. She said her work was not so bad. It paid well and most of the clients were foreigners—"like you, Elena"—lonely visitors who wanted someone to talk to. She had a chance to discuss books, to practice her English.

We hugged at the door to the brothel, and I watched her in, before walking home alone. I told myself, as I walked, that this was simply a choice she'd made. But that's not how it felt. It would be years before it occurred to me that hers had been a straightforward calculation of cost and benefit. Everybody, after all, sold something to preserve their independence—nations sold irreplaceable forests, scholars sold years of research.

I wonder now what I could have done to protect Nelci against the necessity of sale. When I took Nel in, I flattered myself that I was doing something to protect her.

I cannot help but wonder now why we did so little. Why we stood by— the INPA researchers and I—making a career of loss. Why we settled for documentation, taking notes and making calculations. We could have done something, but we didn't. Rationales came easily: prostitution was Nelci's choice; deforestation was an option for the Brazilian government; no one wanted to cultivate dependency. What else could we have done?

If I had given Nelci half my fellowship, she'd have run through it in time. But I might have tried. As we might have tried to save the forest, as we might still try. I might have brought her back with me to the States to finish her schooling or find a job, when it became clear the university would not re-open soon. Instead of studying the ecological consequences of a dam, we might have fought its construction. Put our bodies in front of bulldozers, our lives on the line. The researchers at INPA could have made it difficult to fell the forest if they'd been willing to sacrifice careers and objectivity.

My last weeks in Salvador, I spent money as fast as I could. I would rather use it recklessly rather than return it to Rotary; rather than conserve this bounty, I wanted to be the one to squander it.

In the Porto da Barra, I stopped into a gem shop and bought a ring. I wear it now on my left hand, fourth finger, where a wedding band would be. It is a leaf-green emerald set into a thin gold band. I wanted to bring back something valuable, something precious, to retrieve a tiny scrap of beauty from that year.

On my return to the States, my mother had the ring appraised for insurance purposes and kept it, after that, in a small plastic baggie in her jewelry box. I didn't ask for it back and she didn't return it. I forgot it, as I did so much of that year whose events I'd committed to scraps of paper, put in drawers, walked away from.

Then a few years ago, while visiting my parents in the home where I grew up, I asked my mother if she had the ring and she brought it out and gave it to me in a little plastic Ziploc bag smaller than my palm, in which was a scrap of paper with the appraiser's handwriting on it. The appraiser put the value of the ring at $350—a surprisingly modest price for such a lovely stone. The ring's value, it turns out, was diminished because the stone is full of flaws—cracks that reach the surface and run through—damage unnoticed by me at the time.

As a child—playing imaginary games of adventure in the basement with my best friend, in which dressers became elephants and we rode triumphant through dusty towns and jungles—I loved a piece of costume jewelry made of gold-plated tin and set with fake seed pearls around a large rectangle of deep-green glass. The pendant had once been part of a necklace, but by the time it reached our hands, it was just a fragment, a piece of a broken chain, which nonetheless I loved. I thought it the most beautiful thing I'd seen, that ivy-green glass. Held up to the light, it seemed luminous, magical, and held for me all the promise that I imagined adulthood would, that elegant grownup world I felt sure (from the vantage point of six, seven, eight) would be full of treasures—wondrous, marvelous things.

One evening, I caught the bus to Amaralinha to see a film at the local art film house about the life of Gurdjieff, which someone had recommended to me. I went alone, and stood in line with a crowd of others waiting for the previous show to let out so we could go in.

In front of me stood an enormous blond, big as Texas, or rather, big as a Texan, the same broad barrel chest, the yellow hair, the blue eyes under lids that bore crow's feet at the corners, as if from squinting into sun; he had a large square Teutonic head, the vast appalling health of the overfed. He made me think of cattle, of dust and ranches and Cadillacs, tract housing.

He saw me watching him and smiled back a little shyly, gentle in a manner that seemed vaguely stupid to me at the time. Gentleness had so little use. I felt sure that he was American. No other country grew people large as this. Big. Friendly. Stupid.

I looked away.

—Paulista? he asked, smiling.

I was taken for Brazilian wherever I went by then, so I was not surprised he mistook me for a southerner, for a person from São Paulo, but I was surprised that he spoke Portuguese.

—Americana, I said, glad to be able to say I was not from here. Refusing to claim this place. Refusing to admit I had any part in this.

—You're not really American, he said.

—I am, I said.

—*Mesmo?* Really?

—*Claro,* Clearly, I shrugged. *E voce é de onde?* You're from where?

He told me he was from Rio Grande de Sul, the state where Paulinho lived.

—*Gaucho,* I said, smiling, Cowboy, the nickname for folks from Rio Grande do Sul.

—*Mesmo,* he said.

—*Claro,* I said.

He told me his name was Mario; I told him mine, and for a while we talked about what we were doing here in Salvador. When the line began to move inside, he said he'd like to talk more but that he was here with someone else. He did not specify a gender, a neat trick in a language in which gender is almost always named. He wrote down his number on the back of a business card and handed it to me. He asked me to call him.

—We can go to a movie, he said.

I told him that I was leaving for Rio Grande do Sul soon, that when I returned I'd have only a week before I left for the States.

—We have a week then, he said.

When I returned from seeing Paulinho in Porto Alegre, I dug out Mario's number and called. It was New Year's Eve day and I was alone and I was missing Paulinho.

I asked him what he was doing for New Year's, shamelessly fishing for a date.

He invited me to a New Year's Eve party at the Bahian Yacht Club, a place I'd long wanted to go. From the first time I first rode the bus down the long winding hill to Barra and saw the sparkling white buildings and glistening blue pool of the yacht club, I had wanted to go there. I took comfort in its superfluous wealth, that oasis of ease. He had two tickets, he said, and his date had cancelled.

I told him I'd be delighted to go.

Mario arrived to pick me up wearing a white dinner jacket, looking really very handsome. I wore the green dress that I'd bought to impress Paulinho, which he never saw, a translucent cotton the color of luna moths. The party was held on the patio around the pool. Overdressed people sat at round metal tables and drank too much champagne. A band played. The moon rose. The pool glowed aquamarine. Some were dancing. But the promise of ease was a lie, after all: it looked lovely only from a distance.

I was bored. The party, swank and dull, was disappointing. I spent the first half of the evening swilling champagne and mistaking strangers for Paulinho, though I knew my obsession was useless, a thing I held onto in the place of love.

We sat at a table watching other people dance, until finally Mario suggested that we take a walk on the beach at Barra. As we walked along the beach, Mario stopped by some rocks and kissed me. He smelled of warm cotton, chlorine bleach, and champagne: a comforting smell; his big warm animal body came as a relief, and as we kissed I thought of Paulinho, though they were not alike. Paulo was small and brown and worried. Mario was not worried, not in the least. Mario was a nice big overfed blond guy, likeable, although I didn't like him. I was past liking anyone now. I was just going through the motions, waiting for something to change in me or in the world, to happen, to return me to the living from whom I seemed exiled.

I didn't know then that I would wander like this for years until my heart and all hope had given out, until I had no ambition left, no desire, was done with school, done with everything, done and ready to be dead at twenty-four. I will consider suicide then, and while considering it, I will go camping on the sandy shore of Elephant Butte Reservoir in southern New Mexico, on the edge of White Sands where the first atomic bomb was detonated, the Trinity test.

I will stand on the shore of Elephant Butte Reservoir that first afternoon among a dozen strangers in their Day-Glo nylon jackets and yellow rain slickers, their colorful Guatemalan woolen caps and hiking boots and, inexplicably moved by the loveliness of the pink cliffs across the gray water, I will begin to cry. I will be embarrassed but I will not be surprised.

A few days later, I will be walking alone among the sandy hills beyond camp, among the scrappy creosote that smells of tar, my mind blank as the blue sky, wondering what other people think about when they're alone, imagining others' thoughts more interesting than my own, feeling inadequate even in my solitude, as I pick up rocks and pop them in my mouth and suck them to keep my dry mouth wet and quell my thirst, and I will feel sad, and then I will feel deeply lonely, and then I will shift to something beyond loneliness: I will feel unfamiliar to myself, vacant, as if I were an absence more than a presence and in that instant I will seem merely an empty space, an O, a hollow tube with the world showing through both sides, a mirror with the glass punched out, and I will be terrified by this emptiness and at the same time uncannily calm, becalmed, to feel myself indistinguishable from everything around me, to feel that I am nothing, that I am all of it and nothing at all.

I will stand there, empty, unfamiliar, amidst the tar-stinking creosote and sage, the rocks and sand, under a now gray sky, and as suddenly as I was emptied I will be filled with a great, impersonal joy, overwhelmed by heart-breaking happiness, unearned, unbidden, inexplicable, real as the rock in my mouth. I will feel a sudden great tenderness for all I see—the twisted stink-ing creosote the sage the smooth flat stones the modest plants the sand the cloud-clotted sky the navy blue water capped with wave foam.

It is hard to describe this sort of thing without sounding like you've gone one too many rounds with William James, without sounding like a nut or a salesman. In that moment, I will feel only great joy, profound happiness, as if I am fallen terribly in love with everything and I understand then for the first time that this lovely imperfect world is all there is and it is enough, more than enough. I will feel my senses dilate as they do at the beginning of a love affair, but unlike love this joy will not fade, though it will come and go. Or rather I will come and go from it. This radiance, this joy is like a vast subter-ranean river, there beneath my life, my days, a current I will step into and out of, but that does not leave me as all else must and will.

Only later will I call it grace. In time, I will become convinced that I've been wrong in thinking—as I did throughout my youth, that first quarter century—that we see most clearly when we see through the lens of despair. The truth, I feel now, is that beneath everything is joy: this is the bedrock, that radiance, which, if not precisely god, and certainly not some old man manqué, nevertheless Is, a radiance that feels like desire, that feels like a magnificent longing like *saudades*.

But I am not there yet. In Salvador, I know none of this.

In Salvador, I spent the first day of 1985 alone in my apartment on Rua João Pondé, listening to bad American pop tunes from the seventies. In my diary from the time, I wrote on that first day of the new year, "I am amazed to have survived 1984." I noted that I was listening to Carly Simon's "The Way I've Always Heard It Should Be." I didn't mention whether I grasped the irony of the title juxtaposed with that disastrous year, but how could I not have noted the irony? Nothing was the way I'd heard it should be. Noth-ing even resembled it. Not even close.

I thought a lot that day about what a jerk I'd made of myself in Porto Alegre; I thought a lot about calling Paulinho.

A week later, I gave in and called. Though I knew it would do no good, that it would only compound my humiliation, though I told myself a call would only confirm Paulinho's worst suspicions about me, confirm my worst suspicions about myself, secretly I hoped that he'd tell me that he loved me and that somehow that would put things right.

I sat on the carpeted floor of my apartment, cross-legged, elbows on the coffee table beside the guardaropa, digging my thumb into the nubbly carpeting as I dialed.

—Hey, I said, when he answered. I was just calling to find out how your New Year's was. Talk to you before I leave. Say good-bye.

—Of course, he said. His voice was cool and measured, sleepy maybe. I checked my watch; it wasn't yet 8 o'clock.

—Sorry to have called so early, I said. I wanted to make sure that I caught you in. You said you run at 6, so I figured 7:30 was no problem. I laughed. He didn't.

—It's no problem, Ellen, he said.

I twirled my index finger in the phone cord. So, I said. (It was clear I should not have called.)

—New Year's was good, Paulinho said after a long pause. We got a table at the club, Sylvana, Mande, and I. It was good. And you?

—It was great, I said, overcompensating. Terrific.

Outside the sky had been darkening with clouds since dawn. I found it comforting to watch the clouds' blue bellies beyond the window, the sky growing dim. The line ticked with static and distance.

—My grandfather died on Saturday, Paulinho said.

—The one you were going to spend New Year's with, in Florianopolis.

—That one, yeah.

I tried to imagine his face just then, his eyes red from crying, his soft brown features tight with pain and guilt for not having spent that final New Year's with his grandparents, having called off the trip to spend time with me.

—I'm so sorry, I whispered.

—Yeah.

I rolled little balls of lint across the carpet and stuffed them into the burrow I'd made with my thumb. For a long time we were quiet, listening to the static. Probably one of us should have hung up. Probably it should have been me. But worse than the prospect of saying stupid things was the prospect of not having anyone to say stupid things to, not having anyone I cared enough, longed for enough to be stupid over.

—You know, I said. I mean, I know, rationally, that it ended between us. But, well, I was calling to find out whether maybe you'd thought about us since I left.

Paulinho sighed. This was not a good sign, I knew.

—I really haven't had time to think about anything since Saturday, Ellen.

—Of course, I said. I stabbed at lint balls with my finger.

—But Ellen, he said.

—Yeah?

—I'm not what you lack, he said. I'm not what you need.

I remember the tone of his voice, the brief repeated phrase; I remember the sense of the words and my sense of humiliation, but curiously enough I did not write them down, his final words to me. The rest of our conversation is recorded verbatim in my diary but not his last words to me; still, I feel sure that he used the word *falta*, which means "to lack" as well as "to miss," to err, to fail. To say, as I think he did, *"Não sou o que voce falta"* would thus mean at once I'm not what you lack, what you miss, what you fail.

It is only after I lose all hope that I give in to the simple loveliness of what is and begin to enjoy my last days in Salvador. I begin to go to the beach to tan in the mornings before the sun gets too hot. I buy *sucos* from the ice cream shop in the port, buy coconuts from boys who sell them on the beach and who lop off the ends of the green husks with one clear swing of a machete, leaving a hole in the brown skull through which the boy pushes a straw and I drink warm salty gray milk from the trees.

I begin to visit distant beaches, just to see the beautiful places I have only heard about: Abayaté, Itapoa. I am catching the bus in Barra one morning, on my way to an outlying beach, when I see him, Chequinho, crossing the street toward me with another man. I am standing under the plastic bus shelter as they approach. There is nowhere really to go.

—*Tudo bem,* Elena, he says, coming to stand beside me. *Faz muito tempo, né?* It's been a long time.

I ignore him.

—*Voce é bem Bahiana,* he continues. He looks me up and down. *Tá mas magra, né?* You've lost weight, haven't you?

I have, but oddly after so much effort, it no longer seems important; loss no longer seems a good thing. I am weary of the effort to lose, and not to.

He introduces his friend. A tall, fat, jovial guy, who smiles at me. He looks all right. He doesn't look like a creep, I mean. This has become my standard, creep and non-creep.

—*Tudo bem?* the friend asks. He doesn't hold out a hand, so I do not have to decline it.

—*Tudo bom,* I say. I greet the friend formally, not wanting to appear afraid or even moved by this chance meeting, this reunion.

—*Ta bem loura,* Chequinho says, *bem preto.* You're very blond, he says, very tanned.

I look at him with what I hope is clear contempt.

When the bus comes, I get on; they do too. I sit up front, near the driver, in a long seat that faces the aisle. Chequinho takes a seat across from me. His friend sits beside him, on a seat facing the front.

Chequinho tells me I should come to the racetrack with them. He tells his companion that I am an old friend, then winks at him.

—We are old friends, he brags.

His companion frowns, raises his eyebrows, as if impressed.

—We are not friends, I say, looking Chequinho dead in the eye.

Chequinho loses his smile, then grins, as if it were a joke.

—*Não fica assim*, Elena, he says. Don't be like that. She's just angry, he tells his friend, because I didn't call her.

And that is when I say—slowly, as if speaking to a child or a foreigner who'd not yet mastered the language and needed to be spoken to slowly in order to comprehend, as if what I have to say were of great importance, a thing he needed to understand—

—*Vai pra porra, mal educado.* Meaning Fuck yourself, dirtbag. Literally, Go to the whores, ill-educated one.

I needn't have spoken slowly, of course. The words were familiar, easily understood, spoken in the street all the time here, unmistakable.

Chequinho's friend roars with laughter and rolls in his seat, holding his groin as if he might pee. Chequinho starts up from his seat as if to hit me, but he can't here, not in public. He knows it, and I know it. Instead, he sits watching me. I hold his gaze, refusing to look away, playing that child's game—stare down.

I will not look away.

A few stops later, Chequinho says to his companion, C'mon. Let's get off.

—Why, man? his companion says. We're not even close.

—C'mon, he says, and pulls the cord to signal a stop.

Chequinho's hands are shaking as he stands to get off. He brushes close to me, raising one clenched fist near my face. I raise my chin, daring him to touch me. Never taking my eyes off his. Showing I have no fear. He is nothing to fear anymore.

It is not just his reaction that pleases me, or the piquant flavor of the epithet; it is the unexpectedness and incongruity of a young woman of some education, a well-bred Midwestern girl, saying *Fuck yourself. Fuck* is not the sort of thing a woman like me says. I know this.

And in that moment—for that one moment—I do not wonder what I am supposed to do or be or feel; I am absolutely certain. And in that instant, I seem to have become entirely myself, briefly self-possessed.

On that bus I discover another kind of power than that propriety confers. Propriety's power is authorized, after all, and can be revoked, like a license. The strength I discover on that city bus is my own, no one has given it to me; I am making it up as I go. It is mine. Maybe it has always been there, in me, all along, as Boa Gente suggested when he said I was a *filha de Iañsa*, the warrior, an Amazon after all.

Chequinho and his pal get off the bus in the middle of a stretch of beach nowhere and I ride on alone, watching the lapis lazuli Atlantic beside me and that scrim of aquamarine sky, the sand and the suburbs and the Isle of Itaparica where Isa is, behind a wall capped with broken bottles, trapped now by all she has and by the need to protect it. It takes a while for my heart to slow to a normal rhythm, before I cease to hear its percussive throb. It takes a while after Chequinho and his friend depart the bus before my cheeks lose their flush, before my skin loses the needly electrified feeling I get in a fight.

Meantime, I go on.

I do not know then that it will take me years to make it back from here, to find my way; I do not know it will be years before I grieve all this and learn another way to love and live, another kind of desire than this economy allows. It will take time before I assemble these memories—like something that has been broken, torn apart—and begin to make something whole.

It was a small thing that I learned that day, but it was a start: that moment when I recognized that I did not need permission; I did not need someone else to tell me who I was. The first step to claiming yourself, Jamaica Kincaid once said, is anger. I consider anger a badge of honor. The second step, I'd say, is desire. I will be fully twenty-five before I first go to bed with a woman, and when I do, I will claim myself in another and more lasting way, reaching out in desire, without fear of right or wrong, without thought of utility or avarice, a reaching out that feels like a reaching in, that feels like falling back into my body, embracing a logic beyond the categories I had known, as perhaps we must if we are to find an alternative to the logic of commodities that seems to have so dangerously distracted us of late.

It will be years before I learn the end of Orpheus's story, while rereading Edith Hamilton's *Greek Myths and Legends*. Orpehus, so Ovid's story goes, returned from Hell to the surface of the world and went on alone. One day, he wandered into a forest where he was set upon by maenads. They tore his body limb from limb, severing his torso from his head, scattering his parts. His head, tossed into the Aegean, washed up on the shore of the Isle of Lesbos—made famous by the poet Sappho—and was rescued there. The island's inhabitants brought Orpheus's head to Delphi and laid it to rest. They buried his severed head, understanding what it will take me years to learn after leaving Salvador behind, that the head cannot survive cut off from the body. Calculation cannot save us.

I will never again see Nel or Isa, though I will run into Barbara in the cross-campus library at Yale the following autumn where she will be a graduate student and I will be starting my senior year. We will stand among library stacks and speak lightly, glancingly, of Salvador. Barbara will say that she is hoping to return to study dance. I'll lie and say I'd like to go back too.

In truth, I am relieved to have left it all behind, to have left Salvador, the Amazon, Nel, Isa, that country, my youth, that private history of global loss; I'm relieved to imagine that I have, that I can, that I am safe now. Home.

That autumn, I beg my dean to allow me, a term before I'm scheduled to graduate, to change my major from economics and Latin American studies to history. In the end, after much entreaty, I get my way. I sign up for a ridiculous number of history classes in order to meet the requirements of the major, and opt—in the end—to write the required senior thesis on eschatological narratives—stories, that is, of the world's end.

Specifically, I look at nuclear winter theory to examine whether—despite its scientific grounding—it inadvertently relies on Judeo-Christian myth for the formulation of its predictions. I take my cue from an essay by Perry Miller, the Harvard historian, and argue that though we're inclined to think that faith and science took different paths after the Copernican revolution, we are wrong: as much as the language of natural science informs Christian exegesis of apocalypse, so, sadly, do we find in the history of scientific development a disconcerting reliance on Judeo-Christian myth.

The development of atomic weaponry especially (and the language of nuclear winter theory as well) bears the unmistakable lineaments of Judeo-Christian apocalypse, the vain hope that by bringing about catastrophe we may bring about rebirth. It's not a difficult argument to make, and Perry makes it well: the development of atomic weaponry is crudely adorned with religious imagery—from the naming of the first atomic test (the Trinity) to Oppenheimer's famous quoting of Hindu scripture, the *Bhagavad Gita*, as he watched the first mushroom cloud rise over White Sands. More important than Perry's analysis are the questions he raises: Are we risking destroying the world in the vain unacknowledged hope that cataclysmic destruction will bring about the Kingdom of God? Where is God's judgment if we are the ones to pull the trigger?

Every culture, Mircea Eliade argues, has its myth of the end, a story of the slow steady decline of the peopled world, its degradation and decline from paradise into horror, culminating in flood or fire, apocalypse, from which will come rebirth, a new beginning, a kingdom on earth, cleansed.

We like to think that reasoned science can save us from pursuing myth blindly into hell. But we're wrong to assume that we can keep myth or faith out of scientific inquiry. We can't. Or haven't yet. Newton, the father of modern scientific thought, spent his retirement defining a key to the book of Revelations.

I concluded my hundred-page thesis on a plea, arguing that danger lies less in the threat of nuclear winter than in our attachment to the idea of a perfectible world, in our attachment to the Judeo-Christian notion that destruction can lead to our redemption, can lead us to a greater good, a Blessed

End. I argued that if we are not careful, we may well destroy ourselves and all we love in the pursuit of suspect improvement, specious development, not realizing until it is too late that the world and we are, after all, enough as we are. We must relinquish the hope of perfection, embrace the flawed, settle for safeguarding the miraculous imperfect world, the lovely chaos of things, what is.

Amazon Snapshot #15

When I return to the United States a few months later to complete my senior year of college, I will date a terrifically handsome guy at Yale, a beautiful boy with thick black hair, dense and glossy as a horse's mane (a sweet-tempered and untormented soul who will grow up to be a psychologist in upstate New York), who will tell me in his room late one night when it seems the world is sleeping and we are inventing it all, that I have just explained the philosophy of Martin Buber to him. I hadn't read Buber at the time; I'm not sure that I'd even heard of him (I studied economics, knew little of philosophy). I thought we had been talking about love.

I had been explaining to him that I knew that I loved a person if I could *not* say why I loved him or her. If I were able to enumerate a person's qualities—I knew that it wasn't love I felt (I was describing a prized possession, a commodity). But if I could *not* say why I loved a person—if I could *not* explain or enumerate his or her virtues—I knew it was love, something that existed *between* us, a feeling worthy of the name.

He told me that Buber had said much the same thing in his book *I and Thou*, which my friend had read in a philosophy class the previous term and puzzled over. Buber, a nineteenth-century Jewish mystic and philosopher, describes precisely these two types of relationships, which he terms an I-It relationship (in which we experience the other as an object) and I-Thou (in which we are each a subject, each a being with a soul).

Buber maintains that every time we speak of something separate from ourselves, we conjure a self. So, how we speak of what is *not* ourselves—a woman, a man, a forest—determines the self we bring into being. If we see a world of objects, the self we evoke (the "I") will be an object as well. If we see a world of souls, beings vast and remarkable, the self or "I" that we are invoke is a holy thing, vast and remarkable. "Relation," Buber wrote, "is mutual."

I don't remember how our conversation ended that night; but our relationship ended soon after. Twenty years later, I can see that the conversation that night was the beginning of a change—incremental as loss—or, if not precisely *that* conversation, then ones like it that year that followed my return from the rain forest, when I began to see that the logic of the marketplace and its corrolary self-improvement might not after all be the only or even the best option.

It would be years before I would see that the logic that I applied to myself then was our culture's logic and was wrong. The logic with which I viewed myself at twenty-one was that of the American dream: fueled by that all-American ambition to make something of oneself (as if a life were merely raw material to be made ready for the marketplace, a promising resource), a commodity to be improved upon and sold, like a forest or a body.

I didn't yet know how my time in the Amazon had changed me, and that I had already come to the end of that logic and would have to seek a new one—as perhaps our culture will, too.

Epilogue

Flying into Manaus—the largest city in the Amazon—twenty years after I first visited the rain forest, I was thinking about Manhattan, the city where my father's family lives and which feels to me like my true home, maybe because the city's messy restless yearning feels so like my own, or because that's where I first lived with a woman I loved. Manaus—a city of 3 million people on the bank of the world's largest river—looks like nothing so much as a chunk of Queens shoved like a splinter into the flank of the forest, which stretches out seemingly endlessly to the horizon.

The forest from the air looks rumpled and green, like broccoli crowns or a verdant quilt—from the air, it seems to have largely survived the ravages of development I'd studied twenty years before as an undergraduate at Yale. In fact, the forest has: some 80 percent remains intact, defying the dire predictions of the early 1980s—activism and a lousy economy having slowed deforestation in the last twenty years.

But the forest's future is far from secure. Although deforestation rates have been variable, the loss has been consistent and significant since the 1970s. In 2004, scientists recorded the second largest loss of rain forest on record in more than twenty years. More than 10,000 square miles of forest were destroyed that year in 2004—the equivalent of 500 Manhattans. In just five months in 2007, an area the size of Rhode Island (more than 3,200 square kilometers, or 1,200 square miles) was lost.

Such figures are hard to focus on; to say such loss is more acreage than the tiny contested country of Israel, or so many football fields per minute or hour may be accurate, but it makes my eyes blur. So I imagine the loss this way, as personal:

It is as if *each day* a conflagration were to tear through Manhattan, from the tip of Battery Park to the cloisters on the island's northern tip; as if every twenty-four hours, Manhattan's 23 square miles were to be consumed by fire or bulldozer. Like this: at daybreak, Battery Park would be set on fire, the flames stretching from the Hudson to the East River, consuming ten blocks each hour, as it drifted north; the blaze would claim Wall Street and the little white church down there, scorching Tribeca and Chinatown and Little Italy; bulldozers would tear up the ginkgoes on Perry Street, taking out the White Horse Tavern, the charming Ukrainian restaurants on the lower East Side; by 10:30 a.m. the Flat Iron building, the Chelsea Hotel, and London Terrace would go up in smoke, along with the fashionable galleries, the garment district and Hell's Kitchen, the obscure neighborhoods on the east side in the Thirties; by noon the public library at Forty-second and the lovely shade of Bryant Park would be gone; the MoMA, the Plaza, and the southern edge of Central Park would be ablaze by 1 p.m.; the Frick, the Met, the Guggenheim would be tinder by late afternoon; St. John the Divine would be afire by sunset; into the night Harlem would burn and the Cloisters until everything below 220th Street would be gone by dawn. (Every other month, the fire would consume the other boroughs as well.)

And the next morning—each morning—the destruction would happen again. Every day. Three hundred and sixty-five times a year.

Such destruction would be—as one researcher in the Amazon recently said of the devastation there—"impressive."

Flying over the Amazon, seeing the vast oceanic green of the forest from a plane, it is hard to imagine the forest as finite—just as it has been difficult, despite forty years of warnings—to imagine global climate change, a world warmed or suddenly cooled—but given time, a forest can become a desert (as the Sahara has), a global climate can change. Because we're talking about an area the size of the continental United States, it's hard to imagine the Amazon rain forest as limited, but at the rate of 10,000 square miles per year, what remains of Brazil's rain forest could be gone in less than forty years. A geologic blink of the eye.

"There are few human accomplishments on the planet that are viewable from space," writes Howard Lyman in his 1998 bestseller *Mad Cowboy: Plain Truth from the Cattle Rancher Who Won't Eat Meat.* One, he claims, are "the fires that are burning in the Brazilian rain forest."

Lyman notes that in the late 1990s "as many as seven-thousand [fires] have been detected burning in the Amazon in one day" and that "more of Brazil is aflame now than ever before." Most of the land cleared each year—an area roughly equivalent to the state of Massachusetts—is for cattle pasture, though increasingly for soybeans as well. (In 2003, more than 20 percent of the state of Mato Grosso's forests were converted to cropland. Agricultural production of soya, mainly used to feed animals, has become one of the greatest causes of deforestation.) "Humanity is rich in folly," Lyman writes, "but it's hard to think of a folly more mind-bogglingly stupendous than that of transforming infinitely rich, diverse, dense jungle into desert in a few years time for the sake of a few more hamburgers."

According to the *Concise Oxford Dictionary* on the desk beside me, memory is "related to MOURN." But there is pleasure, too, in remembering.

I remember lying in a hammock on a platform in the Amazon in the heat of a late July afternoon, on my last trip to the Amazon, swinging to catch a breeze, when I heard a sigh, a heavy exhalation of breath, then the slur of water. I looked up, expecting to see my roommate there, but there was no one. They had all gone off to do something useful with the afternoon, while I lay idle.

I heard another cough and turned to the river where I saw the smooth arc of a pink dolphin break the surface, exhale, inhale, and submerge again. The tea-brown river was messy with fluff and leaves, the far bank unruly with foliage—apple green, dark ivy, the white trunks of trees.

There is a sentimental school of thought that maintains that wilderness is a repository of divinity, a source of spiritual rejuvenation, our spiritual fountain of youth. But I don't buy it; I've come to believe that the divinity we seek is in us, that we're at risk of forgetting it in our drive to turn the world into trinkets. Preserving wilderness, we preserve what is best in ourselves, the ability to recognize what is irreducible to commodity or object.

Perhaps wanting to save the rain forest, I was trying to save beings nearer at hand whose peril was less obvious to me: my mother, whose despair was an urgent beacon throughout my youth; or myself, a young woman afraid of where love might lead if she allowed herself to feel. Looking back, it seems clear that I loved Nel, desired Isa, in ways that I could not acknowledge then.

In those days I mistrusted passion; I had not yet experienced the illuminating love that is beyond all judgment or calculation, love like a benediction that makes clear that we do not need to earn our place, calculate our value, that we have an inestimable value all our own before we do a thing, as does a forest or a star. Love like great joy was a thing I would discover late, at twenty-five, in a woman's arms. And when I do, I will realize that my desperate youthful desire to "make something of myself" and "to get somewhere in life" has been misguided; that there is nowhere to get to, that it is all, already, here.

Acknowledgments

I would like to thank Clair Willcox at the University of Missouri Press for his insightful editing, admirable patience, and for giving this book a second chance; the wonderful writer S. L. Wisenberg read this manuscript with generosity and tremendous acuity and gave me the greatest gift a writer could ask—making my work look smarter for her efforts. I owe special thanks to H. Emerson "Chip" Blake at *Orion Magazine,* who accepted and improved upon the essay that would become this book; thanks, too, to the editors at *Writer's Digest* who saw fit on the basis of that slim piece to name me among their twenty-five nonfiction writers to watch in the new millennium. I am tremendously grateful to everyone at the University of Missouri Press, whose great skill and generous efforts have made this book possible and better: Beth Chandler, Sara Davis, Daren Dean, Jennifer Gravley, and Lyn Smith. My thanks to Kathleen Anderson, for her efforts. I owe a debt of deep gratitude to friends and writers who inspired and generously read this in manuscript, and to the organizations that offered funding and shelter to support it: Lauren Fox, Gretchen Legler, Howard Levy, Virginia Levy, Marge and Sy Levy, Sawnie Morris, Nicholas Delbanco, Lisa Schamess, Cheryl Strayed, and the wonderful writing group in Washington (Katharine Davis, Ann McLaughlin, Carolyn Parkhurst, Leslie Pietrzyk, and Amy Stolls), the Sacatar Foundation, the Virginia Center for the Creative Arts, the Millay Colony, the Mid-Atlantic Arts Foundation, and the Mellon Foundation. I want to thank Terry Tempest Williams for her inspiration as an artist and activist, and Philip Fearnside, for his efforts to turn the tide. I am grateful to the extraordinary faculty at Ohio State University: Lee K. Abbott, Michelle Herman, Lee Martin, Bill Roorbach, and Melanie Rae Thon. A special thanks to Cleveland Park Coop friends Dierdre Ball and Philip Benson, without whose milagro and faith this book would not have been completed; Susan Bradfield, whose efforts to protect wild birds inspires me daily; and Kyoko Mori and Andrea Way, who literally gave me shelter. I am most grateful to my dearest friend, Maureen Stanton, a fierce advocate for the environment and a brilliant writer of creative nonfiction, whose remarkable memoirs and literary journalism inspired me to try my hand at this, and without whose help this would not have been begun or finished. Finally, my deepest thanks to my family and to Bill, for helping me find the happy ending.